Practicing Organization Development

The Change Agent Series for Groups and Organizations

MISSION STATEMENT

The books in this series are intended to be cutting-edge, state-of-the-art, and innovative approaches to participative change in organizational settings. They are written for, and written by, organization development (OD) practitioners interested in new approaches to facilitating participative change. They are geared to providing both theory and advice on practical application.

SERIES EDITORS

William J. Rothwell
Roland Sullivan
Kristine Quade

EDITORIAL BOARD

David Bradford
W. Warner Burke
Edith Whitfield Seashore
Robert Tannenbaum
Christopher G. Worley
Shaolin Zhang

Balancing
Individual and
Organizational
Values

Balancing Individual and Organizational Values

Walking the Tightrope
to Success

Ken Hultman

with Bill Gellermann

Forewords by Richard Beckhard and John D. Adams

JOSSEY-BASS/PFEIFFER
A Wiley Company
www.pfeiffer.com

Published by

JOSSEY-BASS/PFEIFFER
A Wiley Company

www.pfeiffer.com

Jossey-Bass/Pfeiffer is a registered trademark of Jossey-Bass Inc., A Wiley Company.

ISBN: 978-0-7879-5720-9

Library of Congress Cataloging-in-Publication Data

Hultman, Ken.
  Balancing individual and organizational values: walking the tightrope
to success / Ken Hultman; with Bill Gellermann.
    p. cm.—(The practicing organization development series)
  ISBN 978-0-7879-5720-9 (alk. paper)
  1. Corporate culture. 2. Organizational change. I. Gellermann,
William. II. Title. III. Series.
  HD58.7 .H84 2002
  912—dc21

2001002022

Copyright page continued on page 241

Acquiring Editor: Matthew Holt
Director of Development: Kathleen Dolan Davies
Developmental Editor: Susan Rachmeler
Editor: Rebecca Taff

Senior Production Editor: Dawn Kilgore
Manufacturing Supervisor: Becky Carreño
Interior and Cover Design: Bruce Lundquist
Illustrations: Richard Sheppard

Printing   10   9   8   7   6   5   4   3   2   1

Contents

List of
Tables, Figures,
and Exhibits

Foreword
to the Series

ON **1967,** Warren Bennis, Ed Schein, and I were faculty members of the Sloan School of Management at MIT. We decided to produce a series of paperback books that collectively would describe the state of the field of organization development (OD). Organization development as a field had been named by myself and several others from our pioneer change effort at General Mills in Minneapolis, Minnesota, some ten years earlier.

Today I define OD as "a systemic and systematic change effort, using behavioral science knowledge and skill, to transform the organization to a new state."

In any case, several books and many articles had been written, but there was no consensus on whether OD was a field of practice, an area of study, or a profession. We had not even established OD as a theory or even as a practice.

We decided that there was a need for something that would describe the state of OD. Our intention was to each write a book and also to recruit three other authors. After some searching, we found a young editor who had just joined the small publishing house of Addison-Wesley. We made contact, and the series was born. Our audience was to be human resource professionals who spent their time consulting with managers in their development through various small-group activities, such as team building. More than thirty books have been published in that series, and the series has had a life of its own. We just celebrated its thirtieth anniversary.

At last year's National OD Network Conference, I said that it was time for the OD profession to change and transform itself. Is that not what we change agents tell our clients to do? This new Jossey-Bass/Pfeiffer series will do just that. It can be seen as:

- A documentation of the re-invention of OD;

- An effort that will take us to the next level; and

- A practical effort to transfer to the world the theory and practice of leading-edge practitioners and theorists.

The books in this new series will thus prove to be valuable resources for change agents to keep current with the new and leading-edge ideas and practices.

May this very exciting change agent series be most creative and innovative. May it give our field a renewed burst of energy and awareness.

Richard Beckhard
Written on Labor Day weekend 1999 from my summer cabin near Bethel, Maine

Introduction
to the Series

"We must become the change we want to see."

—*Mahatma Gandhi*

"We live in a moment of history where change is so speeded up that we begin to see the present only when it is already disappearing."

—*R. D. Laing*

WE CAN EXPECT MORE CHANGE to occur in our lifetimes than has occurred since the beginning of civilization over ten thousand years ago. *Practicing Organization Development: The Change Agent Series for Groups and Organizations* is a new series of books being launched to help those who must cope with or create change in organizational settings. That includes almost everyone.

The Current State of Organization Development

Our view of OD in this series is an optimistic one. We believe that OD is gaining favor as decision makers realize that a balance *must* be struck between the drivers of change and the people involved in it and affected by it. Although OD does have its disadvantages at a time characterized by quantum leap change, it remains prefer-able to such alternative approaches to change as coercion, persuasion, leadership change, and debate.[1] Organization development practitioners are reinventing their approaches, based on certain foundational roots of the field, in combination with emerging principles to ensure that OD will increasingly be recognized as a viable, important, and inherently participative approach to help people in organizations facilitate, anticipate, and manage change.

A Brief History of the Genesis of the OD Series

A few years ago, and as a direct result of the success of *Practicing Organization Development: A Guide for Practitioners* by Rothwell, Sullivan, and McLean, the publisher—feeling that OD was experiencing a rebirth of interest in the United States and in other nations—wanted to launch a new OD series. The goal of this new series was not to replace, or even compete directly with, the well-established Addison-Wesley OD Series (edited by Edgar Schein). Instead, as the editors saw it, this series would provide a means by which the most promising authors in OD whose voices had not previously been heard could share their ideas. The publisher enlisted the support of Bill Rothwell, Roland Sullivan, and Kristine Quade to turn the dream of a series into a reality.

This series was long in the making. After sharing many discussions with the publisher and circulating among themselves several draft descriptions of the series editorial guidelines, the editors were guests of Bob Tannenbaum, one of the field's founders, in Carmel, California, in February 1999 to discuss the series with a group of well-known OD practitioners interested in authoring books. Several especially supportive publisher representatives, including Matt Holt and Josh Blatter, were also present at that weekend-long meeting. It was an opportunity for diverse OD practitioners, representing many philosophical viewpoints, to come together to share their vision for a new book series. In a sense, this series represents an OD inter-vention in the OD field in that it is geared to bringing change to the field most closely associated with change management and facilitation.

---

[1]W. Rothwell, R. Sullivan, & G. McLean. (1995). Introduction (pp. 3–46). In W. Rothwell, R. Sullivan, & G. McLean, *Practicing Organization Development: A Guide for Consultants.* San Francisco, CA: Jossey-Bass/ Pfeiffer.

What Distinguishes the Books in this Series

The books in this series are meant to be cutting-edge and state-of-the-art in their approach to OD. The goal of the series is to provide an outlet for proven authorities in OD who have not put their ideas into print or for up-and-coming writers in OD who have new, sometimes unorthodox, approaches that are stimulating and exciting. Some of the books in this series describe inspirational concepts that can lead to actionable change and purvey ideas so new that they are not fully developed.

Unique to this series is the cutting-edge emphasis, the immediate applicability, and the ease of transferability of the concepts. The aim of this series is nothing less than to reinvent, re-energize, and reinvigorate OD. In each book, we have also recommended that the author(s) provide:

- A research base of some kind, meaning new information derived from practice and/or systematic investigation and

- Practical tools, worksheets, case studies and other ready-to-go approaches that help the authors drag "theory" to "practice" to make these new, cutting-edge approaches more concrete.

Subject Matter That Will (and Will Not) Be Covered

The books in this series are varied in their approach, but they are united by their focus. All share an emphasis on organization development (OD). Hence, books in this series are about participative change efforts. They are not about such other popular topics as leadership, management development, consulting, group dynamics—unless those topics are treated in new, cutting-edge ways and are geared to OD practitioners.

This Book

Balancing Individual and Organizational Values describes how to meet the needs of employees and organizations in ways that serve the mutual interests of both. Values are key because they are driving forces in human motivation and corporate culture, and balance among values is essential to a healthy workplace and to long-term business success. Establishing such a balance and maintaining it have emerged as critical skills for OD practitioners and managers in the new economy. This is a process of continuous improvement—like walking a tightrope. *Balancing Individual and Organizational Values* equips you to walk that tightrope successfully by clearly explaining the dynamics of values and how they often serve as invisible barriers to organizational growth. A variety of powerful tools and instruments presented here allows you to assess and bring about greater balance among values through one-on-one coaching and team and large-scale organizational interventions.

Series Website

For further information and resources about the books in this series and about the current and future practice of organization development, we encourage readers to visit the series website at *www.PracticingOD.Pfeiffer.com.*

William J. Rothwell
University Park, PA

Roland Sullivan
Deephaven, MN

Kristine Quade
Minnetonka, MN

Statement of the Board

IT IS OUR PLEASURE TO PARTICIPATE in and influence the start up of *Practicing Organization Development: The Change Agent Series for Groups and Organizations.* The purpose of the series is to stimulate the profession and influence how OD is defined and practiced. This statement is intended to set the context for the series by addressing three important questions: (1) What is OD? (2) Is the OD profession at a crossroads? and (3) What is the purpose of this series?

What Is Organization Development?

We offer the following definition of OD to stimulate debate:

> Organization development is a system-wide and values-based collaborative process of applying behavioral science knowledge to the adaptive development, improvement, and reinforcement of such organizational features as the strategies, structures, processes, people, and cultures that lead to organization effectiveness.

The definition suggests that OD can be understood in terms of its several foci:

First, *OD is a system-wide process.* It works with whole systems. In the past, the bias has been toward working at the individual and group levels. More recently, the focus has shifted to organizations and multi-organization systems. We support that trend in general but honor and acknowledge the fact that the traditional focus on smaller systems is both legitimate and necessary.

Second, *OD is values-based.* Traditionally, OD has attempted to distinguish itself from other forms of planned change and applied behavioral science by promoting a set of humanistic values and by emphasizing the importance of personal growth as a key to its practice. Today, that focus is blurred and there is much debate about the value base underlying the practice of OD. We support a more formal and direct conversation about what these values are and how the field is related to them.

Third, *OD is collaborative.* Our first value commitment as OD practitioners is to bring about an inclusive, diverse workforce with a focus of integrating differences into a world-wide culture mentality.

Fourth, *OD is based on behavioral science knowledge.* Organization development should incorporate and apply knowledge from sociology, psychology, anthropology, technology, and economics toward the end of making systems more effective. We support the continued emphasis in OD on behavioral science knowledge and believe that OD practitioners should be widely read and comfortable with several of the disciplines.

Fifth, *OD is concerned with the adaptive development, improvement, and reinforcement of strategies, structures, processes, people, culture, and other features of organizational life.* This statement not only describes the organizational elements that are the target of change, but also describes the process by which effectiveness is increased. That is, OD works in a variety of areas, and it is focused on improving these areas. We believe that such a statement of process and content strongly implies that a key feature of OD is the transference of knowledge and skill to the system so that it is more able to handle and manage change in the future.

Sixth and finally, *OD is about improving organization effectiveness.* It is not just about making people happy; it is also concerned with meeting financial goals, improving productivity, and addressing stakeholder satisfaction. We believe that OD's future is closely tied to the incorporation of this value in its purpose and the demonstration of this objective in its practice.

Is the OD Profession at a Crossroads?

For years, OD professionals have said that OD is at a crossroads. From our perspective at the beginning of the new millennium, the field of organization development can be characterized by the following statements:

1. Practitioners today are torn. The professional organizations representing OD practitioners, including the OD Network, the OD Institute, the International OD Association, and the Academy of Management's OD and Change Division, are experiencing tremendous uncertainties in their purposes, practices, and relationships.

2. There are increasing calls for regulation/certification.

3. Many respected practitioners have suggested that people who profess to manage change are behind those who are creating it. Organization development practitioners should lead through influence rather than follow the lead of those who are sometimes coercive in their approach to change.

4. The field is defined by techniques.

5. The values that guide the field are unclear and ill-defined.

6. Too many people are practicing OD without any training in the field.

7. Practitioners are having difficulty figuring out how to market their services.

The situation suggests the following provocative questions:

- How can OD practitioners help formulate strategy, shape the strategy development process, contribute to the content of strategy, and drive how strategy will be implemented?

- How can OD practitioners encourage an open examination of the ways organizations are conceived and managed?

- How can OD focus on the drivers of change external to individuals, such as the external environment, business strategy, organization change, and culture change, as well as on the drivers of change internal to individuals, such as individual interpretations of culture, behavior, style, and mindset?

- How much should OD be part of the competencies of all leaders and how much should it be the sole domain of professionally trained, career-oriented OD practitioners?

What Is the Purpose of This Series?

This series is intended to provide current thinking about OD as a field and to provide practical approaches based on sound theory and research. It is targeted for full-time external or internal OD practitioners; top executives in charge of enterprise-wide change; and managers, HR practitioners, training and development professionals, and others who have responsibility for change in organizational and trans-organizational settings. At the same time, these books will be directed toward cutting-edge thinking and state-of-the-art approaches. In some cases, the ideas, approaches, or techniques described are still evolving, so the books are intended to open up dialogue.

We know that the books in this series will provide a leading forum for thought-provoking dialogue within the OD field.

About the Board Members

David Bradford is senior lecturer in organizational behavior at the Graduate School of Business, Stanford University, Palo Alto, California. He is co-author (with Allan R. Cohen) of *Managing for Excellence, Influence Without Authority*, and *POWER UP: Transforming Organizations Through Shared Leadership.*

W. Warner Burke is professor of psychology and education and chair of the Department of Organization and Leadership at Teachers College, Columbia University, New York, New York. His most recent publication is *Business Profiles of Climate Shifts: Profiles of Change Makers* (with William Trahant and Richard Koonce).

Edith Whitfield Seashore is an organization consultant and co-founder (with Morley Segal) of AUNTL Masters Program in Organization Development. She is co-author of *What Did You Say?* and *The Art of Giving and Receiving Feedback* and co-editor of *The Promise of Diversity.*

Robert Tannenbaum is emeritus professor of development of human systems, Graduate School of Management, University of California, Los Angeles; recipient of Lifetime Achievement Award by the National OD Network. He has published numerous books, including *Human Systems Development* (with Newton Margulies and Fred Massarik).

Christopher G. Worley is director, MSOD Program, Pepperdine University, Malibu, California. He is co-author of *Organization Development and Change* (7th ed.), with Tom Cummings, and of *Integrated Strategic Change,* with David Hitchin and Walter Ross.

Shaolin Zhang is senior manager of organization development for Motorola (China) Electronics Ltd. He received his master's degree in American Studies from Beijing Foreign Studies University, Beijing, China, and holds a Ph.D. in sociology from York University, Toronto, Canada.

Foreword

A **BOOK ON BALANCING INDIVIDUAL** and organizational values is much needed as we head into the 21st Century—especially a book designed to aid the practice of organization development practitioners. Since the beginning of the field in the 1960s, practitioners have espoused a values-based approach. In fact, OD grew out of the shared concerns of a number of corporate managers about how to bring the values they had encountered in their NTL T-group experiences back into their companies. That is, they wanted to see the values they had clarified for themselves as individuals reflected more widely in the organizations for which they worked.

As Ken Hultman points out, Bob Tannenbaum and Shel Davis were among the first to describe these values—the essential importance in the workplace of human development, fairness, openness, choice, and appropriate balances of autonomy and restraint.

Much of our *actual* behavior in the workplace at the end of the 20th Century, however, had little to do with these desirable values and much to do with serving the short-term goals of organizational executives. We are facing great challenges arising in large part from an *absence* of priority being placed on the values articulated by Tannenbaum and Davis. Environmental degradation of many kinds (air, water, climate), resource depletion (fish, forests, minerals), persistent gender and racial inequities, the concentration of wealth with progressively fewer people, and the attitude that we *should do* everything we *can do* with technology are all reflections of our *values* in use today.

In our relentless pursuit of short-term effectiveness, it is easy to lose sight of what matters most to us over the long haul. If our "values" are "our beliefs about what is most important," then it is little wonder that so many people today, in their private conversations, express feelings of alienation and disconnection from their work and from "society."

In many of my courses and workshops over the last several years, I have asked participants to brainstorm adjectives that describe what they experience as the prevailing mindset in their organizations. Then I seek the group's help in sorting the list into related themes. The most frequent themes that emerge have been "short-term," "reactive," "local," "either/or," "blaming," and "doing/having."

Having settled on the theme clusters, I then ask the group to project the results of holding these outlooks over the next twenty to thirty years. The scenarios are uniformly bleak. As Marilyn Ferguson stated in a seminar many years ago:

"If I continue to believe as I have always believed,
I will continue to act as I have always acted.
If I continue to act as I have always acted,
I will continue to get what I have always gotten."

From this we must conclude that the self-reinforcing and self-fulfilling nature of our *values in use* will have a lot to do with the quality of the future we will pass on to our grandchildren. One of the biggest challenges in closing the gap between our *espoused values* and our *values in use* is that, on a day-to-day, moment-to-moment basis, most of us are not aware of how our *values in use* differ from those we truly espouse. Nor are we aware, moment-to-moment, how our *values in use* driven behavior is contributing to our collective future outcomes. As Scottish psychiatrist R.D. Laing said, "The range of what we think and do is limited by what we *fail* to notice. And *because* we fail to notice *that* we fail to notice, there is little we can do to change. *Until* we notice how failing to notice shapes our thoughts and deeds." [my emphases]

I have attempted in my work to help individuals, teams, and whole organizations break out of the six themes I identified above by suggesting that they make each theme the left end of a continuum—and then work to increase the range along each continuum within organizational culture, as shown here.

Short-Term	Long-Term
Reactive	Creative
Local	Global
Either/Or	Both/And
Blaming	Learning
Doing/Having	Being

Integrating individual employees' values with the values an organization actually rewards is a difficult challenge. Perhaps the hardest part of bringing values into alignment in an organizational setting is establishing and maintaining sufficient visible and vocal sponsorship.

A few years ago, I was involved with a massive corporate transformation project that had a strong values base, as well as a compelling business case, supporting the change. The CEO was the primary sponsor of the humanistic values included in the vision and plans for change. However, in the midst of the change effort, after about $100 million had been spent, the CEO decided to retire. His successor reflected a different set of *values in use* (and had a less well-developed systems perspective), with the result that only a few of the initiatives that had been designed were selected for implementation. The change effort just "went away," leaving thousands of employees and millions of customers feeling frustrated and cynical. This was a clear case of how difficult it is for an individual's values to be adopted by a whole organization, especially when the sponsorship for this culture change effort is not sustainable.

It is my hope and expectation that *Balancing Individual and Organizational Values* will be widely adopted by organizational leaders and OD practitioners. This book provides an excellent case for why it is essential to be aware of both individuals' and organizations' espoused values and values in use. It also provides practical processes and valuable tools for bringing values into everyone's awareness, identifying where different values need to be nurtured, and developing plans for supporting and using appropriate values in everyday life for both organizations and individuals.

John D. Adams, Ph.D.
Director, Organizational Systems Ph.D. Program
Saybrook Graduate School
June 2001

To Mike Morris

Mentor, colleague, friend

Preface

OUR **WORLD IS FACING** some mega-value challenges as we enter the new millennium, and the very future of the planet hangs in the balance. These challenges include how to deal with:

- The population explosion,
- Pollution and the threat to public health,
- The risk of global warming,
- The growing gap between the rich and poor,
- The disenfranchised,
- Utilization of dwindling resources,
- Conflict between older Baby Boomers and fast-track twentysomethings,
- Gender and racial inequity, and
- Our increasingly diversified workplace.

Because business organizations are considered by some people to be the most powerful institutions on earth (Korten, 1995), their values will play a crucial role in determining how these issues are addressed. Accordingly, organization development (OD) practitioners and managers are and will continue to be in a position to help shape those values. This represents both an opportunity and an awesome responsibility. For these reasons, a thorough understanding of both the dynamics of values and how to assess and change values is essential.

Throughout modern history, organizations have made productivity and profits their primary values, even when these created negative conditions for workers. Then in the 1950s and 1960s the emerging field of organization development began championing values that added quality of work life to the productivity-profitability equation. Organization development practitioners and other change agents helped organizations make steady progress toward achieving greater balance until globalization shifted the emphasis to efficiency, cost reduction, and short-term profits. And many OD practitioners are now helping organizations downsize and restructure, often with little regard for work-life quality. Consequently, the progress made over the previous decades is in jeopardy.

The key question is "Are we going to be guided by clear inner convictions about what's needed to develop and maintain a healthy workplace or are we going to be influenced primarily by external circumstances and self-serving motives?" Recently, W. Warner Burke (1997) challenged OD practitioners to return to an emphasis on the founding values by fostering human development, fairness, openness, choice, and balance of autonomy (individual freedom) and constraint (organizational requirements).

I believe the biggest challenge facing OD professionals is to foster growth in ways that satisfy the needs of individuals, teams, organizations, and the larger world—not one or two at the expense of others. When I use the term "growth," I don't mean in the narrow sense of financial gain, but in the broader sense of self-actualization and ability to move toward a vision that serves the mutual interests of the organization and the human beings affected by it, which is like walking a tightrope. Considerable research exists showing a relationship between such humanistic values and bottom-line results (see, for example, Collins & Porras, 1994; Kotter & Heskett, 1992), but convincing busy leaders and managers that they must pay attention to both is still a challenge. This book will present some ways that this can be done.

Values can be discussed in terms of *process* and of *content.* Process concerns *how* values impact choice and behavior; content concerns *what* values people hold. In this book, I will examine values from both process and content perspectives. Intended for OD practitioners, change agents, organizational leaders and managers, the book content examines the underlying dynamics of values and motivation, examines dysfunctional values and valuing processes, and offers many practical suggestions for creating and maintaining a vibrant, high performing work environment. In addition, I suggest a set of criteria for assessing values in order to stimulate further discussion and research.

How This Book Is Organized

The book is divided into two parts. Part 1, "Understanding Values," consists of four chapters. Chapter 1 deals with what values are and why they are important. Chapter 2 presents the Motivational System Model, which is used to explain personal, interpersonal, team, and organizational behavior. Chapter 3 contains a discussion of the role of values in personality, while Chapter 4 is focused on values in organizations. Part 2, "Assessing and Changing Values," also consists of four chapters. Chapter 5 outlines four criteria for assessing values: balance, viability, alignment, and authenticity. Chapter 6 describes fifteen values that I believe have particular relevance in the new economy and features an interview with OD values pioneer Dr. Robert Tannenbaum. Chapter 7 contains a discussion on how to develop and implement values-driven interventions aimed at individuals, teams, and organizations. Finally, Chapter 8 describes Motivational System Mapping™, an approach to assessment that can be used with individuals, teams, and organizations.

I invited two colleagues to submit examples of how values were affirmed through an OD intervention. Those examples appear in various places throughout the text. A variety of tools and processes for diagnosing and addressing individual, team, and organizational issues are included.

Ken Hultman
July, 2001

Acknowledgments

① WOULD LIKE TO THANK THE PEOPLE WHO helped me with this project. Melinda Adams-Merino was the first one to suggest that I write the book, right after my last book, *Making Change Irresistible*, was released. I thought I had included everything I knew about organizational behavior in that book, but I greatly appreciate her insisting that I had more to say. I would also like to thank the *Practicing Organization Development* series editors who worked with me on this project: William J. Rothwell, for suggesting the book's structure and for encouraging me to "hang in there" during the revision process; Roland Sullivan, for embracing my book proposal with such enthusiasm and for suggesting that I had an important message to convey about values; and Kristine Quade, for her detailed feedback and for helping me become more sensitive to diversity issues. The Jossey-Bass/Pfeiffer editorial team of Josh Blatter, Kathleen Dolan Davies, Susan Rachmeler, Samya Sattar, and Dawn Kilgore also provided considerable help and assistance during the editorial and production processes.

I greatly appreciate the insightful and supportive foreword written by John D. Adams. I'd also like to thank Robert Tannenbaum and Warner Burke for the one-on-one time they spent with me discussing the organizational value issues. Their input was instrumental in shaping the book's basic message. In addition, I'd like to thank David Nicoll, Joel Finlay, and Frances Baldwin for their helpful feedback during the final stages of manuscript review. I'd also like to thank my colleagues and friends, Mike Morris and Roger McAniff, who submitted examples for inclusion. Their stories help bring the book's message to life, and I'm pleased to showcase the work of these dedicated practitioners.

After working on the manuscript for about a year, I reached an impasse. I had gone as far as I could working alone, but needed to do more in order for the book to reach its full potential. That's when I met Bill Gellermann. Initially, I asked Bill to help me increase the book's relevance to OD practitioners, but we quickly established a level of shared purpose that impacted the entire work. Bill's input and suggestions enhanced the basic conceptual framework, added depth to the main points, made the use of terms more consistent, and increased the book's overall readability. There's no way I could acknowledge his contribution adequately by thanking him here. He helped me over my impasse and was involved every step from then to completion, so I have reflected this by indicating on the cover that the book was written *with* Bill Gellermann. I hope that this volume sparks additional interest in the issues raised by Bill and his co-authors in their important book, *Values and Ethics in Organization and Human Systems Development.*

Finally I'd like to thank my wife, Pat, who bears the burden of being married to a writer. Writers must write, but it takes a special spouse to accept this with grace and dignity. She also provided me with many helpful content and editorial suggestions, along with much love and encouragement throughout the writing process.

Balancing Individual and Organizational Values

Part 1
Understanding Values

1

Why Values
Are Important

❶N THIS CHAPTER, I DEFINE THE TERM *VALUE,* describe changes
in OD values from the 1960s to the present, and summarize some recent research
showing a clear relationship between values and organizational success. Following that, I describe how OD practitioners can find common ground regarding values by focusing on the profession's mission and by identifying criteria for assessing
values. I suggest a set of criteria for assessing values (balance, viability, alignment,
and authenticity) and then offer four case studies to demonstrate their relevance.

What Values Are

Understanding values requires us to understand their relationship to needs. Ani-
mals act on instinct, preprogrammed how to respond by nature; people act on free
will, choosing for themselves how to respond. Our choices are based on values,
which are beliefs about what is important in life. A primary function of values is to
meet needs. According to Abraham Maslow (1954), people have physiological,
safety, social, esteem, and self-actualization needs. These needs are reflected in such

values as "survival," "security," "belonging," "esteem," and "personal growth." Maslow maintains that once people's basic needs (physiological, safety, and social) are met, they focus on their higher-level needs (esteem and self-actualization). Attempting to meet needs brings us face-to-face with the dilemma of choice. This requires us to step into the future, where risk is associated with everything we do. No matter how carefully we plan, we're always aware that things can go wrong.

This dilemma places us between two sets of forces: those pulling toward safety and those pushing toward growth and development. Harrison (1969) described this as a struggle between the need for defenses (security) and the need to know (growth). How people resolve this dilemma depends on their values. Values shape people's preferred ways of satisfying their needs and, whether they're aware of it or not, every action is guided by one or more values. Maslow (1968) distinguished three types of values: *growth values,* *"coasting" values* (healthy regression), and *defensive values* (unhealthy regression). He maintained that people have a natural desire for growth, but they need homeostatic values for peace, rest, and relaxation. He asserted that more mature and healthy people place greater emphasis on growth, but that "coasting" values are always necessary. Defensive values protect against pain, fear, loss, and threat, but they can significantly inhibit growth.

Milton Rokeach (1973) also discussed the relationship between values and needs. He said, "Values are the cognitive representations and transformations of needs, and man is the only animal capable of such representations and transformations" (p. 20). He defined a value and value system this way:

> "A *value* is an enduring belief that a specific mode of conduct or end-state of existence is personally or socially preferable to an opposite or converse mode of conduct or end-state of existence. A *value system* is an enduring organization of beliefs concerning preferable modes of conduct or end-states of existence along a continuum of relative importance." (1973, p.5)

Once embraced, values become our standards of importance (Gellermann, Frankel, & Ladenson, 1990). They also serve as criteria for making decisions and setting priorities and lie behind the explanations and justifications we give for our actions. Without the capacity to formulate and act on values, life on the human level would not exist.

Rokeach (1973) distinguished between *terminal values* (such as world peace, wisdom, and happiness), which are preferred end-states of existence, and *instrumen-*

tal values (such as responsibility, cooperation, and customer service), which are preferred modes of conduct. This distinction is important because it addresses two major questions in life: "What do I want to achieve?" and "How do I want to achieve it?"

Instrumental values focus on either *competence*, which has to do with one's ability, or *integrity*, which has to do with one's character. Values in the latter category (such as honesty, justice, and mercy) are based on ethics and morals. Ethics are standards of good/bad or right/wrong behavior (for example, "Do unto others as you would have them do unto you"), and morals are standards for avoiding or minimizing harmful or bad/wrong behavior (for example, "Do not kill"). Thus, a moral is also an ethic, but not all ethics are morals.

Values perform three primary functions: *defending against perceived threat, adjusting to society*, and *fostering growth*. All three functions are essential. Maslow said that safety is a *sine qua non* precondition for growth, but their relative emphasis and the particular values people embrace to meet their needs are what account for the wide diversity of human behavior. As we will see later, these factors are not only relevant for individuals, but also for interpersonal relationships, teams, and organizations.

Rokeach's definition of values is important conceptually here, but one qualification must be added at the outset. When we think about our values, we can say we prefer one thing over another, for example, honesty over dishonesty. We can even feel strongly for honesty and strongly against dishonesty. The reality is, however, that no one is 100 percent honest. In actual practice, therefore, values are continuous variables, not either/or choices. What's more, dualistic, black-and-white thinking is one of the primary symptoms of defensive values, a subject that will be discussed in Chapter 3. At any point in time, behaviorally we're somewhere between the two poles defined as honest and dishonest. Honesty and all other values are ideals we believe are worth striving for, not states of grace fully embodied.

Finally, values are psychological constructs. They are internal to a person. Organizations as such don't have values but, because they are composed of human beings, their cultures are shaped by values. The values of persons shape organizational behavior and the direction taken by organizations. These values must be largely shared in order for an organization to forge a direction leading to success. Without a reasonably high degree of shared values, organizations and the people in them flounder and fail. For this reason, an understanding of values on the individual, team, and organizational level is crucial to the effectiveness of all OD activity.

OD Values

Nothing was said above about the merits of particular values. However, OD as a profession was founded on a shared set of beliefs and values. First, some background. Tension between individuals and organizations is inevitable and has always existed. The values of organizations and their members are not always in alignment. There's nothing new or shocking about this. During the Industrial Revolution, low wages and poor working conditions kept employees struggling to meet basic needs and created adversarial relationships between labor and management. Many managers perceived laborers as irresponsible slackers who had to be forced to work and used this to justify bureaucratic controls and rigid structures. Organizations functioned a lot like prisons, with managers acting like guards and employees serving time as inmates. Meanwhile, employees placed a high emphasis on security, so they tolerated these conditions.

With the gradual shift to a service economy, the average level of education increased and people enjoyed a higher standard of living. This freed them to focus more on their social, esteem, and self-actualization needs. At the same time, behavioral scientists began challenging some of the underlying assumptions about workers and the oppressive practices stemming from those assumptions. They asserted that people have an intrinsic desire to work, but that certain conditions are necessary to nurture this desire. These conditions, such as psychological safety, trust, and healthy interpersonal relationships, focused attention on group dynamics and organizational culture. Approaches such as sensitivity training (T-groups) were developed to help people assess and change values, beliefs, and behavior, and the field of organization development (OD) was born.

At its beginning, OD was grounded in humanistic values and in the belief that people should have opportunities to develop their full potential. Warren Bennis (1969) said that the basic value underlying OD is *choice.* Organization development interventions were intended to produce a healthier balance between the needs of organizations and the needs of individuals. In a widely reprinted article, Tannenbaum and Davis (1969) described how such balance could be better achieved by moving away from organizational norms based on the bureaucratic model toward norms based on humanistic values. They outlined their preferences for change in twelve norms; in each instance the change is away from what Maslow would identify as defensiveness and toward growth.

In an effort to make the founding values explicit, Warner Burke (1998) summarized them as follows:

- *Human Development.* People in organizations should have opportunities to learn and grow.

- *Fairness.* People in organizations should be treated equitably, with dignity, and without discrimination.

- *Openness.* People in organizations should communicate with one another in a forthright and honest manner.

- *Choice.* People in organizations should not be subject to coercion and the arbitrary use of power and authority.

- *Balance of Autonomy and Constraint.* People in organizations should have sufficient freedom to perform their work responsibilities as they see fit, yet must also support the organization and from time to time conform to organizational demands for the good of the whole. (1998, p. 3–4)

Table 1.1 (see page 8) organizes the norms suggested by Tannenbaum and Davis under the values suggested by Burke. The norms help operationally define the initial OD value system.

During the 1960s and 1970s, working conditions were greatly improved. With the advent of globalization, however, aggressive new companies introduced better products, faster and cheaper. Caught by surprise, many industrial giants struggled to survive, leading to radical changes in beliefs, values, and behaviors—a *paradigm shift.* Massive downsizing and restructuring efforts were initiated, and organizations began backsliding into the behaviors that Tannenbaum and Davis challenged us to move away from. The focus of OD practitioners also began shifting away from improving the quality of work life toward a focus on efficiency, productivity, and profitability (Nicoll, 1998).

These changes have created an identity crisis within the profession, intensified by a generation gap between older practitioners and younger people coming into the field. Warner Burke told me that back in the 1960s OD practitioners were mission-driven—they believed they could change the world, and they still do. In contrast, he said that younger practitioners appear to be more career-oriented. This

Table 1.1. Synthesis of Burke's Values and Tannenbaum and Davis' Norms

Burke's Values ⇓	Tannenbaum and Davis' Norms	
	Away from ←	→ **Toward**
Human Development	Viewing individuals as fixed	Viewing individuals as being in process
Fairness	Avoidance or negative evaluation of individuals	Confirming individuals as human beings
	Resisting and fearing individual differences	Accepting and utilizing individual differences
	Mistrusting people	Trusting people
Openness	Suppression of feelings	Making the expression of feelings appropriate and effective
	Maskmanship and game playing	Authentic behavior
	Avoiding facing others with relevant data	Making appropriate confrontation
	Viewing process work as being unproductive effort	Viewing process work as essential to effective task accomplishment*
Choice	Viewing an individual within the confines of a job description	Viewing an individual as a whole person
	Avoidance of risk taking	Willingness to risk
Balance of Autonomy and Constraint	Using status to maintain power and personal prestige	Using status for organizationally relevant purposes
	Emphasizing competition	Emphasizing collaboration

Note: In this context, process work refers to interpersonal and intergroup processes, not quality improvement or reengineering initiatives.

isn't surprising, however, because the 1960s was an age of idealism, characterized by tremendous social change, while the present age is one of realism and pragmatism. One generation isn't "right" and the other one "wrong." They're just different. Every generation programs a different set of values, a base of larger social, cultural, and economic forces. The culture of the 1960s was more open to sensitivity training; today's culture is more open to global enterprise.

Nevertheless, the generation gap in OD has become polarized and heated. Some older practitioners accuse younger people of lacking concern for individuals, and even "sleeping with the enemy" in order to advance self-serving interests. For example, Schaef and Fassel (1988) claim that many of the processes in organizations today represent addictive behavior disguised as corporate structure and function. They assert that organizations are able to maintain such practices through the same mechanism that addicts use to avoid looking at themselves honestly—denial. In relating this to OD, they say, "These two tendencies—to deny the presence of the effect of addictions and to see addictive behavior and processes as normal—have also been true in the field of organizational development and in the process of organizational consultation" (p. 5). While Schaef and Fassel did not draw distinctions between veteran and younger OD practitioners, their comments clearly reflect the identity crisis within the field (see also, Church, Burke, & Van Eynde, 1994).

Similarly, David Nicoll (1998) warned that OD professionals have drifted away from the humanistic, democratic, and developmental values that defined their essence, and challenged them to return to these roots. He said, "If we think organizations are unhealthy places in which to work, if we see dysfunctionalities and double binds inside the systems to which we consult, if we are aware of structures and procedures that limit, constrain, and misshape people, then we probably will want to take a clear look at our value system and figure out just exactly what it is we do believe. Just exactly what it is that we, as a profession, want to stand for" (p. 7).

Conversely, some younger practitioners accuse veterans of not understanding what it takes for modern organizations to survive and of resisting change. They claim that veteran practitioners long for "the good old days" and are out of touch with current reality. While finger pointing risks dividing practitioners into camps, I believe that the apparent generation gap is actually symptomatic of the timeless and inevitable tension between individuals and organizations—the yin and the yang.

Not Either-Or, But Both-And

To begin with, it isn't either-or, *either* what's good for the organization *or* what's good for people. No one honestly believes that organizations can be successful today by ignoring people. Even if they did, research evidence to the contrary is overwhelming. Consider the following research-based conclusions:

- *Profits are higher when personal and organizational values are aligned.* A Gallup poll found that organizations had higher profits when workers believed (1) they have a chance to do what they do best each day, (2) their opinions matter, (3) their fellow workers care about quality, and (4) a connection exists between their work and the company's mission (Grant, 1998). *Thus, employees perform much better when organizational values are aligned with their personal values.*

- *Values for trust and camaraderie increase shareholder value.* Levering and Moskowitz (2000) reported that shares of fifty-eight publicly traded companies emphasizing such values as trust, pride, and camaraderie rose 37 percent annualized over the last three years, as compared to 25 percent for the S & P 500.

- *Companies with an enduring core ideology outperform the stock market; also, superior market performance is possible without making profit a primary value.* Collins and Porras (1994) found that companies possessing a rock-solid core ideology (purpose and values) outperformed companies that did not by a factor of 6 and outperformed the stock market by a factor of 15. They concluded that making profit a primary value was not necessary for superior market performance in the long run.

- *Firms that consider the interests of employees, customers, and stockholders greatly outperform those that do not.* Research by Kotter and Heskett (1992) found that revenues for firms with cultural values emphasizing the legitimate interests of employees, customers, and stockholders and encouraging leadership at all organizational levels increased by an average of 682 percent over an eleven-year period, as compared to 166 percent for firms that did not have those values.

- *Organization change efforts fail when culture is ignored.* Cameron and Quinn (1999, p. 1) reported that "as many as three quarters of reengineering, total quality management (TQM), strategic planning, and downsizing efforts have failed entirely or have created problems serious enough that the survival of the organizations was threatened. Several studies reported that the most frequently cited reason given for failure was a neglect of the organization's culture. In other words, failure to change the organization's culture doomed the other kinds of organizational changes that were initiated."

- *Values-based leadership increases job satisfaction and bottom-line performance.* Data from twenty-five thousand employees collected by Wilson Learning Corporation found that 69 percent of employee job satisfaction stemmed from the leadership skills of managers, and that 39 percent of bottom-line performance can be attributed to employee satisfaction (Leimbach, 1994). Essentially, leadership skills are values put into action.

Findings such as these suggest that managers who focus primarily on the bottom line and ignore other values do so at their peril. The reality is that, to remain competitive, organizations have to be innovative in caring about people as well as caring about income, cost, and profits—both-and rather than either-or. The demand for qualified workers in many fields far outstrips supply. In a buyers' market, if employees don't like the way they're treated, they can move to organizations that have values more closely aligned with their own.

By the same token, no one honestly believes that we can focus on people and ignore organizations. The view that older practitioners care more about individuals and younger practitioners care more about organizations is an oversimplification. For example, Church, Burke, and Van Eynde (1994) found that, while OD practitioners had indeed become more oriented to results and the bottom-line in a drive to meet quarterly earnings statements, when asked about their "ideal" motives, they said they were more interested in social action and helping people. I suspect that most younger practitioners are concerned about individuals, but convincing busy managers that they need to pay attention to values has become more challenging. This is an issue we must all address. A veteran colleague told me that he'd never find any work if he appealed to values at the beginning. However, he said that, after showing managers how they can improve results, the door is then open to discussing values.

The identity crisis in OD can be resolved, or at least managed, by looking for common ground. After all, OD practitioners help people in organizations do this all the time; now it's time to walk our talk. Conflict resolution through rational means is one of OD's earliest values (see Schein & Bennis, 1965). We're not going to get anywhere if veterans tell younger practitioners that they should embrace humanistic or person-centered values and younger practitioners tell veterans that they should value efficiency and profitability. As soon as the word *should* is invoked, defenses go up and dialogue shuts down.

Nevertheless, it's important to remember that OD is not value-free (Burke, 1982). Even when practitioners choose to function only as facilitators and avoid advocating specific directions for change—this is referred to as the *contingent* approach—they are making a value decision. Those who *only* ask questions are still guiding their processes, consciously or unconsciously, by the questions they ask. There's no such thing as a *neutral* question. Even if there were, you cannot control how it will be perceived. Consequently, the profession cannot avoid the issue of ethics and morals. In my experience, people's clarity about their standards (values, ethics, and morals) ranges from high to low, and people with low clarity are particularly vulnerable to rationalizing their actions based on narrowly defined self-interest, that is, using reason to give the illusion that they are doing the "right" thing. Acting based on high clarity and conviction means applying one's standards consistently across situations without rationalization. In contrast, low clarity and low conviction tend to result in rationalization and situational ethics; that is, one's standards vary in reaction to one's situation. When a person's ethics are totally dependent on the situation, he or she is like a ship without a rudder or, even better, like a captain without a compass.

People with high clarity do what they believe is good or right and avoid what is bad or wrong ("I think this is unethical and I'm not going to do it"); people with low clarity do what's convenient at the time ("What other choice did I have?"). In all relationships, people try to "read" others to determine "where they're coming from." If you're a person of clarity and conviction, I might not agree with you, but I can trust you to act with integrity; if your clarity and conviction are low, I'd have trouble trusting you.

Toward Common Ground

Because the actions of OD practitioners impact human lives for better or for worse, I believe we have an ethical and moral responsibility to be persons of clarity and conviction. A good starting point for building common ground is to focus on OD's mission, which is working for balance between the individual and the organization for their mutual benefit, rather than debating the merits of particular instrumental values. People are fickle; words to describe specific values go in and out of favor. So, while younger people might not relate to terms like "humanistic" or "person-centered," they will probably relate to learning, empowerment, and collaboration. Instead of getting hung up on words, therefore, the important question is, "What is the purpose or mission of OD and how can we serve it?" In this regard, Gellermann, Frankel, and Ladenson (1990, p. 327) quoted Peter Block as saying, "Dialogue about values and ethics is important, but it requires a context of common purpose to give it meaning."

A mission for the profession is cited at the beginning of the "Organization and Human Systems Development Credo," a statement developed beginning in the early 1980s with input from more than six hundred OD professionals in more than twenty-five countries. It has been endorsed as a "working statement" by leading professionals, including Robert Tannenbaum and Richard Beckhard. It reads, "Our purpose as professionals is to facilitate processes by which human beings and human systems live and work together for their mutual benefit and mutual well-being." (See the Appendix or www.odnetwork.org/credo.html.) That mutuality is even reflected in the term "organization development," where "development" emphasizes growth by people, and "organization" places the development within a specific context. When in doubt, go back to purpose.

The Credo also identifies a variety of values and ethics that OD professionals can use as a guide to clarifying their own standards. For example, *values* include "respect for human dignity, integrity, and worth," "freedom, choice, and responsibility," and "justice and fundamental human rights"; *ethics* include "acting with integrity and being true to ourselves" and "accepting responsibility for acting with sensitivity to the fact that our recommendations and actions may alter the lives and well-being of people within our client systems and within the larger systems of which they are sub-systems." (See the Appendix for the entire Credo.)

Advocating balance between individuals and organizations is a *normative* approach to OD, in contrast to the *contingent* approach, where there is no advocacy. Establishing and maintaining such a balance is a process of continuous improvement, which is precisely why a field like OD is necessary. Prior to the 1960s, the pendulum was overbalanced on the organizational side, and early practitioners helped organizations shift it back in the other direction. In some instances, the balance may have even shifted too far toward the individual. Many practitioners who have backgrounds in the behavioral sciences, as I do, have a bias toward the individual, so we must make a conscious effort to remember organizational interests.

Nevertheless, in the current business environment, the pendulum has once again shifted back toward organizations, resulting in a new round of issues impacting individuals. Here are some examples:

- After organizations downsize, remaining employees are pressured to do the work of those who have departed without additional compensation, creating new personal and financial pressures.

- Many downsized middle-aged managers have become unemployable, or can only find work at greatly reduced wages, causing many personal and financial problems.

- Although we've enjoyed a full-employment economy for over a decade, wages for the average worker have not risen, and in many cases have declined. Some workers must hold down two or even three jobs to make what they consider a decent living.

- Gender inequity in pay is still alive and well in many organizations.

- A feeling of expendability pervades the workplace. Many employees are afraid to speak out against organizational practices for fear of losing their jobs.

The fact is that organizations won't be successful in the long term if they allow such practices to continue (Collins & Porras, 1994). Practices that harm or alienate people lower morale and productivity. They also prevent shared values from emerging, and shared values are necessary to bring about alignment toward vision. Gelinas and James (1998, p. 9) framed the challenge this way: "The question is how can organizations generate profits in a way which both sustains and nurtures the humanity and goodness of people in the organization and considers the health and survival of the planet."

Inwardly, managers know they need to pay attention to people, but in the daily rush they forget or they don't know how. It's up to us to remind them or develop them. Even if they don't want to do this based on values, they have no choice if they want to achieve good business results. It would be unethical, then, for OD practitioners not to warn them about the potential negative consequences of their decisions. Failure to do so would violate their profession's mission, which is to promote practices serving the interests of both people *and* organizations. This would be like an accounting firm colluding with their change management brethren to make the change interventions look better than they really are.

You can't make people change their values, but you can help them see the wisdom of changing their behavior. As the civil rights movement showed, behavior change can eventually lead to changes in beliefs, attitudes, and values. So, if the behavioral outcomes of OD practices serve to bring better balance between individuals and organizations, they will be furthering humanistic and person-centered values, even if we don't call it that. With an eye on OD's mission, therefore, some key questions for OD professionals to ask themselves when working with organizations are:

- What impact do OD practices have on individuals? What are the consequences of these practices?
- What impact will OD practices have on the organization's long-range success?
- How can better balance between individuals and the organization be established and maintained?

By focusing on questions such as these, I'm confident that the generation gap in the profession can be bridged. The profession cannot ignore this issue without losing credibility in the eyes of its clients.

Assessing Values

In addition to a focus on mission, another way to build common ground is to specify objective criteria for assessing values. I offer four such criteria: *balance, viability, alignment,* and *authenticity,* presented in this book to stimulate discussion and possible research. I define them as follows:

- *Balance*—the degree to which values are given proper emphasis relative to one another.
- *Viability*—the degree to which values are workable in the current business climate.
- *Alignment*—the degree to which compatibility exists among an individual's values, or among the values of individuals, teams, and the overall organization.
- *Authenticity*—the degree to which values are used in a genuine, sincere manner.

In one way or another, all four criteria impact the relationship between individuals and organizations. As shown in Figure 1.1, each criterion can be placed on a scale extending from ineffective to effective. In this context, *effective* means ability to obtain desired results. Taken together, these scales can be used to assess the values of an individual, team, or organization, identifying strengths and developmental needs. Detailed descriptions of the criteria are provided in Chapter 5.

Figure 1.1. Ineffective and Effective Values

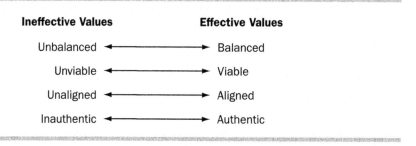

Ineffective Values	Effective Values
Unbalanced	Balanced
Unviable	Viable
Unaligned	Aligned
Inauthentic	Authentic

As a way of introducing the criteria and to show the power of values, it will help to examine four critical incidents where organizations attempted to implement change without considering important values issues. The incidents will be debriefed in terms of the four value scales discussed above. The Values Assessment Inventory (VAI), included in Chapter 5, measures values according to these criteria.

Company A: Unbalanced Values

Company A is a large international management consulting firm with offices located throughout the world. During the 1970s and 1980s, the company expanded rapidly, due to its expertise in helping organizations to restructure after downsizing and implement quality improvement programs. As client organizations became leaner and more efficient, however, Company A experienced a business decline in the early 1990s. After downsizing a quarter of the consultants, the president informed the remaining employees that the company would need to reinvent itself to survive. He said another layoff was likely, but there would always be a place for those who could develop new accounts and who were willing to "go the extra mile."

This meeting struck fear in the attendees, who were experiencing layoff survivor sickness due to the recent downsizing. One veteran consultant remarked, "We help other organizations deal with situations like this all the time with minimum disruption, but when it comes to us they just bring out the machine gun." Over the next few months, consultants worked feverishly to generate new business. While a great deal of camaraderie had existed among them in the past, the new pressures created a climate of internal competition and mistrust. Consultants accused each other of stealing clients and using underhanded tactics. As work demands and pressure continued to mount, one by one the most talented consultants began leaving to start their own businesses or work for other firms. During an exit interview, one of them commented, "The work and travel demands in this field have always been insane, but I'm not going to sacrifice my marriage and health for this business." Another one said bitterly, "I spent many hours nursing a very delicate account over a six-month period, only to have a colleague undercut me to save his own ass."

Alarmed by the exodus of key people, the president administered the Values Assessment Inventory (VAI) the results of which, as shown in Figure 1.2, revealed a lack of balance among the company's values and an inauthentic atmosphere. He knew he needed to act quickly to keep the situation from deteriorating further.

Figure 1.2. Company A Assessment

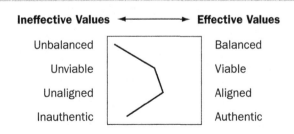

Company B: Unviable Values

Company B is a large manufacturing organization specializing in sophisticated weapon systems for warships. The company came into prominence during World War I and grew rapidly during World War II and the Vietnam Era. When the Cold War ended, the company avoided the massive downsizing other defense contractors experienced by successfully shifting its emphasis from surface vessels to submarines. Also, the company was able to successfully apply its technology to a variety of civilian markets. One insider said with pride, "We bet the farm on these changes and won!"

Over the years, the company built an elaborate hierarchical structure with many layers of management, purportedly to deal with all the checks and balances required by federal agencies. While this slowed the decision-making process considerably, steady revenue growth and minimal competition removed any incentive to change.

In the early 1990s, however, internal and external conditions began catching up to Company B. The organization had experienced minimal turnover in the past, but most of its key managers were well-entrenched Baby Boomers nearing retirement. Also the market was shifting away from conventional weapons systems to laser technology, an area in which the company lacked expertise. After top management decided to enter this market, they hired a group of young, highly educated engineers and scientists. This new crop of creative Generation-Xers had the raw talent and creative zest to make Company B a leader in the emerging laser industry, but many felt stifled by the bureaucracy and slow decision-making process. They clashed with the Baby Boomers who dominated the management structure, whom they viewed as resisting change. Meanwhile, the Baby Boomers complained that their experience wasn't being respected. Some of the most promising younger workers began leaving for start-up companies on the cutting edge of the laser field. When giving his notice, one said, "I didn't get a Ph.D. to sit on my hands and watch a dinosaur die!"

At the same time that the plan for expanding into the laser field was unraveling, competition for Company B's bread and butter products began heating up, and it was losing market share to leaner, far nimbler organizations. Values Assessment Inventory results, shown in Figure 1.3, revealed that Company B's values had become unviable, out of touch with current business realities. The organization needed to reinvent itself quickly or face certain extinction.

Figure 1.3. Company B Assessment

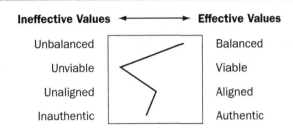

Ineffective Values ◄─────► Effective Values

Unbalanced	Balanced
Unviable	Viable
Unaligned	Aligned
Inauthentic	Authentic

Company C: Unaligned Values

Company C was a computer software business on the cutting edge of the booming e-commerce industry. The market for its products and services had grown so rapidly during its first five years that many aspects of its infrastructure had been simply placed on the back burner. While the company had compensation guidelines and benefits administration, there were, for example, no employee handbooks or new employee orientations. Initially everyone knew everyone else, so personnel issues were handled informally, but now, with over five hundred employees and projections to double in size within three years, this approach became unmanageable. Finally the beleaguered HR manager came to the CEO and said, "We can't just make stuff up as we go along. We'd better get some guidelines fast, or we're a lawsuit waiting to happen."

Alarmed at the situation, the CEO retained an external consultant and took his leadership team on a three-day retreat to carve out a set of company values. This proved to be a very rewarding experience for the participants. Not only did they get to know one another better and build closer working relationships, but they had very dynamic discussions about how they would like to see the company operating as it continued growing. They were unanimous in wanting to preserve the original entrepreneurial spirit, while ensuring that employee issues were handled in a consistent manner. At the end they emerged with a set of five values, which together formed the acronym *focus*. The values were:

F = Fun
O = Optimism
C = Customer-Driven
U = Uniqueness
S = Synergism

The next day the CEO held a company-wide meeting to unveil the new values. While he was very enthusiastic as he described the values and how the team came up with them, there was little reaction from the audience. When someone asked him how they settled on these particular words, the CEO replied, "It was a time of real synergy, as if we were tuned in to the same wave length. It's hard to explain; you just had to be there." As the employees dispersed, they began snickering about the values. Someone asked, "Are we having fun yet?" Several employees laughed, and one of them said, "I'm having fun but not in a unique way." The laughter built as another person added, "I'm having fun now, but I'm not optimistic about it continuing." This attitude quickly became infectious; soon no one could talk about the values and keep a straight face.

The CEO was stunned by this reaction and asked to speak to the consultant, who reminded him of the discussion at the retreat on building alignment. He admitted that in all the excitement he had neglected to do this. "I was so sure they'd catch our vision," he said in disbelief. "Now I've got egg all over my face." They agreed that the consultant would administer the Values Assessment Inventory to the entire workforce and, sure enough, the results, shown in Figure 1.4, revealed a lack of alignment with company values. As the CEO reviewed the results, he started piecing together a plan to correct the damage his oversight had caused.

Figure 1.4. Company C Assessment

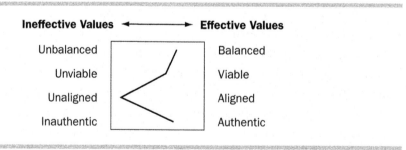

Company D: Inauthentic Values

Company D is a large construction company specializing in office buildings and shopping malls. The company was started by an enterprising architect (Mark) who learned how to bid low on contracts, and still make a profit, through the just-in-time coordination of labor, equipment, and material. He developed a reputation for dependability, so his company grew rapidly. He hired his own work crews and bought heavy-duty equipment, allowing him to keep his operating costs below inflation. In between projects, he subcontracted his workers and equipment to other contractors, which enabled him to maintain steady cash flow during periods of economic downturn. Eventually, the business became too large for him to manage by himself, so Mark hired someone to serve as COO (Sam).

Although Mark was a shrewd businessman, he also had excellent people skills. Workers would rise to the occasion to complete jobs because they felt a personal commitment to Mark. In contrast, Sam was a command-and-control type of manager who prided himself on running "a tight ship." Sam used threats to keep people on track, and mistakes were considered "unacceptable." If someone didn't show up at a work site on time, Sam would fire him or her on the spot. He was also openly critical of workers who didn't follow his orders to the letter. Soon the efficient but congenial organization established by Mark was replaced by one of fear and intimidation. Following a series of complaints by employees, customers, and suppliers, Mark realized he had made a mistake and let Sam go.

Mark replaced Sam with Jim, who had a solid reputation as a people-oriented project manager. During his first employee meeting, Jim said he didn't want people to be reluctant to admit mistakes because his emphasis was going to be on learning, not placing blame. As the weeks went by, everyone was polite to Jim, but no one seemed willing to take responsibility for mistakes. Sensing that they might not trust what he said at the employee meeting, Jim had everyone complete the Values Assessment Instrument. Not surprisingly, the results, presented in Figure 1.5, showed a low level of authenticity, and Jim realized that additional steps would be needed to show employees that his values were genuinely different from Sam's.

Figure 1.5. Company D Assessment

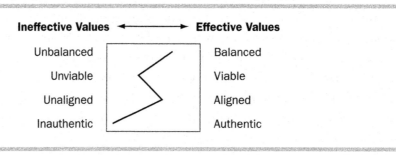

In the next chapter, I introduce the Motivational System Model, which explains the personal, interpersonal, and organizational factors that determine effectiveness. As we shall see, values are a key component of the Motivational System.

② The Motivational System

AT THE BEGINNING OF THIS CHAPTER, I introduce the *Motivational System Model*, which is used throughout the book as a way of thinking about the dynamics of personal, interpersonal, team, and organizational behavior. Following that, I describe some key components of personal motivation: wants and needs; beliefs about self, others, and the external world; and feelings. This provides a foundation for a discussion of the role of values in personality, which is the subject of Chapter 3. I contend that the particular values people choose depend largely on two factors: the degree to which they accept themselves unconditionally and the extent to which they trust others. The Self-Esteem Exercise, which focuses on increasing unconditional self-acceptance, is included at the end of this chapter.

Systems Thinking

As described in Chapter 1, OD's mission is to facilitate processes that serve the balanced interests of individuals and organizations and the larger systems of which they are a part. Doing this requires a systems approach, which is consistent with the OD Network's statement of values: "We demonstrate our appreciation of systems by facilitating connectedness, a holistic approach and community" (see www.odnetwork.org/missionvalues.html). Vaill (1996, p. 109) explained that:

> "Systems thinking is not a reductionistic task through which we search for the one or two factors that 'explain' a phenomenon. Instead, systems thinking asks its practitioner *simultaneously* to hold the whole in mind *and* to investigate the interactions of the component elements of the whole—all the component elements, not just the two or three most obvious and easy to examine—*and* to investigate the relation of the whole to its larger environment."

There are closed and open systems. A closed system is isolated from its environment, while an open system receives inputs from its environment and acts on the environment through outputs. Human systems are open systems; they cannot be understood completely through reductionistic, analytical thinking. Thinking, feeling, and behaving variables all contribute to the motivation of the system. Hallelujah! It isn't necessary to figure out which variables are more important—or even what's a cause and what's an effect. The important thing is to consider them all and to look for their dynamic interconnections. The Motivational System Model does this.

In speaking about organizations, Vaill (1996, p. 109) said, "Because a system is open to its environment, as all human systems are, and because all its internal elements influence each other and the whole in complex and often unpredictable ways, a systems thinker can never know everything there is to know about a system. An open system forever transcends complete understanding." It's foolhardy, therefore, to think you can understand everything there is to know about organizational behavior. The important thing is to find as many ingredients as possible, to understand their dynamics, and to use this knowledge to foster positive change.

The Motivational System Model

Motivation is the energy that moves people to do what they do. It's an expression of our continuing answer to the question, "Why do we do what we do?" The Motivational System Model, depicted in Figure 2.1, will be used throughout this book as a framework for understanding motivation and behavior. It consists of four interrelated loops, focusing on the personal, interpersonal, team, and organizational levels and the larger environmental context within which the four levels function. The larger context, which encompasses everything *outside* impacting the four levels, includes communities, economies, societies, and the world. Each loop contains the following variables: need/want, think, feel, value/decide, and do (adapted from Hultman, 1998a).

Figure 2.1. Motivational System Model

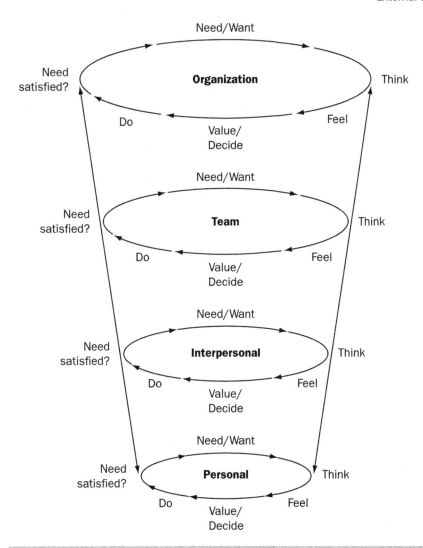

External Environment

Note: The relevant external environment referred to in the model is the system's subjective environment, that is, environment as sensed and perceived. It is not the objective environment, because until environment is sensed and given meaning by perception (based on beliefs and values) it does not "exist" for the Motivational System.

Most definitions of OD concern processes impacting individuals, work groups, and organizations (see, for example, Cummings & Worley, 2000; French & Bell, 1999). Burke (1997) described OD as *inter,* working between people and systems. Argyris (1997) stressed the importance of integrating the individual and the organization. Anderson and Ackerman-Anderson (2001) discussed the importance of focusing on the person and the organization in transformational change.

It is possible to take a detached view and study systems in order to find out how they work, but whether OD practitioners are either internal or external consultants to an organization, they become part of *that* system. Because everything in an organizational system is dynamically interrelated, everything they do has an impact on everything else in one way or another. For this reason, OD practitioners cannot do something that hurts the system or the people in it without hurting themselves.

When discussing the model, I will refer to the personal loop as *personality,* and the interpersonal, team, and organization loops as three levels of organizational *culture.* The four levels become increasingly complex as we move from the personal to the organization. Overall organization culture is the most complex because it includes all the individuals, interpersonal relationships, and teams within a whole organization.

Open systems have a natural tendency toward wholeness or integration, but many factors, such as distorted facts and beliefs, negative feelings, and interpersonal conflict, represent barriers to this. A good way to improve results, therefore, is by identifying and minimizing such barriers so the entire system functions more effectively. This requires an understanding of the personal, interpersonal, team, and organizational loops.

An individual moves around the personal loop thousands or more times a day, usually without awareness of the movement or its underlying motivation. There's constant feedback among the variables as they endeavor to achieve satisfaction. Moreover, because people don't live in a vacuum, complex interrelationships exist among the four loops. They're inextricably linked, representing four interdependent elements of a larger whole. Culture shapes personality; personality shapes culture.

The number of interactions and their complexity increases dramatically as we shift from the personal to the interpersonal and team levels—and becomes incalculable at the organizational level. Knowledge of all variables is necessary to understand the unique role played by values at the personal, interpersonal, team, and whole-system levels of an organization. To be effective, change agents must be able to shift their focus flexibly among the four levels of abstraction.

Let's discuss the first three variables in the personal loop: need/want, think, and feel.

Needing/Wanting

All people have similar kinds of needs and wants; the difference is in how they perceive them and their level of satisfaction. Perceptions are "the way things seem to us," in contrast to "the way they are." Our perceptions guide our thinking, feeling, and valuing, which in turn guide our decisions and doing. The distinction between needing and wanting is useful, because it relates to people's perceptions of why they do what they do. For example, at some level my writing this book may be to satisfy my need for self-actualization, but I perceive myself as *wanting* rather than *needing* to do it.

Abraham Maslow and Milton Rokeach focused primarily on individual needs but their ideas have many implications for interpersonal relationships, teams, and organizations.

As discussed in Chapter 1, Maslow's well-known hierarchy includes physiological, safety, social, esteem, and self-actualization needs. Relatively speaking, physiological and safety needs are being satisfied for most Americans in today's post-modern world, although it is important to recognize that there is still a substantial minority for which this is not true. We are living in the most economically prosperous period in history. As a result, the higher level needs for belonging, esteem, and self-actualization have taken center stage for many organizations. These are the needs those organizations must address effectively in order to achieve and maintain a competitive edge in the new economy.

Richard Barrett (1998, p. 35) spoke about this when he said, "In the next century, the emphasis will be on providing emotional, mental, and spiritual support. People will want to work for organizations that allow them to bring their highest values to work, give them an opportunity to make a positive difference in the world, and encourage them to become all they can become." In other words, people will want satisfaction of their needs for esteem and self-actualization from their work.

This brings us to the important question, "What is our highest need?" Maslow (1968) identified our highest need as self-actualization, becoming everything we can become. Similarly, Rollo May (1967, pp. 81–82) said, "Every organism has one and only one central need in life, to fulfill its own potentialities." I concur with the view. Tension always exists between who we are now and who we're capable of becoming. We can't settle for less than becoming fully ourselves without experiencing frustration and discouragement. How well we succeed at moving toward wholeness and fulfilling our potential, however, largely depends on our sense of self-worth. Let me explain.

As humans, we have the capacity to determine what we value; that is, we can decide what does and does not have *worth* for us. It's part of our essence, the very core of our being. We've all heard stories about people close to death who pulled through because they had unfinished business in their lives. In other words, they had something worth living for, something that gave meaning to their lives, something that gave them the motivation to recover. Viktor Frankl (1963) said this was the key difference between those who did and did not survive the Nazi death camps—they wanted or needed to survive.

The capacity to assign worth is what separates us from other creatures. When you buy something, you choose one product over another because it's worth more to you. You'll even pay more money for something if you view it as having greater worth. More importantly, we assess our own worth as persons; that is, we esteem ourselves. High self-esteem evokes a feeling of hope; low self-esteem evokes a feeling of despair. Everything we do reflects on our sense of worth or self-esteem, one way or another. We seek to validate our worth but, because we can never be sure what's going to happen next, we're also vulnerable to having our self-esteem lowered, particularly by the low esteem others have for us. Consequently, while the need for worth can propel us forward, fear of unworthiness can hold us back.

We pursue self-esteem through the "drive for greatness," which focuses on competence, and the "drive for goodness," which focuses on integrity or character (Rokeach, 1964). To have worth, therefore, people must believe that they are both competent and ethical. Whenever people show exceptional talent in a particular area—athletes are a good example—the next thing others wonder about is their character. Competence and integrity have both a personal and social dimension, allowing us to distinguish four sub-needs that are instrumental to validating our worth: *mastery, a sense of contribution, self-respect*, and *acceptance*. These needs, depicted in Figure 2.2, are described below.

Although I will describe each of these needs separately, it is important to maintain a holistic perspective. They all exert themselves more or less simultaneously, and complex dynamical interactions exist among them.

Figure 2.2. Personal and Social Needs

	Personal	Social
Competence "Abilities"	Mastery	Contribution
	Self-Esteem	
Integrity "Character"	Self-Respect	Acceptance

Mastery (Personal Competence)

People need to view themselves and be viewed by others as being skilled, knowledgeable, and capable. McClelland, Atkinson, Clark, and Lowell (1953) described this as the need for achievement. Frederick Herzberg (1966) identified achievement, responsibility, advancement, and the work itself as four of the five job "satisfiers," all of which are indicators of one's personal competence. Falling short of one's standards for mastery is accompanied by feelings of shame about personal inadequacy.

In addition, every attempt to accomplish something carries with it the possibility of falling short. Consequently, while people have a desire for success, they also contend with fear of failure. May (1967) observed that people would feel as though they no longer existed as persons if their status as a wage earner were threatened. Recently I heard someone reporting the results of a poll say that most men would rather be dead than unemployed. How we orient ourselves to failure plays a key role in how we view our competence and our overall sense of worth.

A Sense of Contribution (Social Competence)

People need to view themselves and be viewed by others as making a contribution—to other individuals, to the team/organization, and to the larger society. People not only need to feel that they've done a good job, but also that their work is important. Herzberg (1966) cited recognition for achievement as the fifth of the job satisfiers; it is an indication that one's efforts make a difference. Hackman and Oldham (1975) asserted that worker satisfaction is a function of (1) the meaningfulness of the work, (2) responsibility for the work and its outcomes, and (3) knowledge of results. Ellinor and Gerard (1998, p. 16) said, "Everyone who works as part of an organization or team today needs to feel how what they do is making a difference to the whole." They went on to say, "When people share in responsibility, they know they make a difference, they participate more creatively, and they have a higher degree of investment in the outcome" (p. 191). While people have a need for contribution, they also have fears that their efforts might not amount to anything significant.

Every book I've read on leadership and change in the past five years has stressed the importance of this need. People with a sense of contribution have higher morale and are more productive than people lacking this. Feeling that your work isn't important can destroy motivation.

Self-Respect (Personal Integrity)

Self-respect has to do with personal character, which relates to ethics and morals. In Chapter 1, ethics were defined as standards of good and bad behavior, such as "tell the truth" and the "Golden Rule," morals were defined as standards of avoiding or minimizing bad behavior, such as "don't lie" and "do no harm." Ethics and morals are standards of behavior based on values.

People need to view themselves as being ethical and moral. Applying the same ethical and moral standards across situations provides people with a basis for self-respect. It also frees them from the need or desire to live up to others' expectations. In contrast, violating one's ethical and moral standards lowers one's self-respect and evokes feelings of guilt.

Self-respect has a social component, because ethical and moral standards are developed during socialization. It's also social in the sense that it's difficult to maintain an image of ourselves as having strong character unless others view us this way. People are afraid of being judged by others as being unethical or immoral. One of the most threatening things you can do to people is attack their character.

Nevertheless, self-respect is primarily personal because, after the standards are internalized, they shape our view of ourselves as ethical and moral beings.

Acceptance (Social Integrity)

People also have a need to be accepted by others. McClelland (1953) discussed this as the need for *affiliation*, while Maslow (1968) referred to it as the need for *belonging*. People can pursue this need in healthy or unhealthy ways. Jerry Harvey (1988) maintained that we seek attachment and fear separation from others. Those with high self-esteem generally have a lower need for others' approval, but they still need a sense of belonging. They are freer psychologically to reach out to others in positive and constructive ways. In contrast, those with low self-esteem often become dependent on others' approval to compensate for perceived inadequacy. They tend to be held back in relationships by fear of rejection or feelings of inferiority. (I will have more to say about this in the section on thinking.) It's not uncommon for people to leave organizations because they don't feel accepted, and this is frequently an underlying reason for morale problems.

You can assess the extent to which these four important needs are being met in your work life by completing the Personal and Social Needs Check-Up in Exhibit 2.1.

Exhibit 2.1. Personal and Social Needs Check-Up

Mastery (Personal Competence)

What am I doing now to satisfy this need?

What else could I do?

A Sense of Contribution (Social Competence)

What am I doing now to satisfy this need?

What else could I do?

Exhibit 2.1. Personal and Social Needs Check-Up, Cont'd

Self-Respect (Personal Integrity)

What am I doing now to satisfy this need?

What else could I do?

Acceptance (Social Integrity)

What am I doing now to satisfy this need?

What else could I do?

Thinking

We don't act on reality, but rather on our perception of it, that is, the way things *seem* to us. We take in information through our five senses—and sometimes a "sixth sense" called *intuition* or *spirit*—and then process it, that is, think about it. The two major aspects of thinking are facts and beliefs. Facts are *objective* realities that can be proven with evidence, whereas beliefs are *subjective* assumptions, conclusions, and predictions.

Our effectiveness in life and at work depends greatly on gathering relevant facts and formulating accurate, reality-based beliefs and systems of beliefs. This is especially true in the networked economy because there's so much more information to process—and a lot of it becomes obsolete in a short period of time. Also, many situations require the ability to comprehend a "whole system." Consequently, people must be able to differentiate the forest from the trees, synthesize information, and look for connections among seemingly unrelated pieces of information.

Three types of beliefs are especially important in determining how we go about meeting our needs and, ultimately, the effectiveness of our values and behavior: beliefs about ourselves, beliefs about other people, and beliefs about the external world. Let's discuss the three types.

Beliefs About Self

Self-esteem can be placed on a continuum, extending from completely conditional at one end to completely unconditional at the other. People at the conditional end compare themselves to some standard or to other people and use this as a measuring stick to judge their worth. Cultural conditioning reinforces conditional self-esteem. From the time children are very young, they're rewarded for their performance and/or personal characteristics. Rarely are children prized for themselves as persons.

This attitude carries over into adulthood and the workplace as people strive for status, recognition, and money to compensate for perceived deficiencies. Peter Senge (1990, p. 156) said, "Most of us hold one of two contradictory beliefs that limit our ability to create what we really want. The most common belief is in our powerlessness—our inability to bring into being all the things we really care about. The other belief centers on unworthiness—that we do not deserve to have what we truly desire."

People with conditional self-esteem are constantly trying to prove their value as human beings, but they can never quite seem to get enough evidence. Because their worth as persons is always on the line, their estimation of themselves rises and falls based on their perception of circumstances. They also tend to be tense and defensive, waiting for the other shoe to drop. Some struggle with feelings of inferiority, while others project themselves as superior in order to hide from underlying feelings of inadequacy. May (1967, pp. 84–85) said, "Self-inflation and conceit are generally the external signs of inner emptiness and self-doubt; a show of pride is one of the most common covers for anxiety."

People with conditional self-esteem frequently have relationship problems. On the one hand they crave approval and validation from others, but they're also sensitive to disapproval and criticism, which makes it difficult for them to receive corrective feedback. They're intimidated by people they view as better than themselves. One way for them to feel more adequate is by putting others down, a practice used in all the organizations I've worked with.

In contrast, people at the unconditional end of the continuum keep their self-esteem separate from their performance and/or personal characteristics, so it remains steady and independent of circumstances. They choose to accept themselves with all of their strengths and weaknesses. Instead of using judgmental terms such as success and failure, they focus on learning. They want to be accepted by others in order to enjoy positive working relationships, but they do not need it to validate their worth. And, because they're not threatened by others' successes, they're more open and self-disclosing, that is, more authentic.

Life presents many opportunities to feel diminished as a person, especially in today's world, which is becoming increasingly impersonal. It takes courage, therefore, to accept yourself as a person. Tillich (1952) defined courage as affirming yourself in spite of disaffirming experiences. People tend to move from an external to an internal focus of self-evaluation as they mature, and many people find a sense of personal worth through their spiritual beliefs, but I've never met anyone who has attained completely unconditional self-esteem. A word of clarification is needed here. Truly unconditional self-esteem is not vulnerable to diminution based on conditions. It involves a shift in kind of self-esteem, not a shift in degree. Although I know people whose self-esteem is high, I know of no one whose self-esteem is truly unconditional. When I use the term "unconditional self-esteem," therefore, I am referring to the developmental process of moving toward this shift in kind of self-esteem.

In addition, self-esteem is dynamic, not static. Even people with strong self-esteem are vulnerable to slipping back. One colleague told me, "Sometimes we leak and need refilling." When dealing with setbacks and failures, I've heard some very bright and successful people say, "I guess this means I'm no good" or "I feel so worthless." That doesn't mean they are "no good" or "worthless," but that is how they feel. It's very important to identify and eliminate beliefs that keep self-esteem conditional because these serve as barriers to effectiveness and success. Some ways to do this include the following:

- Shift from negative self-talk, such as criticizing yourself or putting yourself down, to positive self-talk.

- Don't expect yourself to do the impossible.

- Talk to yourself the way you would to someone coming to you for encouragement.

- Learn from mistakes and then put them behind you.
- Give yourself the benefit of the doubt.
- Remind yourself that you're a "work in progress," and that tomorrow is another day.
- Focus on your strengths instead of dwelling on your weaknesses.
- Celebrate your victories.
- Reflect on past successes.
- Reaffirm that you're a person of value, in spite of life's inevitable ups and downs.
- Keep your eye on your goals, and never give up.
- Remember that you're here for a reason and that you have a lot to offer the world.

For more information on self-talk, I recommend two books: *The Self-Talk Solution* and *What to Say When You Talk to Yourself*, both by Shad Helmstetter.

Beliefs About Others

We not only judge our own worth but also the worth of others. Our beliefs about others, which stem from personal experiences and cultural conditioning, have a tremendous impact on how we relate to them. The first belief we form about people is whether or not they can be trusted. Eric Erikson (1959) described the first development task of childhood as "trust versus mistrust" and said that basic trust is necessary for a healthy personality. He went on to say, "In *adults* the impairment of basic trust is expressed in a *basic mistrust.* It characterizes individuals who withdraw into themselves in particular ways when at odds with themselves and with others" (p. 55). Trust provides a foundation for healthy relationships, while mistrust leads to suspicion and defensive posturing.

Some authors define fear as the opposite of trust (see, for example, Gibb, 1978). I see trust as both a belief and a value, while seeing fear as an emotion. As a belief, trust represents people's views about whether or not others have their best interests at heart. An affirmative answer allows people to feel safe around others; a negative answer evokes feelings of fear. While mistrust is one of the primary causes of fear, as noted above, fear can be triggered by a wide range of beliefs. As a value, trust represents a belief in the importance of being consistent and sincere in relationships.

Negative beliefs about others make it difficult to accept them as persons. There's also a relationship between self-acceptance and accepting others. People who accept themselves are freer to accept others. Because they aren't preoccupied with proving their own worth, it's easier for them to affirm others and to show empathy and compassion, which are essential leadership qualities (Jaworski, 1996).

The degree to which people accept themselves unconditionally has an impact on team performance. One person with low self-esteem and feelings of inadequacy can prevent a team from achieving success. When working with teams, people struggling with low self-esteem are easy to spot. They come across in a defensive manner, creating conflict with others. I try to find ways to work with them individually, pointing out the implications of their actions for themselves and the team. When one member's self-esteem becomes less conditional, it has a positive impact on the team as a functioning system.

Beliefs About the External World

Is the world full of threats or opportunities? From the vantage point of the personal loop in the Motivational System, the external world consists of the interpersonal, team, and organizational loops and the larger context within which the organization functions. To function effectively, therefore, a person must be able to see these parts and their interconnections accurately. Our beliefs about ourselves and other people impact our ability to do this effectively. Negative or limiting beliefs about ourselves and/or others distort our perceptions of the external world, resulting in bad decisions—garbage in, garbage out.

In the later stages of the Watergate scandal, Richard Nixon exercised poor judgment because he was convinced people were out to get him. Similarly, when organizational leaders become paranoid about the competition, they often develop *tunnel vision*, which blocks their ability to formulate effective business strategies. The important thing is to consider information from the external environment in a nondefensive manner and to scrutinize the accuracy of assumptions, conclusions, and predictions based on that information.

Feeling

We aren't simply rational beings who act on logic and data; we're living, breathing creatures with complex feelings or emotions. Thinking has to do with the head; feeling has to do with the heart and soul. Head and heart and soul need to go together.

There isn't just victory and defeat; there's the thrill of victory, the agony of defeat. On a daily basis, people experience a wide range of feelings, including hurt, anxiety, fear, anger, frustration, disappointment, discouragement, joy, happiness, and so on.

Feelings function as both causes and effects. The pain or emotional arousal triggered by unmet needs and wants causes (motivates) us to consider ways of satisfying them. Because we don't know in advance whether or not our efforts will succeed, there's anxiety associated with making and acting on choices. Do I or don't I do this or that? What are the risks? What are the opportunities? Feelings play a crucial role in determining our responses.

While feelings can occur at any point in the process described by the Motivational System Model, for our purposes their most important functions are as outputs of thinking and as inputs into the processes of valuing and deciding. That's why they're placed where they are in the model. Let me explain. By themselves, facts are neutral—they don't elicit any feelings. One person could look at a set of facts and bellow, "The sky is falling!" while someone else asks, "What's the big fuss about?" It is the beliefs (assumptions, conclusions, and predictions) derived from facts that elicit feelings. Inaccurate or distorted beliefs trigger misperceptions and inappropriate feelings, which then have an unfavorable impact on valuing, deciding, and doing. In contrast, accurate, reality-based beliefs trigger accurate perceptions and appropriate feelings, which have a favorable impact on valuing, deciding, and doing. Thus, believing that others are manipulative evokes feelings of apprehension, which leads to values and behaviors emphasizing caution and self-defense. In contrast, believing that others are trustworthy evokes feelings of enthusiasm and excitement, which lead to values emphasizing openness and collaboration.

A dynamic relationship exists between self-esteem (beliefs about self) and feelings. People with unconditional self-esteem handle fear and anger more effectively than people with conditional self-esteem. Bilodeau (1992, p. 32) explained, "A person with [high] self-esteem, seeing that his sense of adequacy is threatened, initially feels fear or anxiety. Because there is no need or means to avoid the situation, or because standing firm in the situation is more advantageous, this feeling changes to anger. The individual then chooses and acts out a behavior that protects his self-concept but won't harm others or self."

In contrast, people with conditional self-esteem handle fear and anger less effectively. To begin with, it's more difficult for them to admit that they're afraid, because such an admission would be seen as a threat to self-worth. They also deal with anger differently. As Bilodeau described it, "The person with low self-esteem seems filled with anger because he interprets and responds in a defensive, angry way to events that are objectively nonthreatening. . . . A person who feels a deep sense of inadequacy responds either aggressively or depressively, directing destructive anger outward or inward" (pp. 48–49). I've conducted a number of workshops on anger management during the past few years. I suggest to participants that when they get angry they should ask themselves, "What are the deeper feelings underlying my anger?" This often helps them identify the cause(s) of their distress, instead of covering it over with anger.

Back in the 1960s when OD was in its youth, focusing on feelings was in vogue; now the focus is on being a savvy thinker. However, both thinking and feeling are facts of life—we don't have to choose between them. If all we needed was thinking, computers could replace humans. From a systems perspective, feelings should be viewed as a source of valuable feedback. When I work with people, I find that getting an initial "read" on their feelings provides clues about the real issues. Feelings alert me to inaccurate perceptions and distorted beliefs. Being open about my own feelings also gives others permission to be open about theirs. A feeling of rightness tells me that I'm heading in the right direction; a sense of uneasiness tells me to slow down and reassess the situation.

Because the degree to which people accept themselves unconditionally has such a strong impact on their feelings and effectiveness, I've included a Self-Esteem Exercise (Exhibit 2.2) here. I suggest that you complete it yourself in order to deepen your understanding of the concept of "self-esteem" and to foster your own personal growth as well as to learn how the exercise can be used with others.

Exhibit 2.2. Self-Esteem Exercise

Purpose

The purpose of this exercise is to help people achieve a greater degree of unconditional self-esteem so they can be more free psychologically to pursue values emphasizing growth and development. The exercise takes about one hour.

Procedures for Group Use

1. **Place** the following continuum on an easel:

Self-Esteem

Completely Conditional   **Completely Unconditional**

2. **Make** the following points:

- "Our self-esteem can be placed on a scale extending from completely conditional at one end to completely unconditional at the other."

- "People at the conditional end of the scale base their self-esteem on performance and/or personal characteristics, so their self-esteem rises and falls with their successes and failures. They are continually trying to prove themselves by striving for recognition, approval, success, and material possessions. Because failure and rejection are always possibilities, however, they are frequently fearful and defensive."

- "In contrast, people at the unconditional end of the continuum keep their self-esteem separate from their performance and/or personal characteristics, so it remains steady, independent of situations. They accept themselves in spite of their weaknesses and limitations. Instead of using judgmental terms such as 'success' and 'failure,' they focus on learning and growth and use their talents and abilities to express who they are as persons."

- "Self-esteem is not static, but changes as we go through life. Although children are born with unconditional self-acceptance, through the process of socialization they soon link their worth as persons to what significant others regard as important: physical attractiveness, school grades, special talents, popularity, excelling in sports, being dutiful and compliant, et cetera."

Exhibit 2.2. Self-Esteem Exercise, Cont'd

- "As people mature, they tend to move from the conditional toward the unconditional end of the scale, but many are still held back by the belief that their worth depends on conditions, by unfavorable social comparisons, and by the perception that they are less worthy than others. For example, when people make mistakes it is commonplace to hear them say such things as, 'I never do anything right' or 'I feel so worthless.' It's important to identify and eliminate the conditions you place on your self-esteem, because these serve as barriers to growth and development."

3. **Divide** participants into groups of four.

4. **Hand out** a copy of the Self-Esteem Worksheet to each participant and give the following instructions:

   "Take a few minutes to complete the Self-Esteem Worksheet individually. When all the people in your group have finished, take turns sharing the information on your worksheet with the others in your small group."

5. **Debrief** key learning points with the full group by asking the following questions and facilitating a dialogue about their answers:

   - "What did you learn about yourselves during this exercise?"
   - "What ideas did you generate for moving toward unconditional self-esteem?"
   - "How do you think unconditional self-esteem could increase your effectiveness?"

6. **Ask** for and **respond** to questions.

Procedures for Individual Use

1. Think about how your self-esteem has changed from your teenage years to the present.

2. Answer the questions on the Self-Esteem Worksheet, identifying how you can move toward unconditional self-esteem.

Exhibit 2.2. Self-Esteem Exercise, Cont'd

Self-Esteem Worksheet

1. A person's self-esteem can range from completely conditional to completely unconditional. On the scale below, circle how you would rate your self-esteem as a teenager.

Completely   Completely
Conditional   Unconditional

    1   2   3   4   5   6   7   8   9   10

2. What factors led to that rating?

3. How would you rate your self-esteem today?

4. What factors caused your self-esteem to change from adolescence to the present?

5. How can you move toward unconditional self-esteem?

6. What would be needed for you to shift to truly unconditional self-esteem, that is, the complete absence of conditions?

This chapter introduced the Motivational System Model and described the first three components in the personal loop of that model: need/want, think, and feel. These components have a profound impact on a person's values and behavior, which are the subjects of Chapter 3.

(3)

Values and Personality

ON THE LAST CHAPTER, WE EXAMINED wanting/needing, thinking, and feeling components of the personal loop of the Motivational System Model. In this chapter we will look at the *valuing, deciding,* and *doing* components in the personal loop, with an emphasis on the role of values. This is important to OD practitioners and managers because many organizational problems can be traced back to people's values. The impact of self-esteem on values will be explained more fully. Understanding the dynamics of values at the personal level is key to understanding them at the interpersonal, team, and organizational levels, which is the subject of Chapter 4. It's also necessary to assessing and changing values, the focus of Chapters 5 through 8. The Personal Vision Exercise is included at the end of this chapter.

Valuing and Deciding

Thinking has to do with the *mind*; valuing and deciding have to do with the *will.* The *New American Heritage Dictionary* defines the will as, "The mental faculty by which one deliberately chooses or decides upon a course of action." Thinking and valuing/deciding are two separate but dynamically interrelated functions. We're able to weigh alternatives and make choices because we have the intrinsic capacity to assign worth. Without this capacity, free will would be impossible. In this process, the mind serves as an advisor or coach to the will. As described earlier, we take in information from the external world and formulate beliefs (assumptions, conclusions, and predictions). Different beliefs evoke different perceptions and feelings. This information is then fed to our will, where it is matched against our values, the standards of importance that guide our process of deciding.

Used in an economic sense, a value means a good deal, well worth the money. Used in a psychological sense, values are conceptions about what's important in life. Rokeach (1973) defined a value as a preferred end-state of existence or mode of conduct. He referred to the former (such as world peace) as *terminal values* and the latter (such as cooperation) as *instrumental values.* Instrumental values guide the process of attaining terminal values.

Once embraced, our values become part of our identity as a person. It's difficult for us to think about ourselves apart from our values. We *care* about our values; we feel positively toward people and experiences that affirm our values and negatively toward people and experiences that negate our values. We also develop a vested interest in our values; we want to believe our values are the right ones, the best ones, even the only ones. Our values have a powerful impact on our choices, serving as criteria for making decisions and setting priorities (Williams, 1968). Every decision we make is based on values, whether we're consciously aware of it or not.

Any particular value, terminal or instrumental, functions to satisfy us in one of three ways: by helping us to defend ourselves against perceived threat, to adjust to society, or to realize our potential. Maslow (1968) referred to these as "defensive" values (unhealthy regression), "coasting" values (healthy regression), and "growth" values. In today's business world, *growth* is usually viewed only in economic terms. In this book, growth means progressing toward full realization of our potential. Individuals, teams, and organizations that do this successfully can expect an economic payoff—and more.

I've modified Maslow's definitions slightly to make them more useful for our purposes:

- *Defensive Values* focus on protecting against perceived threat (for example, security, caution, power, control, territory).

- *Stabilizing Values* focus on maintaining the status quo (for example, reliability, consistency, protocol, procedures).

- *Growth Values* focus on progress or forward movement (for example, creativity, improvement, innovation, learning, flexibility, risk taking).

Now let's discuss terminal and instrumental values separately and show why some people emphasize the defensive or stabilizing function, while others emphasize growth.

Terminal Values

According to Rokeach (1973) beliefs about self (what he called self-conceptions) are at the innermost core of a person's total belief system, followed by terminal and instrumental values, attitudes, and other beliefs. According to his model of cognitive and behavioral change, the ultimate purpose of values, attitudes, and other beliefs is to maintain and enhance a person's self-conceptions, which can be positive or negative. Terminal values do this by serving a person's purpose (personal mission) and dreams (personal vision) for the future.

What is your purpose in life? As I begin to work with someone, this is often my first question. I start there to put the focus on the forest instead of the trees. The trees are safer—easy to hide behind. Usually the person is at a loss for words. Many say they've never been asked this before, and some even say they haven't thought about it. They feel awkward, fidgeting in their chair, inwardly hoping the silence will prompt me to move on. I don't. I acknowledge their discomfort and ask them to wrestle with the question, even if they find it difficult. I assure them that time spent pondering this will be helpful because, as Blanchard and O'Connor (1997, p. 26) said, "The most important thing is to decide what's most important."

While people may feel uncomfortable at first, the question almost always sparks a period of introspection lasting weeks or months. They often discuss it with their spouses or other significant people, which I encourage. The answer seldom comes into focus all at once. An unfolding process occurs. I also find that, although initially they might wish I hadn't asked them, eventually they're glad I did. Being asked about one's purpose is very affirming. It dignifies the person, conveying my interest in the person as a human being.

As humans we have a need for purpose. Purpose represents our reason for living. It answers the question, "Why am I here?" It defines our essence, who we are as people. All behavior is purposeful. Discovering your purpose is like finding treasure. You fall in love with it; you feel passionately about it. Affirming your purpose is celebrating your personhood, and you cannot deny your purpose without pain— a sense of loss. At the core of our being, each of us has a desire to be all we can be as persons, to seek wholeness and completeness—physically, emotionally, mentally, and spiritually.

The next thing I ask the person is about his or her dreams for the future: "What would you like your life to be like?" This is usually an easier question to answer, but there's still a tendency to focus on the trees, mentioning things related to current work and home life: complete a major project, finish raising the family, make retirement plans. I nudge the person to take a forest perspective with respect to dreams. I ask him or her to share any fantasies or wishes that have come to mind over the years, even if these seem capricious or fanciful.

A dream represents one's personal vision for the future. It answers the question, "What do I want to accomplish?" A dream is in service of purpose. It explains how one's purpose will be fulfilled. A clear sense of purpose is needed before one can effectively pursue a dream. As Peter Senge (1990, pp. 148–149) explained, "Purpose is similar to a direction, a general heading. Vision is a specific destination, a picture in your head of a desired future. Purpose is abstract. Vision is concrete." Like an artist standing before a canvas waiting to bring a painting into being, a dream expresses an image of the "picture" you want to paint in your life. It puts your stamp on life. It allows you to say, "I was here." A dream produces hope, buffering us against uncertainty and disappointment. I first had the vision for this book in 1985; even though it took me fifteen years to fulfill the vision, it was never far from my mind.

The relationship between current reality and vision determines direction. Most people have an inner longing, a fantasy, or a wish about their future. It may concern something related to their personal lives, careers, or both. I remember talking to a CEO who initially defined his dream in terms of increased organizational market share. A while later a smile came across his face, however, when he revealed his fantasy about getting out of the rat race and becoming a professional bass fisherman. Another example is the former CEO of a large corporation who resigned "to get a life." We perk up when we hear stories about others who were able to fulfill their dream, but it always seems a little beyond our grasp. The fantasies bring us comfort briefly, but then it's back to reality. They fade into the background, but pop up again later. It's something that doesn't go away, even if you try to ignore it.

When people share their dreams, they often become very animated, saying such things as, "You know, I've always had this idea about. . .," or "If I could do whatever I wanted, I'd. . . ." But when I ask why they haven't done anything about the dream, they offer the standard excuses: no time, no money, too many risks, too impractical. Action is necessary to make a dream real. The artist must take a paint brush to the canvas in order to create a painting. Without action the dream remains a fantasy. The dream and the purpose it expresses remain seeds that never blossom.

Some people make striving for wholeness their purpose, while others do not. What makes the difference? My view is that our beliefs about who we are as persons are the key factors in shaping our terminal values (Rokeach, 1973). People with more conditional self-esteem are held back by fear, while those with more unconditional self-worth are freer to pursue their dreams and develop their potential.

I remember working with an executive who always had to be right. In any conversation in which differing opinions were being expressed, he would argue for his view relentlessly. As a result, he alienated many people and had trouble building collaborative relationships. During our work, he saw that his sense of self-esteem was linked to being right. When he was right, he felt worthwhile; when he was wrong, he felt worthless. As he began to separate his self-worth from being right, he became much more relaxed, his relationships with others improved markedly, and he became more effective.

Unconditional self-esteem means affirming your worth in spite of mistakes, weaknesses, and limitations. It means risking the disapproval of others. It means rejecting the internalized critical parent who keeps bullying you to prove yourself. It means throwing away the measuring stick used to intimidate yourself with social comparisons. It means stopping your judgments about your worth as a human being and claiming your own worth through an act of will.

I once worked with a CEO who felt a desperate need to make decisions that everyone agreed with. She explained that when disagreements arose among her six siblings, she was always the one who was able to restore harmony. When a conflict erupted, her brothers and sisters would say, "We better go get Alice; she'll know what to do." Over time, Alice's sense of self-worth became tied to her conflict-resolution skills. However, this pattern that served her well as a child was making her ineffective as a leader. She had a breakthrough one day when she announced an unpopular decision at an executive team meeting. Talking to me afterward, she said proudly, "I think I became an adult today."

Conditional and unconditional self-esteem serve two very different purposes. For people with conditional self-esteem, maintaining and enhancing self-esteem becomes their purpose. They have difficulty developing a positive vision for their future, which prevents them from moving toward wholeness and integration. For those with unconditional self-esteem, self-actualization or developing their full potential becomes their purpose. They're able to establish a positive vision for their future, and they seek to close the gap between their current reality and vision.

This represents a "Y" in the road, with far-reaching consequences for one's choices—and ultimately for one's satisfaction with life. Let's examine these two purposes more closely.

Maintaining and Enhancing Self-Esteem

People whose purpose is to maintain and enhance self-esteem focus primarily on two objectives: (1) protecting their self-worth from being lowered and (2) striving to prove their worth. Because these objectives are driven by fear triggered by perceived threat, maintaining and enhancing self-esteem is a defensive terminal value. People with this striving evaluate every situation in terms of its potential impact on their self-esteem, and guarding their self-esteem becomes their overriding priority, impacting everything they do.

The defensive striving to maintain and enhance self-esteem greatly limits people both personally and socially. Instead of accepting themselves and embracing growth, they strive relentlessly to prove their worth. Because other people are perceived as potential threats, they're often defensive in interpersonal relationships and have trouble trusting. They screen what others do through its perceived impact on their self-esteem.

They can continue feeling good about themselves in one of two ways: by trying to prove they're better than others or by putting others down. Either way they come out ahead in the comparison, bolstering their self-esteem—at least for the moment. However, this puts a barrier between them and others. They find it difficult to celebrate others' successes or to feel genuine empathy or compassion. People who put others down or have a hidden sense of glee when something bad happens to others reveal their own fragile self-esteem. Unfortunately, dynamics like these are pervasive in many organizations. Standing around the water cooler for a few minutes usually confirms this.

One manager I worked with was continually finding fault with others. Whenever he had a conversation with someone, he would mention negative things about another person. Eventually everyone started avoiding him, and his performance suffered. After reviewing 360-degree feedback, where colleagues characterized him as being ruthless and untrustworthy, he revealed deep feelings of inadequacy. He believed that the only way he could cover up the inadequacy was by putting others down. Once the reasons for his sense of inadequacy became clearer and he was able to move toward more unconditional self-worth, his relationships with others improved dramatically.

Also, many people striving to maintain and enhance self-esteem either don't have a dream or personal vision for their future, or they lack the confidence to achieve it. Consequently, they attach themselves to someone else's vision. They see others—and not themselves—as the key to their future.

Self-Actualization

In contrast to the above, people whose purpose is self-actualization think and act very differently. Because they've accepted themselves as persons and feel no need to prove their worth, they're freed from the crippling need for approval and from the fear of expressing their true selves. Clearly, maintaining and enhancing self-esteem fosters defensiveness, whereas self-actualization fosters growth.

Those pursuing self-actualization avoid evaluating themselves and their experiences in limiting, judgmental terms such as "success" and "failure." Instead, they look forward to life with a sense of excitement and anticipation, focusing on learning. Because they don't view others as threats or need their approval, they're less defensive around them. They have more energy to invest in relationships, take a genuine interest in people, and seek to learn from them. They're also more capable of encouraging others, celebrating their gains and consoling them during their losses.

It's hard to imagine someone who struggles with self-doubt and a sense of inadequacy being an effective leader for any length of time. Leadership means projecting yourself in a way that instills confidence in others. Self-actualizing people are better equipped to do this. I've worked with CEOs who had a deep sense of inadequacy stemming from poor company financial results. I challenge them to identify negative self-conceptions related to performance and the consequences of these beliefs for the future. It's only when they can separate their worth as persons from pressures to produce that they can truly lead. Those who are unable to do this are often overwhelmed by stress, which takes its toll physically, psychologically, and emotionally.

Self-actualizing people are open to their own visions, instead of being dependent on the dreams of others. They're also more willing to face the uncertainties of the future, permitting them to move from images of success to reality. I once worked as an OD practitioner at a continuing care retirement community. During conversations with me, many residents expressed regret because they didn't follow their dreams. They said such things as, "I don't know why I was so afraid" or "If I had it to do over again, I'd have taken more risks." I learned from these people that regret is a cruel teacher. I resolved that when I reflected back on my life I wanted to be able to say, "I went for it!" To help you clarify your dreams, the Personal Vision Exercise (Exhibit 3.1) is included at the end of this chapter.

One time I was helping my daughter develop a game plan for launching her acting career and came up with the following five-step process:

1. What's your dream?
2. What are you afraid of?
3. Set your fears aside.
4. What's left?
5. Go for it!

She looked at it and then said, "This is so simple, yet all the main points are there." Shortly after that, I was coaching a CFO who had an opportunity to take a COO position with another organization. He had been restless in his job for several years and was yearning to try something different. After receiving the other offer, however, he was torn between his current job and the new one. After showing him the five steps, he pointed to number 2 and said, "That's it. I'm afraid if I leave, the people here will be disappointed with me." After discussing this fear more fully, he realized that, while people would be sad to see him go, they would also be happy for him. Relieved, he decided to accept the offer and has enjoyed his new job.

Finally, self-actualizing people are freer to commit themselves to something that makes the world a better place. As Maslow (1976, p. 42) said, "Self-actualizing people are, without one single exception, involved in a cause outside of themselves. They are devoted, working at something which is very precious to them—some calling or vocation. They are working at something that fate has called them to somehow and which they work at and which they love, so the work-joy dichotomy in them disappears."

Self-actualizing people almost always have a commitment to others' actualization, which enables them to transcend the bounds of need and want and act out of love. Each of us is somewhere on the road between the two poles represented by maintaining and enhancing self-esteem and self-actualization, between dependency and realizing one's potential. Often progress is tentative and halting. Sometimes it's one step forward, two steps backward, but any movement away from fear and toward growth is a victory. Experience has taught me that the single most powerful intervention I can make is to help someone achieve a greater sense of unconditional self-esteem. When someone achieves it, it's as though he or she has shifted into a higher gear. This shift is a prerequisite to highly effective interpersonal and organizational functioning.

Instrumental Values

Instrumental values are the standards of importance we use to pursue terminal values. As such, they are means to the end of fulfilling our core terminal value, which, as suggested above, is focused on either maintaining and enhancing self-esteem or on self-actualization. In the work environment, instrumental values focus primarily on four personal and social needs: mastery, contribution, self-respect, and acceptance. Thus, the instrumental values we choose in these four areas are the standards of importance used to either maintain or enhance our self-esteem or actualize our full potential.

It is helpful to think of people as having between thirty and forty instrumental values. Table 3.1 provides examples of common instrumental values in today's world. I've compiled this list over a twenty-five-year period while working with individuals, teams, and organizations. The four categories and the key questions I asked in classifying values into each are listed below:

- *Personal Competence* (mastery): Is it a standard for using or developing my abilities?

- *Social Competence* (contribution): Is it a standard for achieving a larger social purpose?

- *Personal Integrity* (self-respect): Is it a standard for personal character?

- *Social Integrity* (acceptance): Is it a standard for social character?

I don't claim that this list is exhaustive. That would violate my own position against dogmatism, but I'm confident that it can help you gain deeper understanding of the relationship between needs and values, even if you would categorize differently or if you can think of values that I didn't include.

Table 3.1. Instrumental Values Matrix

	Personal		Social	

Competence "Abilities"	Accomplishment
	Achievement
	Adaptability
	Advancement
	Adventurous
	Ambition
	Caution
	Clean
	Comfort
	Competence
	Creativity
	Credentials
	Curiosity
	Delight
	Dependability
	Effectiveness
	Efficiency
	Enthusiasm
	Excellence
	Flexibility
	Freedom
	Growth
	Health
	Humor/fun
	Imagination
	Improvement
	Independence
	Individuality
	Initiative
	Innovation
	Intelligence
	Intuition
		Knowledge
		Learning
		Logical
		Mastery
		Material
		  possessions
		Merit
		Opportunity
		Optimism
		Originality
		Perseverance
		Productivity
		Professionalism
		Quality
		Reliability
		Responsibility
		Responsiveness
		Results
		Risk taking
		Routine
		Security
		Self-discipline
		Self-starter
		Speed
		Spontaneity
		Stability
		Strategic focus
		Success
		Timeliness
		Variety
		Winning
		Wisdom
			Adding value
			Affirmation
			Altruism
			Authority
			Balance home/work
			Boundaryless
			  organization
			Community
			  involvement
			Competition
			Contribution
			Control
			Customer
			  satisfaction
			Developing others
			Empowerment
			Environmentalism
			Financial growth
			Generosity
			Giving something
			  back
			Glory
			Good will
			Harmony
			Honor
			Humanitarianism
			Human rights
			Influence
			Involvement
			Making a difference
			Mentoring
			Mutual interests
				Order
				Organizational growth
				Ownership
				Peace
				Philanthropy
				Power
				Prestige
				Profitability
				Progress
				Recognition
				Self-interest
				Seniority
				Sense of community
				Service
				Social awareness
				Status
				Status quo
				Stewardship
				Synergism
				Territory
				Tradition
				Volunteerism

Integrity "Character"	Authenticity Commitment Congruence Consistency Courage Credibility Dedication Deference Dignity Diligence Discretion Ethics Expediency Faith Genuineness Honesty Humility Integrity Law-abiding Manipulation Morality Obedience Self-control Self-respect Sincerity Situational ethics Spirituality Truth Will power		Accepting others Accountability Alignment Approval Assertiveness Belonging Candor Caring Cohesiveness Collaboration Companionship Compassion Confidentiality Cooperation Coordination Courtesy Diplomacy Diversity Equality Fairness Faithfulness Fellowship Forgiveness Friendship Helpfulness Inclusiveness Interdependence Justice Kindness Love Loyalty	Mercy Networking Openness Participation Partnering Patience Politeness Popularity Respect Tact Teamwork Tolerance Trust

As can be seen in the table, there's a wide variety of instrumental values available for people to choose among. Much of the diversity among people can be explained by the particular values they select and the behaviors used to implement those values.

As with terminal values, any particular instrumental value can be classified as either defensive (D), stabilizing (S), or growth (G), depending on how it functions to satisfy needs and wants. In other words, the standards people employ to pursue their terminal values will emphasize defense, stability, or growth. The instrumental values listed in Table 3.1 are classified as defensive, stabilizing, or growth in Tables 3.2, 3.3, and 3.4.

Categorizing values in this manner will never be an exact science, because a value can mean one thing to one person and something else to another. The name given to a value is less important than the *way* it is experienced and expressed. A "growth" value can be expressed in a dysfunctional manner or in a manner that conflicts with other values. Similarly, a "defensive" value can be expressed in a healthy manner. For example, power is often expressed defensively, but not always. McClelland and Burnham (1976) found that successful managers were characterized by high power motivation, but the power need was socialized, mature, and not used for narrow self-interest.

In any given situation, therefore, the most accurate way to determine a value's function is by asking: What impact does the value have? Does it protect against perceived threat (D), maintain the status quo (S), or provide for forward movement or development (G)? Let's explore the function of D, S, and G values in more detail.

Instrumental Defensive Values

Defensive values aren't "bad," and growth values aren't "good." Judgmental labels such as these don't help us to understand the dynamics of values. Some emphasis on defense is necessary to be safe around others and to guard against exploitation or manipulation. Sometimes it's wise to be cautious. Also, such defensive values as self-control and tact allow people to restrain their anger, which is essential to maintaining constructive relationships.

Nevertheless other defensive values, such as manipulation, expediency, and competition, often have a negative impact on relationships. Research studies have reported a relationship between such values as obedience, politeness, cleanliness, family security, and social recognition, on the one hand, and such measures of defensiveness as dogmatism, authoritarianism, ethnocentrism, and intolerance for ambiguity, on the other (see, for example, Adorno et al., 1950; Feather, 1971; Rim, 1970; and Rokeach, 1973).

Table 3.2. Instrumental Defensive Values

	Personal		Social	
Competence "Abilities"	Caution Clean Independence Logical Material 　possessions Security	Speed Winning	Competition Control Glory Honor Power Prestige Recognition	Self-interest Seniority Status Territory
Integrity "Character"	Deference Expediency Manipulation Obedience Self-control Situational ethics		Approval Courtesy Diplomacy Loyalty Politeness Popularity Tact	

The main problem with defensive values is that their usual function is to protect self-esteem from being lowered. People who emphasize defensive values invest their energy in preventing bad things from happening, rather than in making good things happen. Instead of contributing to the common good, they strive to compensate for perceived inadequacies. They seek to avoid risks rather than to find or create opportunities. When they complete a task successfully, instead of enjoying a sense of accomplishment, they're relieved that they didn't fall on their faces. Each situation is a new risk to self-esteem, so they come across as guarded and tense. They continually seek reassurance and encouragement from others. Preventing a negative does not create a positive, however, so their needs remain largely unsatisfied.

Let's take an example. Tom was a mechanical engineer assigned to a new vehicle launch team with a major automobile manufacturer. Unfortunately, he began clashing with other team members almost immediately. Whenever one of them made a suggestion, he would immediately focus on what could go wrong. Previously he had worked as a trouble shooter, where this kind of behavior was useful. In a creative team that depended on brainstorming and openness to ideas, however, his behavior was very inhibiting. Because he was unable to move from a defensive to a growth orientation, Tom was assigned other work.

Defensive values, and the negative conceptions of self and others behind them, are almost always causal factors in personal, interpersonal, team, and organizational problems, so a thorough understanding of their dynamics is crucial for OD practitioners and managers. This is complicated because the process of acting on values is not an entirely rational one. Subconscious and unconscious forces are often at work, so people are not necessarily aware of the values they use in guiding their decisions and actions. At the same time, people have a need to justify their decisions and actions, and they can use values to serve this purpose. Rokeach (1973) explained that values are used for rational self-justification when possible, but also for rationalized self-justification when necessary to protect self-esteem.

The goal of rationalization is to justify your actions based on "good reasons" in order to maintain your self-esteem or the esteem of others. Here are five common situations in which values can be used as rationalizations:

1. Values can be used to reframe needs into more personally and socially acceptable terms. Needs, such as attention, acceptance, approval, nurturance, and recognition, that are perceived to be less acceptable can be made more noble-sounding by calling them excellence, involvement, cooperation, teamwork, and a sense of accomplishment.

2. Values can be used to rationalize doing something you want to do but believe you should not do, as when you justify unethical business practices in the name of organizational profitability or growth.

3. Values can be used to rationalize doing something you don't want to do but believe you should do, as when you congratulate a competitor for a success.

4. Values can be used to rationalize not doing something you're afraid to do, as when you fail to stand up for something, claiming it's more important to be diplomatic or sensitive to others.

5. Values can be used to rationalize results that fall short of expectations. This is called "C.Y.A.," which is so common that everyone knows what it means by the initials alone.

In Chapter 1, I indicated that people base their decisions on either high or low clarity and conviction about their values. People who act with high clarity can give you a clear explanation for their actions within the context of their convictions. In other words, the actions have integrity. Even if people feel required to make tradeoffs due to complicated circumstances—things are seldom black or white—they can explain the tradeoffs and how these impacted their actions. For example, if I valued honesty and was giving feedback to someone, I might choose not to present data that I believed the person could not receive. I could explain my decision to myself and to colleagues by saying that at this time the data would do more harm than good, and that it would be better to wait until I was more confident that the person could receive the information.

In contrast, people whose values are unclear often rationalize in order to explain why their standards vary from one situation to the next. They often appear to be "making things up as they go along," raising red flags in the process.

People are frequently unaware when they're rationalizing because such awareness would in itself lower self-esteem. It's tough to feel good about yourself when you know you're covering up the truth. In addition to rationalization, people often hold defensive values that they won't admit, either to themselves or others, because such admission would be highly threatening. Some examples are exploitation, manipulation, greed, revenge, racial or ethnic superiority, and so on. You can tell that some people embrace such values by observing their behavior.

Values that are perceived to meet needs resist change, even if they are defensive. If people regard safety as more important than growth, then they will hold on to values consistent with that purpose. It is easier to maintain this type of orientation when security and stability are more available in the external environment. Globalization has changed all that. To be viable in today's workplace, people must find security internally through self-acceptance, freeing them from fear so they can take appropriate risks in responding to change.

When working with individuals, I try to help them move beyond defensiveness by asking such open-ended questions as the following:

- "What is the situation as you see it?"
- "What other factors could be involved?"
- "What have you tried already?"
- "How have those approaches worked?"
- "What else could you try?"
- "What are the pros and cons of those possibilities?"

Organization development consultants and managers may also find such questions useful, both for examining their own options and for encouraging others to do the same.

Sometimes people's defenses are too great, however, and a more directive approach is required. In these situations, it may be necessary to confront people with discrepancies between how they see themselves and how they're perceived by others. Interview data from work associates is often very useful, as long as confidentiality is assured. Both the Values Assessment Inventory (Exhibit 5.1) and the Values Identification Survey (Exhibit 5.2) include a 360-degree feedback option, which can help people improve their self-understanding and their awareness of how others perceive them. More will be said about this in Chapter 8.

Instrumental Stabilizing Values

Stabilizing values provide for necessary rest, relaxation, diversion, and equilibrium. More mature, self-confident people will prefer growth values over stabilizing values, but the latter are still needed for a balanced life (Maslow, 1968). Some stabilizing values, such as accountability, honesty, and reliability, help build a foundation for growth values. However, other stabilizing values, such as comfort, routine, order, and tradition, can cause people to resist positive change. People who place a heavy emphasis on stabilizing values will have trouble keeping up with the changes in today's fast-paced organizations and in their chaotic environments.

Instrumental Growth Values

Instrumental growth values guide people toward realizing their full potential. Because this book takes a systems approach in line with OD's mission, I define a growth value as one that fosters personal, interpersonal, team, and organizational progress toward wholeness and integration. It cannot help one part of the system grow at the expense of other parts. Thus a "growth" value, although it may focus on one level, such as personal growth, must serve the system as a whole or it is not truly a growth value.

A quick glance at the terms in Table 3.4 reveals many synonyms. They're included because people use different words to describe the same thing. It's important that we each use terms that are meaningful to us.

Table 3.3. Instrumental Stabilizing Values

	Personal	Social
Competence "Abilities"	Comfort Credentials Dependability Efficiency Health Productivity Professionalism Reliability Routine Self-discipline Stability	Authority Balance home/work Harmony Order Peace Status quo Tradition
Integrity "Character"	Consistency Dedication Dignity Diligence Discretion Ethics Honesty Humility Integrity Law-abiding Morality Self-respect Sincerity	Accountability Tolerance Belonging Trust Candor Caring Companionship Compassion Confidentiality Cooperation Coordination Faithfulness Fellowship Forgiveness Friendship Helpfulness Justice Kindness Mercy Patience Respect

Table 3.4. Instrumental Growth Values

Competence "Abilities"	Personal		Social	
	Adaptability	Knowledge	Affirmation	Involvement
	Adventurous	Learning	Altruism	Making a
	Competence	Mastery	Boundaryless	difference
	Creativity	Merit	organization	Mentoring
	Curiosity	Opportunity	Community	Mutual
	Delight	Optimism	involvement	interests
	Effectiveness	Originality	Contribution	Organizational
	Enthusiasm	Perseverance	Customer	growth
	Excellence	Quality	satisfaction	Ownership
	Flexibility	Responsibility	Developing others	Philanthropy
	Freedom	Responsiveness	Empowerment	Profitability
	Growth	Results	Environmentalism	Progress
	Humor/fun	Risk taking	Financial growth	Sense of
	Imagination	Self-starter	Generosity	community
	Improvement	Spontaneity	Giving	Service
	Initiative	Strategic focus	something back	Social
	Innovation	Timeliness	Good will	awareness
	Intelligence	Variety	Humanitarianism	Stewardship
	Intuition		Human rights	Synergism
			Influence	Volunteerism
Integrity "Character"	Authenticity		Accepting others	
	Commitment		Alignment	
	Congruence		Cohesiveness	
	Courage		Collaboration	
	Credibility		Diversity	
	Faith		Equality	
	Genuineness		Inclusiveness	
	Spirituality		Interdependence	
	Truth		Love	
			Networking	
			Openness	
			Participation	
			Partnering	
			Teamwork	

One useful way to draw distinctions between values is to think of a value and then try to specify its opposite. For example, the opposite of honesty is dishonesty, the opposite of collaboration is competition, the opposite of risk taking is security, and so on. Tannenbaum and Davis (1969) used this approach to distinguish between what we need to be moving away from and what we need to be moving toward if we are going to grow and develop (see Table 1.1). In almost every instance, the opposite of a growth value is either a defensive or stabilizing value. Helping people notice such contrasts allows them to clarify their values and make conscious choices. Also, just because something is labeled a growth value does not necessarily mean it functions in that manner. It cannot be considered a growth value unless the strategies and behaviors chosen to implement it provide for forward movement in healthy, constructive ways. Growth at any price is always short-sighted.

The Right Combination

Defensive, stabilizing, and growth values are all required for a well-balanced work life. Nevertheless, as Figure 3.1 shows, individuals can differ greatly in the relative emphasis they place on the three types, leading to wide variations in personality and behavior:

- People whose purpose is maintaining and enhancing self-esteem tend to emphasize instrumental defensive values.

- People whose purpose is maintaining things as they are emphasize instrumental stabilizing values.

- People whose purpose is self-actualization tend to emphasize instrumental growth values.

Figure 3.1. Value Differences Among Individuals

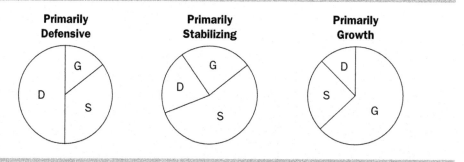

Teams and organizations also show such differences in values, leading to wide variations in culture. Helping organizations move from defensive and stabilizing cultures to growth cultures is a fruitful area for OD practitioners. I'll have much more to say about this in the chapters to come.

Espoused, Actual, and Desired Values

Another important distinction is among espoused, actual, and desired values. *Espoused* values are the ones that people say they value; *actual* values are ones that guide behavior currently; *desired* values are ones that people would like to have guide their behavior. A person with discrepancies between espoused and actual values can be described as not "walking the talk." Discrepancies between actual and desired values reveal opportunities for possible growth.

The Values Identification Survey (VIS), Exhibit 5.2, can be used to help people identify their current values. It can also be used as a 360-degree feedback tool to help them identify discrepancies between actual and espoused values. The VIS has several other possible applications with relationships, teams, and organizations. One way to familiarize yourself with the VIS is by using it to identify your own current values.

The outcome of *valuing*, applying standards of importance, is that decisions are made. All decisions are based on values, and the effectiveness of those decisions depends greatly on the particular values chosen. Among the most important decisions an individual can make concern setting *goals* (general direction), *objectives* (specific results by specific times), and *action plans* (a sequence of steps that will accomplish the objectives).

Doing

Doing has to do with behaving, which is the actual implementation of decisions, goals, objectives, and action plans based on values. Any of the other variables in the Motivational System Model—needs/wants, thinking, feeling, and valuing/deciding—can affect behavior.

Dynamics occurring among the personal, interpersonal, team, and organizational loops, as well as external contingencies, also serve as driving or constraining forces to behavior. Ineffective behaviors are often symptomatic of problems elsewhere in the system. The behavior of people who hold positive beliefs about self, others, and the world and who emphasize growth values will be more effective than will the behavior of people who have negative beliefs and defensive values.

The dynamic interaction among needing/wanting, thinking, feeling, and valuing/deciding is revealed by what we do. There's a lot of talk currently about the difference between espoused and actual values, a topic that will be explored in later chapters. As stated earlier, the former are values people claim to have, while the latter are reflected by what they do. Establishing credibility and trust requires a match between stated values and actions—what we call "walking the talk." Nothing raises a red flag faster than a disconnect between what one says and what one does.

Need Satisfied?

Ways of acting that satisfy needs and wants are reinforced, and people often go along on cruise control. When they start having problems meeting needs, however, they slow down or stop and reassess their situation. This provides them with the incentive to change. People who pay attention to all the variables in the Motivational System and the external environment will be more effective at identifying causes and taking corrective action. Someone can get up on a soap box and champion his or her beliefs and values, but it all boils down to one question: Are you satisfying your needs or not? If your beliefs, values, and behavior don't allow you to satisfy your needs, why hold on to them?

You can gain greater insight into your values by completing the Personal Vision Exercise (Exhibit 3.1) and the Values Identification Survey (Exhibit 5.2).

Exhibit 3.1. Personal Vision Exercise

Purpose

The purpose of this exercise is to help people clarify their personal vision or dreams, and then take steps to fulfill those visions. The exercise is designed to take two hours.

Procedures for Group Use

1. **Say,** "We all have dreams, fantasies, wishes, and hopes about things we'd like to do in our lives, but for one reason or another we don't do them."

2. **Ask,** "What are some of the reasons we don't follow our dreams?"

3. **List** participant responses on an easel, including such responses as the following:

   Lack of time

   Lack of money

   Procrastination

   Laziness

   Dismiss them as unrealistic

   Lack of self-confidence

   Fear of failure

   Fear of criticism or disapproval

   Settling for someone else's vision

4. **Say,** "Regardless of whatever else is going on in our lives, our dreams and fantasies keep tugging at us. The reason is that our dreams are part of who we are as persons. Therefore, neglecting our dreams prevents us from being true to ourselves. Today I'm going to challenge you to develop your dreams into a vision for your future and then to think of ways you can start making that vision a reality."

5. **Divide** participants into pairs.

Exhibit 3.1. Personal Vision Exercise, Cont'd

6. **Hand out** a copy of the pages entitled Coaching Questions and Personal Vision Worksheet to each participant and give the following instructions:

   · "Take some time to complete the Personal Vision Worksheet individually."

   · "Then each pair is to take turns being a Presenter and being a Coach. While you are the Presenter, the two of you will focus on the information you placed on the Personal Vision Worksheet. The Coach will ask a series of questions designed to clarify your vision and the steps required to achieve it."

   · "The coaching questions are designed to encourage risk taking and self-disclosure, which can help the Presenter learn through self-discovery in a setting free from evaluation and judgment."

7. **Debrief** key learning points with the full group by asking these questions:

   · "Who would be willing to share their personal vision?"

   · "What ideas did you generate for making your vision a reality?"

   · "What impact has this exercise had on your views about who you are as a person?"

8. **Ask** for and **Respond** to questions.

Procedures for Individual Use

1. Think about your career dreams and fantasies.

2. Answer the questions on the Personal Vision Worksheet, making sure to identify specific actions you can take to start bringing your vision into reality.

Exhibit 3.1. Personal Vision Exercise, Cont'd

Coaching Questions

1. What is your personal vision for the future?

2. Do you have any beliefs about yourself, other people, or your situation that keep you from following your vision?

3. How did these beliefs originate?

4. Are these beliefs valid currently? If so, what evidence do you have?

5. What would have to change in order for you to follow your vision?

6. How could you go about making these changes?

7. What risks are involved? How could these risks be eliminated?

8. What's the very first step you could take to move toward your vision?

9. When could you take this step?

10. What will you do if you do not succeed? Do you have a back-up plan?

Exhibit 3.1. Personal Vision Exercise, Cont'd

Personal Vision Worksheet

What would your life be like if it were exactly the way you would like it to be?

· What images or thoughts come to you as you think about that question?

· What would you like to have, do, and be?

· What would you like to accomplish?

· How would you like your relationships to be (particularly with family, friends, and co-workers)?

· How would you like your career or profession to be?

· How would you like your organization to be?

· What would your community, country, and world be like if they were exactly as you would like them to be?

You can revisit, review, and revise your answers as the "spirit" moves you! Remember: It's your vision.

Exhibit 3.1. Personal Vision Exercise, Cont'd

What steps can you take to bring your vision into reality?

Don't try for a complete plan. A few steps that move you in the direction of your vision are enough.

In this chapter, we discussed the crucial role of values and behavior in the personal loop of the Motivational System Model. In the next chapter, we will examine the interpersonal, team, and organizational loops of the model, with an emphasis on the key role played by values.

(4)

Values and Organizations

AT **THE PERSONAL LEVEL, VALUES ARE KEY** aspects of personality; at the interpersonal, team, and organizational levels, values are key aspects of culture. Culture will be discussed in terms of the various components of the interpersonal, team, and organizational loops of the Motivational System Model, presented in Chapter 2, with emphasis on the crucial role played by values (standards of importance). Terminal values are standards for conceiving and defining mission and vision; instrumental values are standards for serving mission and vision. More specifically, instrumental values guide the development and implementation of goals, objectives, and action plans. Team and organizational applications of the Values Identification Survey (Exhibit 5.2) will be described. The Value-Centered Planning Worksheet (Exhibit 4.1) is included at the end of this chapter.

A Systems Approach to Culture

What is culture and what is its purpose? If we didn't have needs or wants, culture wouldn't be necessary. We obviously do have needs and wants, however, and we're required to face constant change and uncertainty as we attempt to satisfy them. Culture allows us to organize our efforts with others to meet needs in the midst of change and uncertainty. It emerges whenever people join together to satisfy needs and wants and clarifies how this will be accomplished. The larger society has a culture and many subcultures; teams and organizations develop cultures as well.

A great deal has been written about organizational culture recently. Cameron and Quinn (1999, p. 15) defined culture this way: "An organization's culture is reflected by what it values, the dominant leadership styles, the language and symbols, the procedures and routines, and the definitions of success that make an organization unique." Other writers identify different levels of culture. For example, Kotter and Heskett (1992) talk about two levels of culture: the surface level, represented by behavior patterns or styles employees are encouraged to adopt, and the deeper level, represented by shared values that persist over time. Edgar Schein (1992) identified three levels: artifacts, an organization's visible processes; espoused values, an organization's strategies and goals; and basic underlying assumptions, an organization's unconscious beliefs that are largely taken for granted.

In Chapters 2 and 3, I defined personality in terms of the variables within the personal loop of the Motivational System Model: needing/wanting, thinking, feeling, valuing/deciding, and doing. Consistent with that formulation, I define culture in terms of the same variables within the interpersonal, team, and organizational loops. One way to simplify this is to think of culture as "the way we do things around here" (Deal & Kennedy, 1982). More specifically, it can be conceived of as the values, beliefs, and norms that shape "the way we do things." These variables are defined as follows:

- Beliefs are subjective assumptions, conclusions, and predictions,
- Values are standards of importance, and
- Norms are standards of behavior based on beliefs and values.

In teams and organizations, norms operationally define values. Norms can be explicit or implicit. Explicit norms ("We always start our meetings on time," "We have an open-door policy") are standards to which people conform consciously; implicit norms ("Feelings are kept private," "We take care of our own") are standards to which people conform unconsciously.

Thus, needs and wants motivate people to organize for a shared mission and vision. They work toward these ends by establishing shared values, beliefs, and norms. For example, the motivation for a start-up organization might be to develop or improve a product or service, based on needs or wants. Those starting the venture would make assumptions, conclusions, and predictions about the market, their chances of success, necessary resources, and so on. They would also clarify their mission and vision (based on terminal values), as well as their standards of importance for serving the mission and moving toward the vision (instrumental values). These standards would then shape the development of norms, defining acceptable and unacceptable behavior. Over time, a distinctive way of doing things develops and, if effective, it will be reflected, at least to some extent, in policies, procedures, and corporate mythology. When members talk about their culture, they might say such things as, "This is who we are" or "This is what works for us." But more importantly, the culture will be reflected in what they do.

There's constant interaction among the personal, interpersonal, team, and organizational loops of the Motivational System Model—like particles of an atom and atoms in a molecule—although these usually remain "invisible" until problems occur. Strictly speaking, beliefs and values are personal. They become part of team and organizational culture when they're shared by individuals and passed down by people through the years by words and actions. Because I take a systems approach, I don't believe it's necessary to specify which variables are deeper or more important than others. Needs/wants, beliefs, feelings, values, and norms all have subtle and hidden aspects. The key thing is to be alert to relevant information within the four loops and the dynamics of their interrelationships.

Culture can be used to refer to the interpersonal, team, and organizational levels. Individuals develop interpersonal relationships (both formal and informal) and are members of a team or teams. The organization is a dynamic whole composed of all the interrelated individuals, interpersonal relationships, and teams. Individuals are the basic raw material of an organization—its human capital. Without individuals, there'd be no teams or organizations. Interpersonal relationships and teams are the primary supportive units within organizations. The focus at these levels is on communication, encouragement, and collaboration. This is where people have their closest relationships, where they are known most fully, where they satisfy their need for belonging, and where most of the organization's work is done.

As the focus shifts from teams to the organization, the complexity increases and relationships become less personal. The larger culture is the glue that holds all the individuals, interpersonal relationships, and teams together. It gives cohesion to the entity through which people can collaborate to achieve a larger purpose. At this level, the effectiveness of culture depends on the amount of integration or consistency among individuals, interpersonal relationships, teams, and the overall organization. When I go into an organization, I ask myself four questions:

- "What's happening at the individual level?"
- "What's happening at the interpersonal level?"
- "What's happening at the team level?"
- "What's happening at the organizational level?"

Spotting "disconnects" among levels allows me to focus my attention. For example, disconnects often exist between functional areas (engineering and production, sales and marketing) or between geographical areas (corporate and local, region to region, national and international). The key is thinking about the system and looking for functional and dysfunctional interrelationships. Complete integration is an unachievable goal; moving toward greater integration is a dynamic process of continuous improvement.

Now let's examine the components of culture as they relate to the five variables in the Motivational System Model: needing/wanting, thinking, feeling, valuing/deciding, and doing.

Needing/Wanting

Like individuals, teams and organizations have physiological, safety, social, esteem, and self-actualization needs. Like an individual's, a team or organization's core need is to keep growing—grow or die, that is the choice. Physiological needs for organizations have to do with pay and benefits, while safety needs concern potential dangers in the workplace. These needs are generally met in today's workplace, but they can never be taken for granted. Employee dissatisfaction with wages and/or benefits can threaten survival and growth. When attempting to make a plane reservation recently, I was told I couldn't use my frequent flyer miles because of a possible strike over wages. The reservationist said if there were a strike the airline planned to shut down operations. At this point in time, therefore, the airline was functioning at the bottom of its need hierarchy, with the possibility of losing a great deal of money.

Many safety problems have been eliminated or drastically reduced in organizations by government regulations, but the potential always exists for new threats to appear. Safety problems are symptoms of other problems with the culture that need to be identified and eliminated. For example, there has been an increase in workplace violence during the past few years. I see this as symptomatic of the added pressure many employees feel because they're expected to do more work with less help. Also, recent pressures to cut costs have led some organizations to compromise on safety for their employees and their customers.

A culture must respond to the needs of individuals, teams, and the overall organization. Organizations can no longer satisfy their needs at the expense of employees—at least not for long. Gone are the days when employees would tolerate poor working conditions or limited opportunities just to draw a paycheck. Recruiting and retaining capable employees is one of the most pressing issues many organizations face today. The demand for qualified workers is far greater than supply—especially in the technical, computer, health care, and education fields—and it will continue, giving these employees considerable bargaining power. For example, according to the U.S. Department of Labor's *Occupational Outlook Handbook,* computer systems analysts, engineers, and scientists are expected to be the fastest growing occupations between now and 2008 (see http://stats.bls.gov/oco/ocos042.html#outlook). If these workers' needs are not met, they'll go across the street or around the world.

Although it's necessary to pay attention to physiological and safety needs, the primary focus of culture today is on meeting social, psychological, and self-actualization needs. In previous chapters I categorized these as needs for *competence* and *integrity.* Thus, people in organizations need opportunities to use their skills (personal competence) and to make a contribution (social competence), within an atmosphere conducive to self-respect (personal integrity) and acceptance (social integrity). Surveys show that, as workers feel a sense of satisfaction and a belief that their work is meaningful, the motivational influence of salary and benefits becomes less important (Barrett, 1998). In addition, research findings reveal that organizations that respond to these needs will outperform organizations that do not by a large margin (see, for example, Collins & Porras, 1994; Grant, 1998; Kotter & Heskett, 1992).

At the same time, teams and organizations need a competent and ethical workforce in order to achieve their objectives. Table 4.1 summarizes some of the specific requirements in the current business environment.

Table 4.1. Organizational Needs

	Personal	Social

Competence	Adaptability
	Capable workforce
	Fast learners
	Intellectual leverage
	Openness to change
	Speed
	Responsiveness
		Involvement
		Mutual interests
		Opportunities for growth
		Participation
		Satisfied employees,
		   customers, and stakeholders
		Sense of ownership
		Value-added products or
		   services

Integrity	Commitment to the truth Dependability Honesty	Collaborative partnering Cooperation Emotional intelligence Free flow of information Healthy interpersonal relationships Trust

When I meet with a leadership team struggling with performance issues, I often ask them to describe the organization's needs and wants and jot these down on easel paper. Then I ask them which needs or wants are not being satisfied. Once these have been identified, the focus shifts to how the needs and wants can be satisfied more fully.

Thinking

Just because employees have good wages and feel physically safe doesn't ensure that they'll be free from fear. Their needs for mastery, a sense of contribution, self-respect, and acceptance push them forward but, because the future is always unknown, they can be held back by fears of failure, insignificance, being judged, and rejection. To be effective, therefore, a culture must help employees meet these needs and assuage their fears. Many employees never feel safe, but they get so used to this over a period of time they simply take it for granted—almost as if it's supposed to be that way. Breaking this pattern often requires a combination of encouragement and reassurance—and trust.

The first question job applicants ask themselves, usually subconsciously, is, "What would I have to do to survive here?" They start gathering this information during the interview process, and this continues during new employee orientation and the early stages of employment. Everything that members of an organization say to job applicants and new employees, both formally and informally, conveys information about the culture. The assumptions and conclusions drawn will determine whether someone accepts a job offer, and whether a new employee feels safe.

As Schein and others have pointed out, a lot of the basic beliefs underlying culture are taken so much for granted that they're simply assumed to be true. Just because people share these beliefs, however, doesn't make the beliefs effective or healthy. There's a psychiatric condition called folie´ a deux, referring to people who share the same delusional system—they believe each other's distortions. On more than one occasion, I've gone home from a consulting assignment thinking, "These people really believe each other's illusions." I prefer working with at least one other consultant on projects, so I have a reality check for what I've seen. Otherwise, I'm vulnerable to wondering whether it's them or me.

Jerry Harvey (1988) used a parable to describe how people collude to do things they don't want to do as individuals. Kets de Vries and Miller (1984) used psychoanalytic concepts to describe five common dysfunctional organizational styles: paranoid, compulsive, dramatic, depressive, and schizoid. Similarly Morgan (1986) used metaphorical language to describe organizations as psychic prisons and instruments of domination. These parables, styles, and metaphors concern distorted beliefs that result in unhealthy organizational cultures and practices.

People are quite capable of seeing threats and opportunities that aren't really there and making a persuasive case to others that they are. Similarly, beliefs that were accurate in the past may no longer be true. An example is the belief that organizations can guarantee employment as long as a person's performance is adequate. This was accurate right after World War II, but is now part of history. If people assume their beliefs are "true," they will not be open to scrutinizing and changing them.

The three most important types of beliefs that shape culture are beliefs about self, beliefs about others in the organization, and beliefs about the outside world.

Beliefs About Self

In Chapter 2, I indicated that people's sense of self-worth varies from completely conditional to completely unconditional. Those with conditional self-worth tend to be more fearful and defensive than those with more unconditional self-worth. When individuals form themselves into groups, teams, and organizations, a shared sense of worth evolves over time. On these levels, the differences between conditional and unconditional worth can be quite dramatic. Groups and teams with conditional worth compare themselves with others, forming judgments regarding superiority and inferiority. This results in stereotypes, prejudice, and discrimination. In contrast, groups and teams with a less conditional sense of worth show more tolerance and acceptance of differences.

Barrett (1998, p. 35) said, "The emotional well-being of an organization is determined by how good it feels about itself and the quality of its relationships." I've consulted with teams and organizations struggling with low self-esteem. In fact, some people were even ashamed to tell me where they worked. My impression is that many HR teams struggle with low self-esteem, believing that their contribution to the organization isn't appreciated. Human resource team members often spend time consoling one another ("I know, they treat me the same way") and complaining about the rest of the organization ("They don't realize how tough they make our job"). Staff teams tend to have a lower sense of worth than line teams—except for IS and legal services—rooted in deeply held assumptions about whose work is more important. Ideas originating from the "wrong" department or people low in the chain of command are often dismissed, forming invisible barriers.

The recent emphasis on empowerment and cross-functional and virtual teams challenges arbitrary distinctions among people. Interventions designed to tear down distorted or narrow beliefs often encounter stiff resistance, however, showing just how powerful these components of culture can be.

Beliefs About Others in the Organization

The most important conceptions about others in the organization concern people's basic views about human nature and about whether or not others can be trusted.

In terms of human nature, it comes down to this question: Do you believe that you have to motivate people to do their work, or do you believe that people want to work and your role is to help create the conditions under which they will motivate themselves? This is the old Theory X (people are lazy and have to be coerced or intimidated to work) and Theory Y (people want to work and enjoy using their talents and abilities) debate.

Although we've moved away from Theory X toward Theory Y since Douglas McGregor's book, *The Human Side of Enterprise,* was published in 1960, Theory X still has many proponents. In cultures dominated by negative views of human nature, the emphasis is on "command and control"; in cultures dominated by positive views of human nature, the emphasis is on empowerment and supervisors function more like coaches and resource people. The issue is whether people need to be policed or can be turned loose to do what needs to be done. The choice plays a huge role in defining culture.

I define trust as believing others have your best interests at heart. Cultures vary widely in the amount of trust that exists. Just as conditional self-esteem is the single biggest barrier to personal effectiveness, lack of trust is the single biggest barrier to interpersonal, team, and organizational effectiveness. Although unconditional self-esteem must be claimed as a birthright, however, trust must be nurtured. Few people automatically trust others; proving thrustworthiness is the unspoken code governing relationships.

Just how big an issue is mistrust? It's an insidious and pervasive problem, robbing organizations of much-needed commitment and performance. In a survey conducted by the Lausanne Institute (1998), 91 percent of 474 government supervisors reported that lack of trust negatively impacts productivity. When trust is low, people focus on protecting themselves from each other instead of focusing on accomplishing organizational goals. Individuals with conditional self-esteem have more difficulty trusting others. They tend to project their negative views about themselves onto others, preventing teams and organizations from achieving their potential. Unless trust issues are brought to the surface and dealt with, they remain deeply ingrained, negative aspects of culture.

When I work with teams struggling with mistrust, I hit the issues fast and hard. Mistrust never goes away by itself and doesn't fade with time. To be resolved, mistrust must be brought out in the open. Usually team members don't address trust issues directly, but act more like card sharks playing a game of poker. The climate is adversarial, and every move is carefully calculated. I challenge people to lay down their cards and confront the mistrust, explaining that until they do this they can forget about accomplishing working together effectively.

Beliefs About the Outside World

The third major type of beliefs are conceptions about the world outside. Remember that the external environment is part of the Motivational System Model (see Figure 2.1). This is a vital source of information about conditions and trends that have organizational relevance. The survival and growth of organizations depends largely on their ability to gather and accurately interpret such information.

Organizations plagued by low self-worth and mistrust often take a defensive stance toward the outside world. Consequently they're either hyper-vigilant about the competition, convinced that others are "out to get us," or they don't pay enough attention to what others are doing and are unprepared. To avoid these risks, organizations must be willing and able to scrutinize outside information nondefensively and update their culture when necessary to remain viable. Kotter and Heskett (1992) explained, "In corporate cultures that promote useful change, managers pay close attention to relevant changes in a firm's context and then implement incremental changes in strategies and practices to keep firms and cultures in line with environmental realities."

GE's Work-Out is a good example of how this can be done. Jacquie Vierling-Huang, manager of Work-Out and Change Acceleration at GE Crotonville, described the process this way: "Work-Out, which was launched in 1989, was named for the idea of taking excess 'work out' of the system, thus eliminating bureaucracy and freeing up people's time. It was deliberately designed to focus on the cultural side of change: helping people change their attitudes about their work and the ways they approached their jobs" (Vierling-Huang, 1999, p. 75). In a continuous effort to increase effectiveness, people are challenged to ask themselves and others, "Why do we do it that way?" Jack Welch, GE's CEO, has said that a GE business must be either number one or two in its industry to remain part of the corporation, so considerable incentive exists to ensure cultural effectiveness.

One manufacturing organization I consulted with has a two-year, four-rotation training program whereby new engineers rotate through engineering, sourcing, production, and sales and marketing. Trainees worked together well during training, but conflict emerged after they were assigned to functional areas. They wanted to get away from "functional thinking," so they set up regular "Integrated Product Team" meetings to keep the focus on the product rather than on functions. Efforts such as this have allowed the organization to adapt its culture to changing conditions.

Feeling

Teams and organizations vary widely in terms of how they view feelings and their expression. In some cultures, people remain on a head level and feelings are seldom expressed; in other cultures, people are more open about their feelings. Once I was doing team building for a large oil company where everyone had just taken the Myers-Briggs Type Indicator®, which identified people's preferences along four scales: introversion-extroversion, sensing-intuition, thinking-feeling, and judging-perception. In this organization, it was considered the kiss of death for males to come out an F on the Thinking/Feeling scale. While this scale distinguishes between a preference for objective or subjective factors in decision making, in this culture F was perceived as a weakness—they connected it with a stereotyped view of femininity—so the males deliberately faked their answers to make sure they were identified as T's. This is the kind of distorted thinking that can hamper a team or organizational culture.

In some cultures the only acceptable feelings to express are frustration and anger. These cultures tend to be characterized by low trust, so anger is viewed as the only "safe" emotion. Being open about other feelings is viewed as a risk, so people keep them private.

Often teams and organizations seek an OD intervention because unhappy workers are having a negative impact on customers and business results. In cultures in which people are more formal and closed, people compensate for the lack of emotional data by making inferences about others' motives and feelings. Often these inferences are inaccurate, fueling fear and mistrust. I explain to clients that feelings are an important source of data and that negative feelings often stem from distorted and inaccurate beliefs. I also warn them that unexpressed feelings based on inaccurate beliefs can sabotage the decision-making process. Then I work to establish a climate in which people feel safe to express feelings, so that the assumptions and conclusions behind them can be identified and assessed. Interventions like this often have a very positive impact on culture, increasing people's emotional intelligence. People learn that they don't have to be afraid of feelings, and they're more aware of the risks of keeping feelings hidden. Over time, the greater openness among people serves to raise the level of trust.

Valuing/Deciding

As standards of importance, values are crucial cultural components, because they're the criteria used to make decisions, set priorities, and develop strategies. Values are also standards that allow teams and organizations to make comparisons ("We're a better supplier because our customer service is second to none"). Because tradeoffs exist with every choice, values define what teams and organizations want to get out of their decisions and plans. As such, values perform a leadership function within culture. Needing, thinking, and feeling all provide input, but values are the most compelling factors in the decision-making process.

Like individuals, teams and organizations have both terminal and instrumental values. Terminal values are preferred ends, and instrumental values are preferred means for accomplishing those ends. Terminal values are fundamental to mission and vision. A team's mission and vision might differ somewhat from those of the overall organization but, to avoid conflict, there must be enough alignment for progress toward the overall mission and vision to be made.

A lot of authors make a distinction between mission and vision, on the one hand, and values on the other. When they discuss values, however, they're actually referring to instrumental values. I believe, consistent with Rokeach's (1973) value theory, that mission and vision are based on terminal values. Values are superordinate concepts encompassing both preferred ends and means. The reason many OD activities fail is that the consultants are blind to an organization's prevailing values and are therefore unsuccessful in having a significant impact on them. Let's talk about terminal and instrumental values separately.

Terminal Values

Mission represents a team or organization's purpose, its reason for existence. C. William Pollard, chairman of the ServiceMaster Company said, "People want to work for a cause, not just for a living. When there is alignment between the cause of the firm and the cause of its people, move over—because there will be extraordinary performance" (Pollard, 1996, p. 45). Vision represents a team or organization's dreams for the future. Broholm (1990, p. 6) said, "I would choose to define 'vision' as 'a valued image of the future which connects to our sense of purpose and draws forth the commitment of our energy.'. . . It has the power to motivate and empower us to make that image a reality."

Employees must be committed to the mission and vision, because their efforts will determine ultimate success or failure. For this reason, it's important for an organization's mission and vision to overlap with the purpose (personal mission), dreams (personal vision), and goals of employees. This is often referred to as organizational alignment, an ongoing process of building a cohesive culture. The satisfaction and motivation of employees depends considerably on the "fit" between their personal values and the values of their team and organization. Cultivating this fit is an ongoing process. As Peter Senge (1990, p. 311) said, "Experience suggests that visions that are genuinely shared require ongoing conversation where individuals not only feel free to express their dreams, but learn how to listen to each other's dreams."

Unfortunately, many organizational leaders either do not care about or, at least, do not take the time to sit down with employees and ask them about their hopes and dreams. Consequently, they miss opportunities to show employees the connection between what they want and what the organization wants. Making this connection strengthens integration. To do this effectively, leaders must genuinely care about the wants and aspirations of employees. Commitment cannot be coerced through fear and intimidation, but must be gained through mutual consent.

To a large extent, the ability of leaders to develop and gain commitment to an organization's mission, vision, and goals depends on their beliefs about themselves and their beliefs about others. Leaders struggling with low self-esteem and trust issues have trouble inspiring others because they cannot establish the type of climate necessary to meet the personal and social needs of employees. As Kotter (1990, p. 63) said, "Achieving grand visions despite the obstacles always requires an occasional burst of energy, the kind that certain motivational and inspirational processes can provide. Such processes accomplish their energizing effect, not by pushing people in the right direction, as a control mechanism often does, but by satisfying very basic human needs: for achievement, belonging, recognition, self-esteem, a sense of control over one's life, and living up to one's ideals."

Think of it this way. If an organization is like a rocket, fuel is necessary for the rocket to fly. Providing for employee need satisfaction releases the energy necessary for the rocket to blast off, and maintaining alignment of organizational and personal visions guides the rocket in the right direction. Leaders with low self-esteem are too self-absorbed and defensive to do this effectively. In contrast, leaders with high self-esteem not only have more freedom to see that employees' needs are satisfied, but they're often capable of creating conditions within which they are motivated to achieve more than employees ever thought possible. Employees respond to such leaders with enthusiastic support.

Most organizations start out with a grand mission and vision for the future but, over time, the mission and vision can in fact become defensive. Survival takes the place of growth. Such an organization becomes reactive instead of proactive. In the new economy, however, organizations lacking a vision based on growth-oriented terminal values will not survive.

Terminal values also shape goals and objectives, allowing the mission and vision to be fulfilled. About goals, Senge (1990, pp. 217–218) said, "Just setting goals without a genuine vision will likely lead to backsliding when the goals prove difficult to realize." Similarly, Schein (1992, p. 56) said, "Goals concretize the mission and facilitate the decisions on means."

Instrumental Values

Instrumental values are reflected in preferred modes of conduct for achieving terminal values. Broholm (1990, p. 15) said, "Values are the fuel which drive the engine of desire to make vision a reality. Vision is first and foremost concerned with values." Recall that instrumental values can be classified as defensive (power, control), stabilizing (routine, predictability), and growth (creativity, risk taking), depending on how they function to meet needs. Defensive values protect against perceived threat; stabilizing values maintain the status quo; growth values provide for movement forward. (Tables 3.2, 3.3, and 3.4 in Chapter 3 list defensive, stabilizing, and growth values.) Values are not defined by the labels used to describe them, but by their results. Regardless of the particular words that are used, therefore, in actual practice any value can function as either D, S, or G. Similar to those of individuals, the value systems of teams and organizations will contain a combination of D, S, and G values, and their cultures will vary greatly based on that mix.

Once values become part of a team or organizational culture, they resist change. There's also pressure on people to conform to the values. An attitude can develop in an organization that its values are the best ones, even the only ones. Potential employees are screened in terms of their willingness to embrace the values, and existing members are rewarded or punished for adhering to the values. While shared values provide order and consistency, a dogmatic and rigid stance toward values can create an intolerant culture. In today's increasingly pluralistic society, an organization must be open to a diversity of values while maintaining its basic integrity. The large number of discrimination and sexual harassment lawsuits that have been filed over the past two decades reveal how difficult maintaining this balance can be.

When I use the term "growth value," I don't simply mean financial gain. A growth value is one providing *forward movement that meets system needs.* In other words, it meets the needs of individuals, teams, and the overall organization, not one at the expense of others. In organizations that emphasize growth values, financial success occurs as a by-product of their operating values (Collins & Porras, 1994). Ironically, many companies currently enjoying financial success are actually defensive organizations. Driven by short-term profits and stock market evaluations, their employees live under constant fear of being fired unless they perform better and faster. Although these organizations may be able to continue their methods for a period of time, at some point they'll come to a grinding halt.

If the external environment changes, organizations may have to change their values in order to survive. Inwardly this is experienced as a discrepancy between "what we have to do" and "what we want to do." In these situations, organizations often shift to more defensive values, which may be necessary to deal with the immediate threat.

While some emphasis on defense is always necessary—survival is prerequisite to growth—cultures weighted down by defensive values often contain major barriers to progress. In an early article, for example, Jack Gibb (1961) described the impact of defensive communication on organizational behavior. Defensive teams and organizations tend to be characterized by low self-esteem and mistrust. Their primary focus is on compensating for perceived inadequacy, not on striving to fulfill their potential. Consequently, people are reactive and become bogged down by internal competition and politics. So much energy is spent on infighting that employees have trouble mounting a unified effort to deal with the competition. Teams and organizations lose to the extent that they perform at less than their full potential. Defensive values tend to widen this gap, not close it.

In defensive teams and organizations, power tends to be the prerogative of management. Consequently, many others feel powerless. Rosabeth Moss Kanter (1977) explained that, when people feel powerless, they protect and defend themselves by attempting to control others. For this reason, empowerment—which is a growth value—is usually more effective than consolidating power in the hands of a few.

Defensive teams and organizations often have many of the characteristics of unadaptive cultures described by Kotter and Heskett. They said, "Cultures that are not adaptive take many forms. In large corporations, they are often characterized by some arrogance, insularity, and bureaucratic centralization, all supported by a value system that cares more about self-interest than about customers, stockholders, employees, or good leadership. In such cultures, managers tend to ignore relevant contextual changes and to cling to outmoded strategies and ossified practices. They make it difficult for anyone else, especially those below them in the hierarchy, to implement new and better strategies and practices. And they tend to turn people off—particularly those individuals whose personal values include an emphasis on integrity, trust, and caring for other human beings" (Kotter & Heskett, 1992, p. 142). Obviously, such teams and organizations will have trouble surviving in the global economy.

The focus of stabilizing values is on keeping things the way they are currently. As with defensive values, some emphasis on stabilizing values is necessary to provide balance—no one can cope with constant change—but too much emphasis on stabilizing values can stifle growth. Kotter's distinction between management and leadership provides some insight into the difference between stabilizing and growth values. He said, "The basic function of management is homeostatic; it is to keep a system alive by making sure that critical variables remain within tolerable ranges constantly. . . . An important aspect of any homeostatic process is control" (Kotter, 1990, p. 63). In contrast to management, which focuses on homeostasis, leadership focuses on movement or change.

Another way to look at this is to contrast order with creativity. While stabilizing values provide for consistency and order, growth values provide for creativity, which is essential to progress. In discussing the environmental conditions of organizations, Morgan (1986, p. 39) said, "We find that bureaucratic organizations tend to work most effectively in environments that are stable or protected in some way and that very different species are found in more competitive and turbulent regions, such as environments of high-tech firms in the aerospace and microelectronics industries."

In the years ahead, fewer organizations will be able to find a stable or protected environment, which will in turn place a higher premium on creativity. The question is how to achieve organizational creativity. Change has developed a negative connotation over the past decade, so I avoid using the term in my practice. When evoked, it conjures up images of struggle, uncertainty, and loss. An emphasis on growth is a more effective way of initiating change because people don't perceive growth as change (even though it is). People will pursue growth naturally if they feel safe.

When I work with teams or organizations on values issues, I often ask them to complete the Values Identification Survey (Exhibit 5.2). After identifying their values, participants label them as defensive, stabilizing, and growth. Then I ask them to think of ways to shift from defensive values to more growth values. This often deepens people's understanding of organizational issues and generates many useful suggestions for dealing with them. I used this exercise with two groups of business process consultants at Boeing Commercial Airplane Group. The organization, which had been losing market share to Airbus, needed a cultural change to spark revitalization. Six subgroups working independently were remarkably consistent in estimating the overall organizational values to be about 50 percent defensive, 20 percent stabilizing, and 30 percent growth. These consultants agreed that the percentages for defensive and growth values should be reversed in order to deal with the competition; their challenge was to figure out how this could be done proactively to avert a potential income crisis.

The best way to gain support for culture change is to show people how it will enhance their growth. This means teams and organizations must be characterized by high self-esteem and trust; they must be able to look past their fears to affirm their highest aspirations. Along with this, the timing and pacing of change must be managed effectively, so it doesn't lead to instability and trigger a slide back into defensive values. I did some work with a small firm that had been growing about 30 percent a year. Their challenge was to figure out how to continue growing without lowering service quality. They decided to slow their rate of growth slightly until they could build a stronger infrastructure for hiring and training new employees.

Espoused, Actual, and Desired Values

Another cultural distinction is between espoused, actual, and desired values. Espoused values are the ones teams and organizations say they hold, whereas actual values are the ones they act on. Desired values are the ones they would like to be moving toward. I view espoused values as part of a team's or organization's mythology, not part of its operating culture. Espoused values that are not reflected in actual practice are either ignored or looked on with cynicism. Discrepancies between what people say and do are a significant factor in creating a climate of suspicion and mistrust.

In contrast, actual values are revealed by what teams and organizations reward and punish. These actions make it crystal clear what a team or organization really cares about and will have a tremendous impact on what employees do and do not do. Identifying desired values can be helpful because they point the direction toward change. In a sense, desired values are reflected in team and organizational visions. It's important to close the gap between actual and desired values; otherwise desired values end up generating the same kinds of problems as espoused values.

The Values Identification Survey (Exhibit 5.2) can be used to establish team or organizational values and identify discrepancies between espoused and actual values. It can also be used to identify discrepancies among individual, team, and organizational values. This shows the degree of integration existing within a culture. The Values Assessment Inventory (Exhibit 5.1) can also be employed to assess team and organizational values against four criteria: balance, viability, alignment, and authenticity (as described in Chapters 1 and 5).

As with individuals, the key outcome of valuing (applying standards of importance) for a team or organization is that decisions are made. Every decision is based on values, and the effectiveness of those decisions hinges on the values selected. Therefore, it's always important to consider how values impact decisions, and vice versa. Strategic planning is a process of making decisions about goals (general direction), objectives (specific results by specific times), and action plans (a sequence of steps that will accomplish the objectives). The entire strategic planning process is value-centered, serving the larger mission and vision. Teams and organizations that fail to consider values during strategic planning risk selecting methods that aren't aligned with their goals.

Doing

Behavior represents the actual implementation of value-centered decisions and action plans to actualize visions. As such, they are the tangible result of decisions. For this reason it's very important that values be related to specific behavioral norms. One way to relate norms to values and to assess norms is by asking a series of questions, such as the following:

- What are your explicit (discussed) and implicit (undiscussed) norms?
- What values do these norms serve?

- Which norms serve your values effectively?

- Which norms serve your values ineffectively?

- How could you make your norms more effective?

After effective norms serving values have been established, everyone from the top down should be held accountable for acting in accordance with the behavioral standards. Ideally, they will hold themselves accountable. Simply put, everyone must be on the same page. Behavior problems in teams and organizations can be caused by (1) lack of alignment within the culture, (2) lack of clarity regarding expectations, and/or (3) poor execution. It's important to identify the specific cause because the solutions for each problem will be different. Alignment can be increased by relating organizational values to personal values; clarity can be increased by specifying acceptable and unacceptable behaviors; execution can be increased by providing coaching, mentoring, or other learning opportunities.

Need Satisfied?

The real bottom line for a culture is how well it satisfies needs. The question here is, "Whose needs are being satisfied?" Argyris (1962) maintained that the key challenge is satisfying the relationship between the individual and the organization. He argued that in order to accomplish this, the organization must adjust its value system toward helping employees become more psychologically healthy, and employees must adjust their value system toward greater commitment to organizational goals. Thus, an effective culture is one that successfully balances individual and organizational values, that is, walking the tightrope to success.

Also, just because a culture satisfied individual and organizational needs at one point doesn't guarantee that it will be able to do so at another point. With the knowledge explosion and worldwide access to information, teams and organizations must continuously reassess their cultures and adapt to changing conditions (see Nadler, 1985). How effectively they do this will determine their ability to survive and grow.

The Value-Centered Planning Worksheet (Exhibit 4.1) can help you pull the points presented in this chapter together into a strategy for integrating means to accomplish the ends. It can be used to facilitate individual, team, or organizational planning. This exercise may be completed by itself or in conjunction with tools described elsewhere in the book.

Exhibit 4.1. Value-Centered Planning Worksheet

Purpose

The Value-Centered Planning Worksheet provides an efficient tool for applying the concepts presented in this chapter, whether for an individual, a team, or an organization.

Background

Values pertain to ends and to means for accomplishing these ends. Thus, values guide all the key components in the planning process and allow a consistent and integrated approach to management. Organizational values guide decisions about mission, vision, culture, strategy, and action. Of course, you must be alert to the complexity and changing dynamics of the market and other elements in the situation within which you are functioning. In other words, think strategically. Something is strategic if it:

- Establishes direction,
- Impacts organizational values,
- Has organization-wide implications,
- Impacts the future,
- Affects competitive position,
- Has a long-term perspective,
- Involves calculated risks, and/or
- Guides action.

In the past, it was possible to map out relatively firm five-year strategic plans, but in the networked economy that is no longer realistic. Situational changes may require changes in goals, objectives, and/or plans. Because of this, clarity about mission, vision, and values takes on added significance. And clarity about values is important because values are fundamental.

A variety of tools, instruments, and processes can be used. I encourage you to use whatever processes you have found effective to accomplish these tasks and to experi-

Exhibit 4.1. Value-Centered Planning Worksheet, Cont'd

ment with new ones. This worksheet provides a way to consolidate information about the key elements involved in formulating strategy.

Instructions

This worksheet can be used by an individual for personal planning or by a group to facilitate team or organizational planning. In actual practice, the responses for mission, vision, and values may each be recorded on one or two sheets of paper (easel paper for a team or an organization). Then a separate set of sheets can be prepared for each goal, the objectives related to the goal, and action steps.

When used as a large group intervention, the worksheet allows the entire system to operate "on the same page" (actually several pages). Once the process is complete, relevant information for individuals, teams, and the overall organization can be placed on a computer to facilitate communication, revision, and accountability. (For examples of specific statements of mission, vision, and values, see *The Mission Statement Book: 301 Corporate Mission Statements from America's Top Companies,* by Jeffrey Abrams, 1999.)

Exhibit 4.1. Value-Centered Planning Worksheet, Cont'd

Value-Centered Planning Worksheet

Focus of Attention: ☐ Myself   ☐ The team   ☐ The organization

Mission (Purpose, reason for existing)

Vision (Dreams for the future)

Values (Standards of importance for moving toward vision)

Goals, objectives, and action plans:

· Goals (general directions for moving toward vision)

· Objectives (specific results for each goal by a specific time)

· Action plans (sequence of actions that will accomplish each objective, which generally include "who," "what action," and " by when")

(Note: Add additional goals, objectives, and action plans as needed.)

Exhibit 4.1. Value-Centered Planning Worksheet, Cont'd

Goal #1:

Objective:

Action Plans:

Objective:

Action Plans:

Goal #2:

Objective:

Action Plans:

Objective:

Action Plans:

Goal #3:

Objective:

Action Plans:

Objective:

Action Plans:

Summary of Part 1

We are finished with Part 1 of the book, which has focused on understanding motivation within the personal, interpersonal, team, and organizational loops of the Motivational System Model. Special attention has been given to the role of values in motivation. The key points to remember about values are as follows:

- The reason for behavior is to satisfy needs and wants; values orient us to preferred ways of doing that.

- Values are standards of importance. Once embraced, values serve as criteria for making decisions and setting priorities.

- A value is a preference for one thing over its opposite. While we can say we're *for* something and *against* something else, values are not dichotomous, but rather continuous variables.

- Values are ideals. They point a direction, and moving toward the ideal represented by a value is a continuous process.

- Values are concerned with preferred ends (terminal values) and preferred means for achieving the ends (instrumental values).

- Values are organized into a value system; they are best understood systemically.

- Everyone needs a sense of purpose in life, and our specific purpose affects our choice of terminal values and vice versa.

- One's beliefs about self and others have a major impact on one's choice of purpose and that choice, in turn, affects one's personal vision of life as we would like it to be.

- People who have conditional self-esteem and have trouble trusting others strive to maintain and enhance their self-esteem, while people who have more unconditional self-esteem strive for psychological integration, wholeness, and self-actualization.

- Maintaining and enhancing self-esteem is a defensive terminal value driven by fear rooted in conditional self-esteem; self-actualization is a growth terminal value energized by a desire to express one's uniqueness and develop one's potential to the fullest.

- People fulfill their terminal values—which manifest in their purpose and vision—by acting on needs for mastery (personal competence), a sense of contribution (social competence), self-respect (personal integrity), and acceptance (social integrity).

- Instrumental values function in three ways to help people satisfy their needs for competence and integrity: defensive (D) values protect against perceived threat; stabilizing (S) values maintain the status quo; growth (G) values provide for development and are fundamental to OD.

- People with defensive terminal values tend to choose defensive instrumental values; people with growth terminal values tend to choose growth instrumental values.

- One of the best ways to increase individual effectiveness is by helping people move toward unconditional self-esteem, ideally to a state of true self-acceptance, that is, no conditions.

- One of the best way to increase interpersonal effectiveness is to raise the level of trust among people.

- Values that are shared become part of team and organizational culture. Teams and organizations characterized by low self-esteem and mistrust emphasize defensive values; teams and organizations characterized by high self-esteem and trust emphasize growth values.

- Like individuals, organizations must have both competence and integrity to satisfy their needs. The best way to foster organizational growth is to create conditions whereby people can use their abilities and gain a sense of contribution in an atmosphere conducive to self-respect and acceptance (mutual respect).

- Working in a climate that enhances self-respect and mutual respect paves the way for greater self-esteem and trust.

- Satisfying basic personal and social needs for self-esteem and trust are mutually reinforcing and, simultaneously, support high levels of organizational achievement.

Although values are crucial components in motivation, it's important to remember that values do not exist in isolation. A dynamic relationship exists between values and the other variables within each loop of the Motivational System Model: needs and wants, thinking, feeling, and doing. Part 2 focuses on assessing and changing the various components of the model, with an emphasis on values.

Part 2

Assessing and Changing Values

(5) Assessing Values

ON **THIS CHAPTER I WILL** describe in detail four criteria for assessing values: *balance, viability, alignment,* and *authenticity.* The Values Assessment Inventory (VAI), based on these criteria, and the Values Identification Survey (VIS), are included at the end of the chapter.

Why Specify Criteria?

Historically, OD practitioners have been the champions of healthy work values, serving the mutual interests of human beings and organizations. But today we are under intense pressure to help organizations increase productivity, efficiency, and short-term profits at all costs, with little regard for other values. The risk is that we will become co-opted, tearing down the values that the profession has emphasized in the past. Is it possible to help today's fast-paced organizations achieve their goals while continuing to advocate the humanistic, democratic, and developmental values upon which the field was founded? I believe it is, if we articulate objective criteria that align the energies of individuals and teams with the organizations of which they are parts.

Putting values under a microscope conjures up images of scrutinizing motherhood, the flag, and apple pie. Many people become defensive when you question their values, regarding this as a personal affront. They expect you to show deference toward their values simply because they embrace them, and they are easily offended if you don't. People develop a vested interest in their values, sometimes to the point of fanatical allegiance. When listening to these people, it often becomes clear that they believe their values are the right ones, the best ones, the *only* ones.

Values must be scrutinized, however, because they have either a positive or negative impact on decisions, priorities, strategies, plans, and behavior—there's no such thing as a value with a neutral impact. Visions are beacons, but their light is limited by people's perceptions, beliefs, and values. Throughout history, values have been used to justify everything from the noble to the heinous. Each day we read about atrocities being committed in the name of national security, religious freedom, patriotism, ethnic or racial pride, and other values. Similarly, organizations justify downsizing, restructuring, plant closings, mergers, acquisitions, and hostile takeovers in the name of corporate survival, profitability, efficiency, and shareholder value. We can engage in endless debate about whether these are the best or even the real values, only to remain adrift in a sea of subjectivity. The fact that globalization has made organizations such powerful institutions and that their decisions affect us all, however, dramatizes the need to assess values.

In my view, values must meet four requirements in order to be effective: balance, viability, alignment, and authenticity. I define *effective* as the ability to get desired results. These criteria, which themselves are values, should be viewed from a systems perspective—used to assess values in the personal, interpersonal, team, and organizational loops of the Motivational System. They should also be viewed as a useful source of hypotheses, open for discussion and research. The Values Assessment Inventory (Exhibit 5.1) is a nonstandardized instrument that can help serve these purposes. I will now describe each criterion separately.

Balance

Balance can be defined as the degree to which values are given proper emphasis relative to one another. There are four types of balance: *balance between opposites, balanced representation, balanced emphasis,* and *value tempering.* The four kinds of balance are discussed below.

Balance Between Value Opposites

When we think about our personal values, it's usually easy to identify their opposites. Standing for something means being against its opposite. While this sort of thinking makes values appear to be dichotomous, as noted previously, they are continuous variables. Thus, although we might say we value mutual interest, no one is completely free of narrowly defined self-interest. To be emotionally healthy, mutual interests must be balanced by self-interests; each has its proper place. Although there are exceptions—honesty isn't balanced by dishonesty, it is tempered by sensitivity—in most cases it is appropriate for values to be balanced by their opposites. Low self-esteem and mistrust often cause people to hold values in rigid and dogmatic ways, interfering with personal and interpersonal flexibility and effectiveness.

Balanced Value Representation

A balanced value system *must* contain values relating to the four categories of personal and social needs: *mastery* (personal competence), *a sense of contribution* (social competence), *self-respect* (personal integrity), and *acceptance* (social integrity). This ensures that the important areas of human functioning are covered and provides for accountability. Imagine what it would be like if an organization lacked standards of importance for individual performance (personal competence), or if no effort were made to show employees how their efforts contribute to the whole (social competence). Similarly, imagine an organization putting pressure on people to compromise their ethical standards (personal integrity), or people feeling marginalized by their color, age, sex, or ethnicity (social integrity). It doesn't take long to realize that all four value categories are crucial to effective functioning.

Burke (1997) articulated five values on which the profession of OD was founded: *human development, fairness, openness, choice,* and *balance of autonomy and constraint.* They can be categorized as follows (see Chapter 1): human development (personal competence), balance of autonomy and constraint (social competence), openness and choice (personal integrity), and fairness (social integrity). Thus, OD was founded intuitively on a balanced set of values.

Similarly, I categorize the OD Network's current values this way: professional development and knowledge of self (personal competence); systems orientation/approach/wholeness and social responsibility (social competence); cooperation, inclusion, collaboration, and social justice (social integrity). Although none of the values fits neatly in the category of personal integrity, this standard is implicit in the definitions of several values (see www.odnetwork.org/missionvalues.html).

I've worked with organizations that lacked values in one or more key areas, which resulted in a variety of personal and interpersonal problems. For example, one organization had three stated values: excellence (personal competence), customer success (social competence), and teamwork (social integrity). They did not have any stated values in the area of personal integrity, however, which resulted in questionable business practices and customer complaints. Another organization had five values: trying your best (personal competence), developing your potential (personal competence), delighting the customer (social competence), contributing to society (social competence), and being honest (personal integrity). They did not have any values in the area of social integrity, however, and this surfaced as petty bickering and in-fighting.

In contrast, at Menno Haven, Inc., a progressive continuing care retirement community where I facilitated the establishment of organizational values, the values chosen were excellence (personal competence), service and stewardship (social competence), integrity (personal integrity), and teamwork (social integrity). At Messiah Village, a collaborative partner of Menno Haven, where I also facilitated the establishment of organizational values, the values selected were creativity and efficiency (personal competence), enthusiasm (social competence), honesty (personal integrity), and compassion (social integrity). Having all four categories represented allowed these organizations to develop consistent and effective human resource systems.

Balanced Value Emphasis

Balanced emphasis or priority must exist among values in a value system. Many writers have stressed the importance of balancing tasks and relationships (see, for example, Blake & Mouton, 1978). I've consulted with organizations that placed such a high emphasis on performance (personal competence) that people failed to develop the cohesiveness (social integrity) needed for effective teamwork and with others that emphasized speed at the expense of quality (both personal competence values).

In today's fast-paced organizations, many employees lack balance among the different areas of their lives. Placing too high a priority on one value can supplant other values. I've done executive coaching with people struggling with compulsive productivity, which will be discussed further in the next chapter. Burning the candle at both ends, they neglected their home lives, resulting in personal and interpersonal problems.

During the past decade, the importance of balance between work and home life has been given increased attention in the literature (see, for example, Sherwood, 1998). However, this is not a new issue. Weisskopt (1959, p. 115) said, "Most of our spiritual, psychological and social problems can be traced back to a lack of integration and union. . . . Under the impact of technology and business we have become concerned exclusively with activity directed towards change and control of the external world, with things to be produced and consumed, with money, possessions and their power. The inner life has been neglected. . . . The same one-sidedness and lack of integrative union can be found in our interpersonal relations." Weisskopt made these statements in 1959, but they're just as relevant today.

Finding the right balance among values is an ongoing challenge for organizations. Barrett (1998, pp. 104–105) said, "Visionary organizations find a dynamic balance between the organization's needs for survival and growth, the employee's needs for personal fulfillment, and the local community's and society's needs for economic, social, and environmental sustainability." OD practitioners can make an important contribution by helping individuals and organizations achieve such balance.

Value Tempering

Finally, healthy functioning requires that values be tempered or moderated by each other. Thus, honesty is tempered by tact (brutal honesty is seldom effective), openness is tempered by discretion, ambition is tempered by cooperation, justice is tempered by mercy. Such tempering guards against dogmatic, unthinking imposition of values. As discussed in Chapter 1, balance between freedom and constraint was a founding value of the OD profession, and balance between the individual and organization is cited at the beginning of the "Organization and Human Systems Development Credo" (see Appendix). Table 5.1 summarizes some consequences of overemphasizing and under-emphasizing values, along with suggestions for improving balance. I encourage you to think of your own examples.

Table 5.1. Consequences of Lack of Balance and Ways to Achieve Balance

Value	Overemphasis	Under-Emphasis	Ways to Achieve Balance
Mastery (Personal Competence)	Fear of failure	Poor quality	Set performance goals that are meaningful, achievable, measurable, and controllable
	Unrealistic goals, deadlines	Inefficiency	Emphasize developing one's potential
	Insecurity	Customer complaints	Focus on learning, instead of labeling performance in terms of success or failure
	Stress, frustration	Lack of performance goals	Strive for excellence
	Anger, resentment	Carelessness, mistakes	Balance work/home life
	Feeling used	Loss of business	Think creatively
	Feel treated like a number	Waste of talent, ability	
	Internal competition	Under-utilizing people	
	Exploitation	Tension between productive and unproductive employees	
	Emphasis on tasks at the expense of relationships		
	Sabotage, rebellion		
	Unionization, strikes		
A Sense of Contribution (Social Competence)	Fear of insignificance	Lack of fulfillment	Praise good performance
	Making arbitrary distinctions between the importance of jobs	Indifference, complacency	Point out how a person's work contributes to the whole
	Status issues	View job as just a paycheck	Stress mutual interests
	Emphasis on "hype"	Lack of recognition	Strive to add value
		Lack of commitment	Give credit where credit's due
		Lack of ownership	Avoid minimizing contributions
		Cynicism	Emphasize customer success
			Focus on stewardship

Self-Respect (Personal Integrity)	Fear of being judged Emphasis on formality Lack of spontaneity Fear of offending people	Hostile work environment Harassment Insensitivity Lack of accountability Labeling people Lack of trust	Clarify acceptable and unacceptable behaviors Hold people accountable Follow the "Golden Rule" Do the right thing, even if it's unpopular Present yourself as someone worthy of trust Deal with issues directly Maintain a commitment to the truth Honor commitments
Acceptance (Social Integrity)	Fear of rejection Social club atmosphere Emphasis on relationships at the expense of tasks Deadlines are missed Compromising honesty to maintain acceptance Pressure to conform Office politics	Prejudice, discrimination Alienation Cliques, in-groups, out-groups Favoritism Lack of cohesiveness Lack of cooperation Lack of teamwork Communication problems Lack of diversity, inclusiveness Lack of participation, involvement Lack of trust	Invite participation and involvement Stress team success Champion inclusiveness and diversity Avoid unhealthy competition Strive for cohesiveness and cooperation Foster open communication Eliminate discrimination Challenge stereotypes

The following questions can be asked to determine whether balance exists:

- Are the values balanced by their opposites when appropriate?
- Are there values representing all four personal and social needs?
- Are values pertaining to the four needs given proper emphasis?
- Are values tempered or moderated by each other in appropriate ways?

Viability

Viability can be defined as the degree to which values are workable in the current business climate. To be viable, values must allow people to use and develop their abilities and make a contribution within an atmosphere conducive to self-respect and acceptance. Unless values provide such a foundation, anything else they might do will be severely limited. In addition, viable values must be based on accurate beliefs, in tune with current realities, and must produce the desired results. It's not enough for values to be balanced. Balance can exist among a set of unhealthy values.

People's values aren't defined by what they say, but by what they do. In order to be viable, therefore, these behaviors must produce effective outcomes. The Values Assessment Inventory (Exhibit 5.1) uses behavioral terms to evaluate viability and the other three criteria. When an organization establishes or changes its values, it's very important to give those values specific behavioral definitions, so employees will know what's expected of them. It's also important to build those behaviors into key management processes, such as employee selection and performance evaluation. Embedding values in this way makes them *real.* Table 5.2 provides a checklist to determine the viability of a value.

Table 5.2. Viable Value Checklist

- Is it favorable to growth?
- Does it contribute to a sense of wholeness and completeness?
- Does it encourage people to achieve their potential?
- Does it foster a positive sense of self-esteem?
- Does it free people to pursue their aspirations?
- Does it take a long-range perspective?
- Is it based on accurate beliefs?

Table 5.2. Viable Value Checklist, Cont'd

- Is it based on trust?
- Is it in tune with current business realities?
- Is it defined clearly?
- Are the behaviors chosen to pursue it effective?
- Does it produce the desired results?
- Are potential consequences taken into consideration?
- Does it have the intended impact?
- Does it satisfy people's needs and wants?

Defensive and stabilizing values are not necessarily unviable. It depends on their impact. Also, some values might be viable in certain organizations but not in others. Kotter and Heskett (1992) found, for example, that the business context of a culture was related to performance. Table 5.3 offers some examples of viable and unviable values in the contemporary business climate. Again, I encourage you to think of some of your own. Many of the values in the unviable column were once standard practices in organizations, but shifts in the external environment required radical change. Gone are the days when bureaucrats, stacked on top of one another in elaborate hierarchies, can demand loyalty, control information, and use threats to force compliance. Today's organizations have to be flatter and leaner to remain competitive, so values emphasizing collaboration and influence without authority have become essential.

Table 5.3. Unviable and Viable Organizational Values in Today's World

Unviable	Viable
Security	Risk taking/courage
Tenure/seniority	Adding value
Conformity	Innovation
Predictability	Flexibility
Control	Empowerment/self-control
Independence/dependence	Interdependence
Internal competition	Internal collaboration

Table 5.3. Unviable and Viable Organizational Values in Today's World, Cont'd

Unviable	Viable
Outcome focus	Process focus
Reactive	Proactive
Formality	Informality
Routine	Responsiveness
Privilege/special interests	Inclusiveness
Bureaucracy	Boundaryless
Similarity	Diversity
Traditional education	Life-long learning
Hierarchical leadership	Leadership at all levels
Tactical thinking	Strategic thinking
Compliance	Commitment
Meeting standards	Continuous improvement

Alignment

Alignment can be defined as the degree to which compatibility exists among values. There are two types of alignment, *intrapersonal* and *interpersonal.* Intrapersonal alignment, or what many people call congruence, is consistency or integration among a person's beliefs, values, and behaviors—they guide the person in one direction. Interpersonal alignment is consistency or integration among these variables at the interpersonal, team, and organizational levels. In either case, alignment also refers to consistency between espoused and actual values.

The opposite of alignment is misalignment—namely lack of consistency or integration. Both imbalance and misalignment cause conflict, but for different reasons. With imbalance, the conflict stems from either overemphasizing or under-emphasizing important values; with misalignment, the conflict stems from a fundamental incompatibility among beliefs, values, and/or behavior—like mixing oil and water. These conflicts can either be intrapersonal (within a person) or interpersonal (between or among people). Let's talk about each type separately.

Intrapersonal Conflict

Recall that a person's self-esteem can be placed on a continuum extending from completely conditional at one end to completely unconditional at the other. Although some people lean toward the conditional and others lean toward the unconditional, most of us have a mixture of beliefs about self representing both types. Also, beliefs about self are dynamic, not static. People's self-conceptions change from day to day depending on what's happening. We notice, for example, how a person's self-confidence rises and falls with his or her performance. Moving from conditional to unconditional self-acceptance is a process that unfolds over the course of a lifetime.

People who have a mixture of conditional and unconditional beliefs about self often find themselves struggling with internal conflict. They may want to do something, but are held back by self-doubt and uncertainty. Their internal dialogue goes something like this:

"I can do that job; I think I'll apply for it."

"No, what makes me think I can do it?"

"I'm just as qualified as anyone else."

"You're just kidding yourself; they'd never select you."

"Well, there's nothing wrong with trying."

"You'll just make a fool out of yourself."

As people struggle with such competing beliefs about self, they go back and forth between confidence and fear, hope and despair. If the conditional beliefs prevail, they tend to settle for defensive or stabilizing values and behaviors, even though their innermost desires might be toward growth. In the same way, if their more unconditional beliefs prevail, they are freer to choose more growth-oriented values and behaviors. That's why making progress toward unconditional self-acceptance is so important.

Sometimes people have trouble identifying the source of their internal conflicts, and coaching is needed to help them to uncover and resolve these conflicts. One time, for example, a supervisor who was terminated for failure to meet project deadlines came to me for help. He had always exuded self-confidence, so the dejected person sitting across from me was quite a contrast. As he worked with me, he revealed that his family raised him to present an optimistic, can-do attitude to others. His self-esteem was based on being positive and optimistic. Whenever his manager asked whether a project was on schedule, therefore, he always said yes, even if there was no way it could be completed on time. Over the period of a few meetings, he realized that his need to be optimistic prevented him from being honest with himself or others. Separating his self-worth from being optimistic freed him to make more realistic assessments.

Intrapersonal conflicts can also stem from competition among the values within a person's value system. Rokeach (1973) explained that a person can have conflict between two moral values (honesty and sensitivity), between two competence values (logic and creativity), or between a moral and a competence value (humility and ambition). It's important for conflicts such as these to be identified and resolved so that they do not limit a person's personal and interpersonal functioning.

Also, there are tradeoffs with every choice, because making one choice means foregoing or de-emphasizing others. Parenting, for example, involves a tradeoff of personal freedom to raise a family. Technicians who become supervisors take on additional responsibility to pursue their careers. If people are prepared to make the tradeoffs associated with a choice, they can still remain congruent. If they're not prepared, however, they'll feel trapped by the choice. It's crucial, therefore, to identify the tradeoffs involved with choices and determine whether or not they're acceptable.

Interpersonal Conflict

When people with different levels of self-esteem come together in a team or organization, the stage is set for interpersonal conflicts. Those with lower self-esteem pull toward defensive or stabilizing values and behaviors, while those with higher self-esteem push toward growth values and behaviors. These differences manifest themselves as disagreements about goals, priorities, and methods, resulting in power struggles, hidden agendas, manipulation, internal competition, and mistrust.

Conflict of this kind can be understood as lack of alignment or a poor fit between personal, interpersonal, team, and/or organizational values. The concept of alignment can be controversial. Some people view alignment as manipulating employees to achieve organizational goals. However, attempts to force alignment never work for long; they only serve to increase conflict. They drive values issues underground, and they later resurface as passive-aggressive behavior, open defiance, sabotage, morale problems, and turnover.

There's nothing wrong with seeking alignment per se. Efforts to increase consistency among the four loops in the Motivational System Model can lower conflict and increase effectiveness. The issue is not whether or not to work toward alignment, but *how.* I believe the best way is to create a *shared* vision with which people can freely align themselves based on their personal visions; that is, to align individual, team, and organizational visions. Regarding this Senge (1990, p. 206) said, "A shared vision is a vision that many people are truly committed to, because it reflects their own personal vision." Similarly, Broholm (1990, p. 4) said, "Less willing to invest loyalty in an organization, people are more inclined to invest their loyalty in an 'end result' which holds meaning for them and which, at some level, reflects their deeply held values. A shared and valued organizational vision holds promise in securing commitment."

Alignment based on value integration is an ongoing process. Rokeach (1973) estimated that the average person has between thirty and forty values in his or her value system. A team or organization would reflect a much larger number. As with personal alignment, therefore, it's unrealistic to think that a team or organization could achieve complete integration. Also even when people agree on values, they often disagree on their priority. For these reasons, alignment is better seen as a dynamic process. I've consulted in situations in which there was alignment at the team level, but disconnects between team and organizational values. Increasing integration among the four loops of the Motivational System Model requires an atmosphere in which people can discuss their differences openly and honestly, identify tradeoffs involved with decisions, and manage them effectively. People are more willing to support decisions they don't agree with if they've been given an opportunity for input and they trust that their input will be considered.

Discrepancies Between Espoused and Actual Values

Further explanation is required about misalignment between espoused and actual values; such misalignment often accompanies both intrapersonal and interpersonal conflicts. Regardless of what values people espouse, others will infer their real values from what they do. Dyer (1976, p. 8) said, "Social systems that do not support congruent behavior may need to be changed before people in the system can become congruent. In order to build greater trust in organizations, it is important for managers to develop greater congruence in their own behavior. Nothing undermines trust more rapidly or thoroughly than an awareness that someone is not what he pretends to be—that his behavior is not congruent with what he thinks and feels."

A team or organization's values are revealed by what it rewards and punishes, regardless of lofty value statements to the contrary. Schein (1992, p. 242) said, "Leaders can quickly get across their own priorities, values, and assumptions by consistently linking rewards and punishments to the behavior they are concerned with." Leaders who fail to do this create confusion. I remember standing next to an employee once who pointed to a list of the organization's noble-sounding values and said cynically, "All they really care about is getting us to do the most work for the least amount of pay." Sometimes discrepancies between espoused and actual values represent hypocrisy—not "walking the talk"—while at other times they represent a lack of skill or poor execution. In the former case, people should be held accountable for choosing behavior consistent with the values; in the latter case, clarification of expected behaviors and/or training is indicated.

Inconsistencies between two behaviors—such as being supportive on one occasion and critical on another—could reflect a value conflict or other issues. It is symptomatic of underlying issues that may not be clear. More information is usually necessary to identify reasons for such inconsistencies. Finally, differences between actual and desired values pose no problem, as long as people are actively working toward the latter. Values are ideals; people can accept inconsistency as long as they sense progress in working toward those ideals.

Authenticity

Authenticity can be defined as the degree to which values are expressed—both verbally and behaviorally—in a genuine, sincere manner. In their study of visionary companies, Collins and Porras (1994) concluded that the authenticity of the ideology (values and purpose) and alignment with the ideology are more important than the content of the ideology. Earlier I said that people's core need is to have a sense of self-esteem. We're not only motivated to enhance our self-esteem, but also to protect it from perceived threat. Here's where authenticity comes into play. Authenticity means offering the *real* reasons for our actions; inauthenticity means giving plausible but false reasons for what we do ("I did it out of fairness"). Authenticity is similar to Senge's concept of a commitment to the truth, which he identifies as a criterion for the discipline of personal mastery (Senge, 1990). It's also related to what Roger McAniff (1999) calls level four truth—where rational and emotional intelligence combine (see McAniff's example, "Valuing the Truth," in this section). Inauthentic values manifest themselves as defensive behavior, which leads to interpersonal conflict, mistrust and, ultimately, blocks alignment toward vision.

▶ Valuing the Truth

ROGER MCANIFF, PRESIDENT, MCBLISS LEADERSHIP CO.

One of my clients was a Fortune 500 manufacturer and constructor of major environmental equipment for the electric utility industry. After reviewing year-end financial data, the CFO was uncomfortable signing off on them because he wasn't sure that the projected profits for ongoing design and build projects were achievable. The construction portion of the projects had just begun, and the CFO didn't believe the company had the expertise necessary to complete them on time and within budget. To study the situation further, a team of forty or fifty design, construction, estimating, and project administration experts was assembled to provide an independent analysis of current project status and completion costs. Team findings supported the CFO's concerns: estimated completion costs were $10 million to $15 million higher than originally projected, with a corresponding reduction in profits.

Two divisions operate and manage these construction projects. One division manager was territorial and defensive. He refused to accept the findings and ended up losing $10 million the next year. The other division manager was collaborative and had a strong commitment to the truth. After discussing the findings with his team, he implemented a new control system and a new construction project organization was hired. These initiatives put their projects back on schedule and brought costs back under control within six months, turning their losses into profits.

The corporate CEO was uneasy with conflict and allowed the two division managers to make their own decisions. This proved very costly. Losses from the first division wiped out the gains realized by the second; both divisions were sold to cover the losses, but the corporation never recovered financially.

The four key players in the company had different and, in some cases, conflicting values. The CFO valued truth and had the courage to question financial results before reporting them. His instincts were correct, and he moved on to other positions of responsibility. The CEO valued independence, but this prevented him from intervening to prevent financial disaster. He subsequently retired in disgrace. The collaborative division manager went on to become a highly valued member of the acquiring company, while the territorial division manager was let go. ◄

A relationship exists between authenticity and self-justification. People use both authentic and rationalized self-justification. Asking people *why* they did something is a potential threat to these people's self-esteem, so they must decide whether to be authentic or to rationalize. If they decide to rationalize, maintaining self-esteem is the real value and the explanation is based on a defensive value. Elsewhere, I refer to the latter as *bogus* values (see Hultman, 1979). All defense mechanisms serve the purpose of helping people maintain a sense of self-esteem, which is why they're called ego-defenses. Rationalization is the defense mechanism most closely tied to values, however, because values are offered as justifications for decisions and actions.

People often rationalize when confronted with discrepancies between espoused and actual values. There is, however, a difference between intrapersonal misalignment (incongruence) and rationalizing. With intrapersonal misalignment, a conflict exists among values (cooperation and competition) or between values and behavior (honesty and telling "white lies"); with rationalization, a false value underlies the reasons offered, while the real value—maintaining self-esteem—remains hidden. No one says, "I'm doing this to salvage my self-image," but in reality this is the underlying motivation for many actions. Establishing a nonthreatening climate in which people can relax their defenses and be honest is a prerequisite to coaching and other OD interventions. If a manager sends a person to you to be "fixed," forget it; you'll never get off of ground zero. "Fixing" can only be done by the people themselves. The most a manager or coach can do is support that process.

At first glance, this issue might seem limited to individuals, but I've worked with teams and organizations that have a predominantly defensive value system. You can sense this because people come across as closed and guarded, making interactions awkward and uncomfortable. In contrast, people with authentic value systems tend to be more open and relaxed, allowing interactions to flow more freely. Lack of authenticity is a major barrier to effectiveness. It creates misalignment and a climate of mistrust and defensiveness.

Separating self-esteem from performance allows people to be more authentic. In addition, self-confrontation is a useful method. Self-confrontation means asking yourself before acting: "What's the real reason I want to do this?" or "What am I really trying to accomplish here?" These questions allow people to be more honest with themselves and others, which can prevent them from slipping into self-deception.

On a team or organizational level, fostering greater authenticity requires a culture in which people can admit mistakes and still maintain their self-esteem. The emphasis should be on learning and continuous improvement, not on blaming oneself or others. A shared commitment to such values as trust, mutual respect, honesty, openness, cooperation, collaborative partnering, and taking responsibility for one's actions is essential to creating a more authentic culture.

Organizations are like ships on a stormy sea, battered on all sides by the winds of change. Values function as a rudder or, even better, as a compass. By ensuring that values are balanced, viable, congruent, and authentic, change agents and leaders can help individuals, teams, and organizations successfully navigate the rough waters through which they must pass. In the next chapter, I will highlight fifteen specific growth values that can point the way toward a more enlightened future.

Value Assessment Tools

Two tools for assessing values are included at the end of this chapter: the Values Assessment Inventory (VAI) and the Values Identification Survey (VIS). Both tools have instructions for personal, team, and organization uses, and include a 360-degree feedback component. The VAI assesses values according to the four criteria discussed in this chapter. I strongly recommend that you complete the VAI (Regular Form) now as a way of assessing the effectiveness of your values in the current business climate.

The Values Identification Survey (VIS) can be used for the following:

- To identify the actual values of organizations, teams, and individuals;

- To establish desired personal, team, or organizational values;

- To make the following comparisons among organizational, team, and personal values:

Personal Values

To compare current with desired personal values

To compare personal with actual team values

To compare personal with actual organizational values

To compare self, supervisor, peer, and subordinate perceptions of current personal values

Team Values

To compare actual with espoused team values

To compare actual with desired team values

To compare actual team with actual organizational values

Organizational Values

To compare actual with espoused organizational values

To compare actual with desired organizational values

A good way to learn how to use the VIS is by clarifying your personal values. To do this, follow the Procedures for Personal Use and employ Instruction Sheet Number 1.

Exhibit 5.1. Values Assessment Inventory

Purpose

The Values Assessment Inventory (VAI) assesses current values according to four variables: balance, viability, alignment, and authenticity. The variables are defined as follows:

- *Balance*—the degree to which values are given proper emphasis.
- *Viability*—the degree to which values are workable in the current business climate.
- *Alignment*—the degree to which compatibility exists among an individual's values, or among the values of individuals, teams, and the overall organization.
- *Authenticity*—the degree to which values are used in a genuine, sincere manner.

The VAI (Regular Form) provides a general assessment of current personal, team, and organizational values, while the VAI (360-Degree Feedback Form) allows individuals to compare self, supervisor, peer, and subordinate value ratings. Mean scores can range from 0 to 60. High mean scores show that values are effective, while low mean scores show that values are ineffective. Scores less than 30 should be viewed as cause for concern. Also, even if the mean score for a variable is high, items consistently receiving scores of 0 or 1 are indicative of problems. The VAI can be completed by itself or in conjunction with the Values Identification Survey (see Exhibit 5.2) and/or Motivational System Mapping™ (see Chapter 8).

Procedures for Organizational Use

The VAI (Regular Form) can be copied and given to everyone in an organization, to a representative sample, or to members of the leadership team. Check the "Your Organization" box on the first page so that respondents understand that the *overall organization* is the focus of assessment. Inform respondents that their results will be confidential. Follow the instructions for calculating scores. Then meet with organizational leaders, display the completed Values Assessment Profile, facilitate a discussion of the results, and develop strategies for dealing with organizational values issues.

Exhibit 5.1. Values Assessment Inventory, Cont'd

Procedures for Team Use

The VAI (Regular Form) can be copied and given to everyone on a team to assess current team values. Check the "Your Team" box on the front page so that respondents understand that the *team* is the focus of assessment. Inform respondents that their results will be confidential. Follow the instructions for calculating scores. Then meet with the team, display the completed Values Assessment Profile, facilitate a discussion of the results, and develop strategies for dealing with team values issues.

Procedures for Personal Use

The VAI (Regular Form) can be copied and completed by individuals to assess their current values. Each person should check the "Yourself" box on the front page, respond to the sixty items, calculate his or her scores, and place the scores on the Values Assessment Profile. Following this, the person should examine the Profile, reflect on the results, and develop strategies for dealing with personal values issues.

Procedures for 360-Degree Feedback

The VAI (360-Degree Feedback Form) can be copied and used with an individual to compare self, supervisor, peer, and subordinate ratings. When administering the inventory, a sample of peers and all subordinates should be included. A cover letter should be provided to those in the sample, indicating the person to be evaluated, the purpose of the assessment, and where to return completed inventories. Inform respondents that their results will remain anonymous. Follow the instructions for calculating scores. Then meet with the individual, review the completed Values Assessment Profile, discuss similarities and differences among self, supervisor, peer, and subordinate ratings, and develop strategies for dealing with individual values issues.

Exhibit 5.1. Values Assessment Inventory, Cont'd

Values Assessment Inventory (Regular Form)

Ken Hultman

Name: **Date:**

Position:

Team:

Organization:

Note: As you complete this inventory, you will be assessing:

☐ **Yourself**   ☐ **Your team**   ☐ **Your organization**

Instructions: The Values Assessment Inventory (Regular Form) evaluates the effectiveness of values in the current business climate. Read each item on the next two pages and circle the number that best expresses your opinion. Note that, in some cases, the scale is reversed; thus strong agreement can be either "4" or "0," depending on the specific statement.

These are tough items, requiring careful thought and introspection. Please give your honest opinion; otherwise the results will be meaningless. Team and organizational ratings will be grouped together and all ratings will remain anonymous.

Thank You for Completing This Inventory

Please turn the page and begin.

Exhibit 5.1. Values Assessment Inventory, Cont'd

Read each item and answer carefully based on whether you agree or disagree. Note that strong agreement can be either "4" or "0," depending on the specific statement.

	Strongly Disagree				Strongly Agree

Balance

1. Have trouble coping with stress.	4	3	2	1	0
2. Care about others' interests as well as self-interest (win-win).	0	1	2	3	4
3. Present opinions dogmatically.	4	3	2	1	0
4. Compromise on issues when appropriate.	0	1	2	3	4
5. Care primarily about self-interests; not about others' interests (win-lose).	4	3	2	1	0
6. Keep an open mind when opinions differ.	0	1	2	3	4
7. Maintain balance between tasks and people.	0	1	2	3	4
8. Maintain balance between work and other aspects of life.	0	1	2	3	4
9. Place too little emphasis on some important priorities.	4	3	2	1	0
10. Don't consider the views of others.	4	3	2	1	0
11. Balance short-term and long-range needs.	0	1	2	3	4
12. Show a willingness to be flexible.	0	1	2	3	4
13. Listen carefully to others' views.	0	1	2	3	4
14. Have symptoms of burnout.	4	3	2	1	0
15. Pay attention to all relevant factors.	0	1	2	3	4

Total for Balance: _____

Viability

16. Place a low priority on learning.	4	3	2	1	0
17. Give others the benefit of the doubt.	0	1	2	3	4
18. Treat others with respect.	0	1	2	3	4
19. Have difficulty adapting to change.	4	3	2	1	0
20. Have a strong desire for growth.	0	1	2	3	4
21. Weigh the potential consequences of decisions.	0	1	2	3	4
22. Resist change.	4	3	2	1	0
23. Demonstrate creativity and innovativeness.	0	1	2	3	4
24. Long for the "good old days."	4	3	2	1	0
25. Emphasize personal development.	0	1	2	3	4
26. Avoid taking risks.	4	3	2	1	0
27. Articulate values clearly.	0	1	2	3	4
28. Fail to produce effective results.	4	3	2	1	0
29. Don't back up opinions with data.	4	3	2	1	0
30. Encourage others to grow.	0	1	2	3	4

Total for Viability: _____

Exhibit 5.1. Values Assessment Inventory, Cont'd

Read each item and answer carefully based on whether you agree or disagree. Note that strong agreement can be either "4" or "0," depending on the specific statement.

Alignment

	Strongly Disagree			Strongly Agree
31. Choose behaviors that are inconsistent with stated values.	4	3	2	1	0
32. Don't respect value differences among people.	4	3	2	1	0
33. Emphasize inclusiveness.	0	1	2	3	4
34. Don't walk the talk.	4	3	2	1	0
35. Match methods with goals effectively.	0	1	2	3	4
36. Waffle on issues.	4	3	2	1	0
37. Identify and manage tradeoffs effectively.	0	1	2	3	4
38. Work toward decisions that are acceptable to everyone involved when possible.	0	1	2	3	4
39. Emphasize compliance among co-workers.	4	3	2	1	0
40. Stand up for convictions.	0	1	2	3	4
41. Give in to pressures to conform.	4	3	2	1	0
42. Seek win-win outcomes.	0	1	2	3	4
43. Act with integrity in the face of opposition.	0	1	2	3	4
44. Impose values on others.	4	3	2	1	0
45. Strive to achieve compatibility among values, goals, and objectives.	0	1	2	3	4

Total for Alignment: _____

Authenticity

	Strongly Disagree			Strongly Agree
46. Avoid manipulating others.	0	1	2	3	4
47. Seek the truth, while respecting others' views.	0	1	2	3	4
48. Avoid dealing with conflicts.	4	3	2	1	0
49. Respond defensively to criticism.	4	3	2	1	0
50. Honor agreements.	0	1	2	3	4
51. Have hidden agendas.	4	3	2	1	0
52. Don't share information freely.	4	3	2	1	0
53. Emphasize learning, not blaming.	0	1	2	3	4
54. Misrepresent what others say.	4	3	2	1	0
55. Acknowledge responsibility for mistakes.	0	1	2	3	4
56. Face issues openly and honestly.	0	1	2	3	4
57. Convey the same message to everybody.	0	1	2	3	4
58. Don't level with people.	4	3	2	1	0
59. Admit mistakes reluctantly.	4	3	2	1	0
60. Can be trusted.	0	1	2	3	4

Total for Authenticity: _____

Exhibit 5.1. Values Assessment Inventory, Cont'd

Instructions for Completing the Values Assessment Profile

If you are rating yourself:

1. Total the scores you gave yourself for the four variables (balance, viability, alignment, and authenticity),

2. Place a dot on the Profile at the corresponding point on the continuum for each of the four scores, and

3. Connect the dots with a line.

If you are rating your team or organization:

1. Add the totals of all respondents together for each variable,

2. Divide these scores by the number of respondents completing the inventory (this will give you the average or mean scores for the four variables), and

3. Follow procedures 2 and 3 above (under rating yourself).

Values Assessment Profile

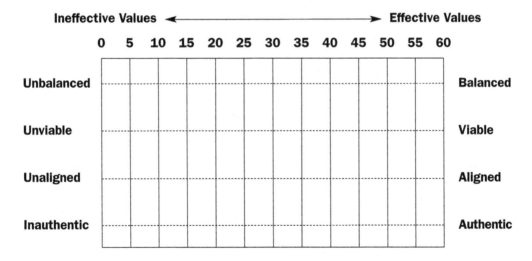

Develop Strategies for Value Change

After studying the Values Assessment Profile, think of ways that the effectiveness of values can be increased by addressing the following questions:

1. How can you bring about greater balance among values?

2. How can you make values more viable?

3. How can you bring about greater alignment among values?

4. How can you make values more authentic?

Exhibit 5.1. Values Assessment Inventory, Cont'd

**Values Assessment Inventory
(360-Degree Feedback Form)**

Ken Hultman

Name: **Date:**

Position:

Team:

Organization:

Note: Your ratings on this inventory are for the following person:

Instructions: The Values Assessment Inventory (360-Degree Feedback Form) is a developmental tool intended to help people evaluate the effectiveness of their values in the current business climate.

Read each item on the next two pages carefully and circle the number that best expresses your opinion about the person named above. Note that in some cases, the scale is reversed; thus strong agreement can be either "4" or "0," depending on the specific statement.

These are tough items, requiring careful thought and introspection. Please give your honest opinion; otherwise the results will be meaningless. Peer and subordinate ratings will be grouped together and individual ratings will remain anonymous.

Thank You for Completing This Inventory

Please turn the page and begin.

Exhibit 5.1. Values Assessment Inventory, Cont'd

Read each item and answer carefully based on whether you agree or disagree. Note that strong agreement can be either "4" or "0," depending on the specific statement.

	Strongly Disagree				Strongly Agree

Balance

1. Has trouble coping with stress.	4	3	2	1	0
2. Cares about others' interests as well as self-interest (win-win).	0	1	2	3	4
3. Presents opinions dogmatically.	4	3	2	1	0
4. Compromises on issues when appropriate.	0	1	2	3	4
5. Cares primarily about self-interest; not about others' interests.	4	3	2	1	0
6. Keeps an open mind when opinions differ.	0	1	2	3	4
7. Maintains balance between tasks and people.	0	1	2	3	4
8. Maintains balance between work and other aspects of life.	0	1	2	3	4
9. Places too little emphasis on some important priorities.	4	3	2	1	0
10. Doesn't consider the views of others.	4	3	2	1	0
11. Balances short-term and long-range needs.	0	1	2	3	4
12. Shows a willingness to be flexible.	0	1	2	3	4
13. Listens carefully to others' views.	0	1	2	3	4
14. Has symptoms of burnout.	4	3	2	1	0
15. Pays attention to all relevant factors.	0	1	2	3	4

Total for Balance: _____

Viability

16. Places a low priority on learning.	4	3	2	1	0
17. Gives others the benefit of the doubt.	0	1	2	3	4
18. Treats others with respect.	0	1	2	3	4
19. Has difficulty adapting to change.	4	3	2	1	0
20. Has a strong desire for growth.	0	1	2	3	4
21. Weighs the potential consequences of decisions.	0	1	2	3	4
22. Resists change.	4	3	2	1	0
23. Demonstrates creativity and innovativeness.	0	1	2	3	4
24. Longs for the "good old days."	4	3	2	1	0
25. Emphasizes personal development.	0	1	2	3	4
26. Avoid taking risks.	4	3	2	1	0
27. Articulates values clearly.	0	1	2	3	4
28. Fails to produce effective results.	4	3	2	1	0
29. Does not back up opinions with data.	4	3	2	1	0
30. Encourages others to grow.	0	1	2	3	4

Total for Viability: _____

Exhibit 5.1. Values Assessment Inventory, Cont'd

Read each item and answer carefully based on whether you agree or disagree. Note that strong agreement can be either "4" or "0," depending on the specific statement.

	Strongly Disagree			Strongly Agree

Alignment

31. Chooses behaviors that are inconsistent with stated values.	4	3	2	1	0
32. Does not respect value differences among people.	4	3	2	1	0
33. Emphasizes inclusiveness.	0	1	2	3	4
34. Does not walk the talk.	4	3	2	1	0
35. Matches methods with goals effectively.	0	1	2	3	4
36. Waffles on issues.	4	3	2	1	0
37. Identifies and manages tradeoffs effectively.	0	1	2	3	4
38. Works toward decisions that are acceptable to everyone involved when possible.	0	1	2	3	4
39. Emphasizes compliance among co-workers.	4	3	2	1	0
40. Stands up for convictions.	0	1	2	3	4
41. Gives in to pressures to conform.	4	3	2	1	0
42. Seeks win-win outcomes.	0	1	2	3	4
43. Acts with integrity in the face of opposition.	0	1	2	3	4
44. Imposes values on others.	4	3	2	1	0
45. Strives to achieve compatibility among values, goals, and objectives.	0	1	2	3	4

Total for Alignment: _____

Authenticity

46. Avoids manipulating others.	0	1	2	3	4
47. Seeks the truth, while respecting others' views.	0	1	2	3	4
48. Avoids dealing with conflicts.	4	3	2	1	0
49. Responds defensively to criticism.	4	3	2	1	0
50. Honors agreements.	0	1	2	3	4
51. Has hidden agendas.	4	3	2	1	0
52. Doesn't share information freely.	4	3	2	1	0
53. Emphasizes learning, not blaming.	0	1	2	3	4
54. Misrepresents what others say.	4	3	2	1	0
55. Acknowledges responsibility for mistakes.	0	1	2	3	4
56. Faces issues openly and honestly.	0	1	2	3	4
57. Conveys the same message to everybody.	0	1	2	3	4
58. Doesn't level with people.	4	3	2	1	0
59. Admits mistakes reluctantly.	4	3	2	1	0
60. Can be trusted.	0	1	2	3	4

Total for Authenticity: _____

Exhibit 5.1. Values Assessment Inventory, Cont'd

Instructions for Completing the Values Assessment Profile

There are four types of ratings that should be placed on the Profile: self, supervisor, peer, and subordinate. (*Note:* color code the four types of ratings, so they can be distinguished from one another.)

- Self-ratings can be listed by placing a dot at the corresponding point for the four total scores (balance, viability, alignment, and authenticity) and connecting the dots with a line. The same procedure can be used for supervisor ratings if one supervisor completed the inventory. (If more than one supervisor responded, use the procedures outlined below for peers and subordinates.)

- Peer ratings can be listed by adding the totals of all peers together for each variable and dividing these scores by the number of peers responding. This will give you the average or mean scores for peers. The same procedure can be used for subordinates.

Values Assessment Profile

Person's Name:

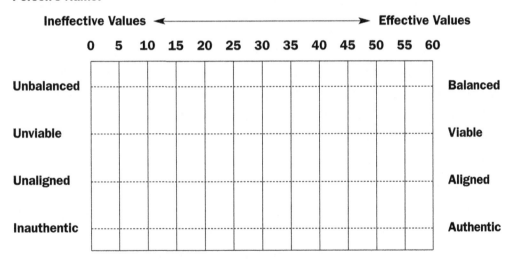

Develop Strategies for Value Change

After studying the Values Assessment Profile, think of ways that the effectiveness of values can be increased by addressing the following questions:

1. How can you bring about greater balance among values?
2. How can you make values more viable?
3. How can you bring about greater alignment among values?
4. How can you make values more authentic?

Exhibit 5.2. Values Identification Survey

Purpose

The purpose of the Values Identification Survey (VIS) is to clarify the values of individuals, teams, and organizations. The VIS consists of three forms—Actual Values, Espoused Values, and Desired Values—each containing a list of 186 values in alphabetical order. This list is not intended to be exhaustive, so space is provided on each form to write in other values. The three types of values are defined as follows:

- *Actual Values*—standards that guide behavior currently.
- *Espoused Values*—standards that people say they value.
- *Desired Values*—standards that people would like to have guide their behavior.

The VIS can be administered by itself or in conjunction with the Values Assessment Inventory (see Exhibit 5.1) and Motivational System Mapping (see Chapter 8) to assess and deal with values issues.

Instructions: The VIS has a number of personal, team, and organizational uses that are keyed to detailed instruction sheets. The instruction sheets allow a facilitator to consolidate data, assess values, and conduct feedback meetings during which values are discussed and decisions regarding values are made. To accomplish these tasks, the facilitator should:

- Follow the procedures for organizational, team, personal, and 360-degree feedback uses.
- Consolidate data and complete steps 1 and 2 on the appropriate instruction sheet.
- Make copies of the instruction sheet and distribute them at the beginning of a feedback session.
- Summarize the data and answer questions.
- Facilitate discussion pertaining to the remaining steps on the instruction sheet.

Table 5.4 summarizes the materials needed for various uses of the VIS at the personal, team, and organizational levels.

Exhibit 5.2. Values Identification Survey, Cont'd

Table 5.4. Using the VIS with Individuals, Teams, and Organizations

Level → Uses ↓	Individual	Team	Organization
Identify actual values	Actual Values Form Instruction Sheet 1	Actual Values Form Instruction Sheet 1	Actual Values Form Instruction Sheet 1
Establish values	Desired Values Form Instruction Sheet 2	Desired Values Form Instruction Sheet 2	Desired Values Form Instruction Sheet 2
Compare actual with espoused values		Actual Values Form Espoused Values Form Instruction Sheet 3	Actual Values Form Espoused Values Form Instruction Sheet 3
Compare actual with desired values	Actual Values Form Desired Values Form Instruction Sheet 4	Actual Values Form Desired Values Form Instruction Sheet 4	Actual Values Form Desired Values Form Instruction Sheet 4
Compare actual personal with actual team values	Two Actual Values Forms Instruction Sheet 5		
Compare actual personal with actual organizational values	Two Actual Values Forms Instruction Sheet 5		
360-degree feedback	Actual Values Form Instruction Sheet 6		
Compare actual team with actual organizational values		Two Actual Values Forms Instruction Sheet 5	

Exhibit 5.2. Values Identification Survey, Cont'd

Procedures for Organizational Use

The Actual Values Form can be used by itself to identify current organizational values or in conjunction with (1) the Espoused Values Form to compare current with verbally touted organizational values or (2) the Desired Values Form to compare current with ideal organizational values. The Desired Values Form can be used by itself to establish organizational values.

The VIS can be given to everyone in an organization, to a representative sample, or to members of the leadership team. Check the appropriate box on the first page of the VIS form(s) and distribute them as appropriate. Then follow the instructions for listing results and facilitating discussion.

Procedures for Team Use

The Actual Values Form can be used by itself to identify current team values or in conjunction with (1) the Espoused Values Form to compare current with verbally touted team values, (2) the Desired Values Form to compare current with ideal team values, or (3) the Actual Values Form for organizations to compare current team and organizational values. The Desired Values Form can be used by itself to establish team values.

Check the appropriate box on the front page of the VIS form(s) and distribute them to team members. Then follow the instructions for listing results and facilitating discussion.

Procedures for Personal Use

The Actual Values Form can be used by itself to identify current personal values or in conjunction with (1) the Desired Values Form to compare current with desired personal values, (2) the Actual Values Form for a team to compare current personal and team values, or (3) the Actual Values Form for an organization to compare current personal and organizational values. Also, the Desired Values Form can be used by itself to establish desired personal values.

Check the appropriate box on the front page on the VIS form(s) and distribute them as appropriate. Then follow the instructions for listing results and facilitating discussion.

Procedures for 360-Degree Feedback

The Actual Values Form can be used to compare self, supervisor, peer, and subordinate perceptions of current individual values. When conducting this assessment, a sample of peers and all subordinates should be included. A cover letter should be provided to those in the sample, indicating the purpose of the assessment and where to return completed surveys.

Write the person's name on the front page of the Actual Values Form, so respondents understand who is the focus of assessment. Summarize results on Instruction Sheet 6. Then meet with the individual and review the findings, discuss similarities and differences among self, supervisor, peer, and subordinate perceptions, and develop strategies for dealing with identified values issues.

Exhibit 5.2. Values Identification Survey, Cont'd

Values Identification Survey (Actual Values)

Name: Position:

Organization: Team: Date:

Instructions: Circle the ten most important values that actually guide:

☐ **Your Team's Behavior**

☐ **Your Organization's Behavior**

☐ **Your Behavior**

☐ **The Behavior of (Person's Name):**

Accepting others	Deference	Influence	Profitability
Accomplishment	Delight	Initiative	Progress
Accountability	Dependability	Innovation	Quality
Achievement	Developing others	Integrity	Recognition
Adaptability	Dignity	Intelligence	Reliability
Adding value	Diligence	Interdependence	Respect
Advancement	Diplomacy	Intuition	Responsibility
Adventurous	Discretion	Involvement	Responsiveness
Affirmation	Diversity	Justice	Results
Alignment	Effectiveness	Kindness	Risk taking
Altruism	Efficiency	Knowledge	Routine
Ambition	Empowerment	Law abiding	Security
Approval	Enthusiasm	Learning	Self-control
Assertiveness	Environmentalism	Logical	Self-interest
Authenticity	Ethics	Love	Self-discipline
Authority	Equality	Loyalty	Self-respect
Balance home/work	Excellence	Making a difference	Self-starter
Belonging	Expediency	Manipulation	Seniority
Boundaryless organization	Fairness	Mastery	Sense of community
Candor	Faith	Material possessions	Service
Caring	Faithfulness	Mentoring	Sincerity
Caution	Fellowship	Mercy	Social awareness
Clean	Financial growth	Merit	Speed
Cohesiveness	Flexibility	Morality	Spirituality
Collaboration	Forgiveness	Mutual interests	Spontaneity
Comfort	Friendship	Networking	Stability
Commitment	Freedom	Obedience	Status
Community involvement	Generosity	Openness	Status quo
Companionship	Genuineness	Opportunity	Stewardship
Compassion	Giving something back	Optimism	Strategic focus
Competence	Glory	Order	Success
Competition	Good will	Organizational growth	Synergism
Confidentiality	Growth	Originality	Tact
Congruence	Harmony	Ownership	Teamwork
Consistency	Health	Participation	Territory
Contribution	Helpfulness	Partnering	Timeliness
Control	Honesty	Patience	Tolerance
Cooperation	Honor	Peace	Tradition
Coordination	Humanitarianism	Perseverance	Trust
Courtesy	Human rights	Philanthropy	Truth
Courage	Humility	Politeness	Ultruism
Creativity	Humor/fun	Popularity	Variety
Credentials	Imagination	Power	Volunteerism
Credibility	Improvement	Prestige	Willpower
Curiosity	Inclusiveness	Productivity	Winning
Customer satisfaction	Independence	Professionalism	Wisdom
Dedication	Individuality		
Other: _____	_____	_____	_____
_____	_____	_____	_____

Exhibit 5.2. Values Identification Survey, Cont'd

Values Identification Survey (Espoused Values)

Name: **Position:**

Organization: **Team:**   **Date:**

Instructions: Circle the ten most important values verbally espoused in:

- ☐ **Your Team**
- ☐ **Your Organization**

Accepting others	Deference	Influence	Profitability
Accomplishment	Delight	Initiative	Progress
Accountability	Dependability	Innovation	Quality
Achievement	Developing others	Integrity	Recognition
Adaptability	Dignity	Intelligence	Reliability
Adding value	Diligence	Interdependence	Respect
Advancement	Diplomacy	Intuition	Responsibility
Adventurous	Discretion	Involvement	Responsiveness
Affirmation	Diversity	Justice	Results
Alignment	Effectiveness	Kindness	Risk taking
Altruism	Efficiency	Knowledge	Routine
Ambition	Empowerment	Law abiding	Security
Approval	Enthusiasm	Learning	Self-control
Assertiveness	Environmentalism	Logical	Self-interest
Authenticity	Ethics	Love	Self-discipline
Authority	Equality	Loyalty	Self-respect
Balance home/work	Excellence	Making a difference	Self-starter
Belonging	Expediency	Manipulation	Seniority
Boundaryless organization	Fairness	Mastery	Sense of community
Candor	Faith	Material possessions	Service
Caring	Faithfulness	Mentoring	Sincerity
Caution	Fellowship	Mercy	Social awareness
Clean	Financial growth	Merit	Speed
Cohesiveness	Flexibility	Morality	Spirituality
Collaboration	Forgiveness	Mutual interests	Spontaneity
Comfort	Friendship	Networking	Stability
Commitment	Freedom	Obedience	Status
Community involvement	Generosity	Openness	Status quo
Companionship	Genuineness	Opportunity	Stewardship
Compassion	Giving something back	Optimism	Strategic focus
Competence	Glory	Order	Success
Competition	Good will	Organizational growth	Synergism
Confidentiality	Growth	Originality	Tact
Congruence	Harmony	Ownership	Teamwork
Consistency	Health	Participation	Territory
Contribution	Helpfulness	Partnering	Timeliness
Control	Honesty	Patience	Tolerance
Cooperation	Honor	Peace	Tradition
Coordination	Humanitarianism	Perseverance	Trust
Courtesy	Human rights	Philanthropy	Truth
Courage	Humility	Politeness	Ultruism
Creativity	Humor/fun	Popularity	Variety
Credentials	Imagination	Power	Volunteerism
Credibility	Improvement	Prestige	Willpower
Curiosity	Inclusiveness	Productivity	Winning
Customer satisfaction	Independence	Professionalism	Wisdom
Dedication	Individuality		
Other: _____	_____	_____	_____
_____	_____	_____	_____

Exhibit 5.2. Values Identification Survey, Cont'd

Values Identification Survey (Desired Values)

Name: **Position:**

Organization: **Team:**   **Date:**

Instructions: Circle the four to ten most important values you think should guide behavior for:

☐ **Your Team**

☐ **Your Organization**

☐ **Yourself**

Accepting others	Deference	Influence	Profitability
Accomplishment	Delight	Initiative	Progress
Accountability	Dependability	Innovation	Quality
Achievement	Developing others	Integrity	Recognition
Adaptability	Dignity	Intelligence	Reliability
Adding value	Diligence	Interdependence	Respect
Advancement	Diplomacy	Intuition	Responsibility
Adventurous	Discretion	Involvement	Responsiveness
Affirmation	Diversity	Justice	Results
Alignment	Effectiveness	Kindness	Risk taking
Altruism	Efficiency	Knowledge	Routine
Ambition	Empowerment	Law abiding	Security
Approval	Enthusiasm	Learning	Self-control
Assertiveness	Environmentalism	Logical	Self-interest
Authenticity	Ethics	Love	Self-discipline
Authority	Equality	Loyalty	Self-respect
Balance home/work	Excellence	Making a difference	Self-starter
Belonging	Expediency	Manipulation	Seniority
Boundaryless organization	Fairness	Mastery	Sense of community
Candor	Faith	Material possessions	Service
Caring	Faithfulness	Mentoring	Sincerity
Caution	Fellowship	Mercy	Social awareness
Clean	Financial growth	Merit	Speed
Cohesiveness	Flexibility	Morality	Spirituality
Collaboration	Forgiveness	Mutual interests	Spontaneity
Comfort	Friendship	Networking	Stability
Commitment	Freedom	Obedience	Status
Community involvement	Generosity	Openness	Status quo
Companionship	Genuineness	Opportunity	Stewardship
Compassion	Giving something back	Optimism	Strategic focus
Competence	Glory	Order	Success
Competition	Good will	Organizational growth	Synergism
Confidentiality	Growth	Originality	Tact
Congruence	Harmony	Ownership	Teamwork
Consistency	Health	Participation	Territory
Contribution	Helpfulness	Partnering	Timeliness
Control	Honesty	Patience	Tolerance
Cooperation	Honor	Peace	Tradition
Coordination	Humanitarianism	Perseverance	Trust
Courtesy	Human rights	Philanthropy	Truth
Courage	Humility	Politeness	Ultruism
Creativity	Humor/fun	Popularity	Variety
Credentials	Imagination	Power	Volunteerism
Credibility	Improvement	Prestige	Willpower
Curiosity	Inclusiveness	Productivity	Winning
Customer satisfaction	Independence	Professionalism	Wisdom
Dedication	Individuality		
Other: _____	_____	_____	_____
_____	_____	_____	_____

Exhibit 5.2. Values Identification Survey, Cont'd

Values Identification Survey: Instruction Sheet 1

Use: To identify Actual Values for:

☐ **Your Organization**   ☐ **Your Team**   ☐ **Yourself**

1. *List* the top ten Actual Values. (*Note:* List an individual's values in alphabetical order; list a team or organization's values in rank order, indicating how many people selected each one).

Actual Values:

1.
2.
3.
4.
5.
6.
7.
8.
9.
10.

2. *Label* each value according to its function: defensive (D), which focus on protecting against perceived threat; stabilizing (S), which focus on maintaining the status quo; or growth (G), which provide for forward movement.

3. *Evaluate* the values according to the following criteria:

   Balance

   Are there values pertaining to all four needs (mastery, contribution, self-respect, acceptance)?

   Viability

   Are the values workable in the current business climate?

   How can defensive and stabilizing values be decreased?

   How can growth values be increased?

   Alignment

   Are the values compatible with one another?

   Authenticity

   Are the values used in a genuine, sincere manner?

4. *Decide* on changes needed with Actual Values and how these changes will be made.

Exhibit 5.2. Values Identification Survey, Cont'd

Values Identification Survey: Instruction Sheet 2

Use: To establish Desired Values for:

☐ **Your Organization**   ☐ **Your Team**   ☐ **Yourself**

1. *List* the top ten Desired Values in rank order (indicating how many people selected each one in case of team or organizational rankings).

Desired Values:

1.
2.
3.
4.
5.
6.
7.
8.
9.
10.

2. *Label* each value according to its function: defensive (D), which focus on protecting against perceived threat; stabilizing (S), which focus on maintaining the status quo; or growth (G), which provide for forward movement.

3. *Evaluate* the values according to the following criteria:

Balance

Are there values pertaining to all four needs (mastery, contribution, self-respect, acceptance)?

Viability

Are the values workable in the current business climate?

How can defensive and stabilizing values be decreased?

How can growth values be increased?

Alignment

Are the values compatible with one another?

Authenticity

Are the values used in a genuine, sincere manner?

4. *Decide* on final list of values and develop behavioral definitions.

Exhibit 5.2. Values Identification Survey, Cont'd

Values Identification Survey: Instruction Sheet 3

Use: To compare Actual with Espoused Values for:

☐ **Your Organization**   ☐ **Your Team**

1. *List* the top ten Actual and Espoused Values in rank order, indicating how many people selected each one.

Actual Values for:	**Espoused Values for:**
1.	1.
2.	2.
3.	3.
4.	4.
5.	5.
6.	6.
7.	7.
8.	8.
9.	9.
10.	10.

2. *Label* each value according to its function: defensive (D), which focus on protecting against perceived threat; stabilizing (S), which focus on maintaining the status quo; or growth (G), which provide for forward movement.

3. *Compare* the similarities and differences among Actual and Espoused Values.

4. *Discuss* how to bring about greater alignment between Actual and Espoused Values.

5. *Lay out* goals, objectives, and plans for improving alignment.

Exhibit 5.2. Values Identification Survey, Cont'd

Values Identification Survey: Instruction Sheet 4

Use: To compare Actual with Desired Values for:

□ **Your Organization**   □ **Your Team**   □ **Yourself**

1. *List* the top ten Actual and Desired Values in rank order (indicating how many people selected each one in case of team or organizational ranking).

Actual Values of:	Desired Values of:
1.	1.
2.	2.
3.	3.
4.	4.
5.	5.
6.	6.
7.	7.
8.	8.
9.	9.
10.	10.

2. *Label* each value according to its function: defensive (D), which focus on protecting against perceived threat; stabilizing (S), which focus on maintaining the status quo; or growth (G), which provide for forward movement.

3. *Compare* the similarities and differences among Actual and Desired Values.

4. *Discuss* how to move from Actual to Desired Values.

   How can defensive and stabilizing values be decreased?

   How can growth values be increased?

5. *Lay out* goals, objectives, and plans for moving toward Desired Values.

Exhibit 5.2. Values Identification Survey, Cont'd

Values Identification Survey: Instruction Sheet 5

Use: To compare Actual Values between:

☐ **Yourself and your team**
☐ **Yourself and your organization**
☐ **Your team and your organization**

1. *List* the two sets of top ten Actual Values for the comparison checked above (*Note:* If the comparison is between yourself and your team or organization, list your values in alphabetical order and the team or organization's values in rank order, indicating how many people selected each one. If the comparison is between your team and organization, list the values in rank order).

Actual Values of:	**Actual Values of:**
1.	1.
2.	2.
3.	3.
4.	4.
5.	5.
6.	6.
7.	7.
8.	8.
9.	9.
10.	10.

2. *Label* each value according to its function: defensive (D), which focus on protecting against perceived threat; stabilizing (S), which focus on maintaining the status quo; or growth (G), which provide for forward movement.

3. *Compare* the similarities and differences between Actual Values.

4. *Discuss* how to bring about greater alignment among Actual Values.

5. *Lay out* goals, objectives, and plans for increasing alignment.

Exhibit 5.2. Values Identification Survey, Cont'd

Values Identification Survey: Instruction Sheet 6

Use: To compare self, supervisor, peer, and subordinate perceptions of Actual Values for (Person's Name):

1. *List* the top ten values for self, supervisor, peers, and subordinates. (*Note:* List self and supervisor values in alphabetical order, but list peer and subordinate values in rank order, indicating how many people selected each one.)

Self:	Supervisor:	Peer:	Subordinate:
1.	1.	1.	1.
2.	2.	2.	2.
3.	3.	3.	3.
4.	4.	4.	4.
5.	5.	5.	5.
6.	6.	6.	6.
7.	7.	7.	7.
8.	8.	8.	8.
9.	9.	9.	9.
10.	10.	10.	10.

2. *Label* each value according to its function: defensive (D), which focus on protecting against perceived threat; stabilizing (S), which focus on maintaining the status quo; or growth (G), which provide for forward movement.

3. *Compare* the similarities and differences between self, supervisor, peer, and subordinate perceptions of values.

4. *Discuss* value changes needed and how these changes will be made.

   How can defensive and stabilizing values be decreased?

   How can growth values be increased?

5. *Lay out* goals, objectives, and plans for value changes.

6

Toward
Growth Values

WE HAVE JUST LOOKED AT FOUR CRITERIA for assessing values, namely balance, viability, alignment, and authenticity. Defensive, stabilizing, and growth values can all meet these criteria. The emphasis in today's business climate, however, needs to be on values fostering growth. The chapter begins with an interview I conducted with Dr. Robert Tannenbaum focusing on values changes in organizations during the past thirty years and the challenges current value issues pose for OD practitioners and other change leaders. Next we look at fifteen growth values that I believe have particular relevance for success in the current business climate, showing how they relate to Warner Burke's summary of OD values and Tannenbaum and Davis's list of norms that organizations should be moving toward (see Table 1.1). The chapter ends with the Growth Values Exercise, which allows individuals, teams, and organizations to assess where they are now in terms of the fifteen values and to make plans for change.

Introduction

So far I've discussed the role of values in personality and culture and offered a set of criteria for evaluating values. Although deepening your understanding in these areas is one of this book's goals, it is not my intention to remain entirely neutral. Another goal is to build a case for specific values that I consider promising for establishing and maintaining balance between individuals and organizations—in other words, to make a case for values that I think should be normative in organizations. Warner Burke (1982) argued that OD practitioners should advocate certain values when he said, "Since individual and group behavior in an organization is largely determined by group norms (part of the organization's culture), the changing of certain of these norms and their accompanying values should be a major focus of an OD effort" (p. 75).

Robert Tannenbaum and Sheldon Davis were among the first OD practitioners to articulate a normative position regarding organizational values. In their widely reprinted 1969 article, "Values, Man, and Organizations," they suggested a direction for change in twelve norms based on humanistic values (see Table 1.1). They stated that such values were then resonating with increasing numbers of people, and that they were also highly consistent with the effective functioning of organizations built on the rapidly emerging organic model of organizations as living systems rather than as machines. One of the goals I had for this book was to bridge my work to theirs, so on April 6, 2000, I conducted an extensive interview with Bob at his home. Here is my summary of his remarks.

▶ From Fragmentation Toward Wholeness: An Interview with Bob Tannenbaum

Dr. Robert (Bob) Tannenbaum was a professor at the UCLA Graduate School of Management from 1948 to 1977. In 1952 he was part of an interdisciplinary team that planned and conducted the first group development labs on the West Coast—summer programs that were often called "West Coast Bethels" (after the town in Maine where such programs started). As one of the founders of the OD profession, Bob has had a profound impact on many people in the field.

KH: Bob, what progress do you think organizations have made since the publication of your 1969 article, "Values, Man, and Organizations"?

BT: "For many years now, there has been a widespread move away from Theory X organizational characteristics (top-down authority, tight control, rigid structures, et cetera) to Theory Y characteristics (consultation, collaboration, flexibility, flow, and so forth). As I reflect on this direction of change, I think it has occurred primarily as a response to changes that have been taking place in the environment of organizations, that is, in the larger society. For example, many companies have come to a realization that they can't create productive innovative organizations if they don't permit people at different levels to talk to each other and to cross the boundaries of organizational units. Also, fostering organizational flow has greater payoff than managing through command and control. Changes such as these are occurring, not because of deep organizational concern about values, but because changes are occurring in the environment that make such organizational changes imperative for survival.

"Many organizations now have developed values statements, but I wonder whether their stated values reflect what they now deeply believe, or if they are only a pragmatic response to realities in the larger environment. I suspect most of it is the latter. I am certainly not aware of many companies that are really taking a values stance in the direction suggested by our article because of a deeply held commitment to those values for their own sake."

KH: What values issues do you think organizations need to be facing as we enter the new millennium?

BT: "A central one I think is the time pressures workers are under and the pressures that employers face on hiring and retention. These go hand in hand because, if a worker becomes ill due to the pace of work, it puts pressure on the employer to find a replacement. There's tremendous pressure on families today. The change to two-worker households has raised all kinds of questions that people have to deal with in terms of child rearing and so on. The roles of men and women have changed drastically. Men are now expected to share many domestic responsibilities. Women are under greater pressure at work, and this has led for them to an increased incidence of heart and other diseases. Organizations have responded to these issues by offering maternity leave, child day care, and other benefits. Again, does this represent a change in what organizations consider important in value terms, or is it primarily due to larger changes in society? I suspect it's the latter.

"Another change is in the area of diversity. Organizations are emphasizing diversity now, but this is largely in response to demographic changes in society. Here in California, in a few years Caucasians will be in the minority. My hunch is that minorities will be more accepted in the future than they are now. People from different races will have to work together in order for organizations to achieve their goals. Now when we think about diversity it often connotes race and ethnicity, but in a broader sense working with anyone requires you to deal with differences.

"Another issue is that there's been a rapid breakdown in boundaries of all kinds in recent years. It's happening internationally. The Euro dollar serving many countries is a good example. Mergers and acquisitions have also broken down barriers. Companies are recognizing that to be successful in the new environment, they have to add new competence. Rather than taking the time to build competence themselves, they find a company that already has it and add it on. This has tremendous boundary-breaking implications.

"On a personal level, our underlying psychological issues represent boundaries to wholeness within ourselves. The challenge of personal growth is to become more whole. It seems to me that the current thrust toward spirituality represents getting beyond ego and becoming one with the larger whole. This may have to do with where I am in life, but the notion of wholeness is very much with me. A lot of the earlier OD work had to do with encouraging people in sales, production, research, and other departments to talk to each other and become more whole. This is happening now in so many different aspects of life—moving away from fragmentation toward wholeness. But again, I wonder whether this is happening for pragmatic reasons or because organizations are placing a higher value on wholeness.

"Of course, there's no quick path to wholeness. I've been very troubled by a lot of the recent books on leadership, which list the characteristics of a transformational leader. The implication is that if you're aware of the characteristics, you can go out and become compassionate and accepting, drop your defensiveness, control your anger, and so on. However, my experience tells me that major behavioral change does not occur as a product of a week-end workshop. The path toward personal wholeness requires deep inner work over a long period of time. The journey is well worth it, however, because people who move toward wholeness can both raise the level of their professional performance and savor life itself more fully."

KH: What values do you think should define OD as a profession?

BT: "My personal bias is toward humanistic, person-centered values. One of the concerns I have is that, while people who are really involved in creating new technology are probably getting the degree of satisfaction they want out of their work, the larger number of people view work as just making a living. One measure of that I think is the increasing interest in spirituality. There are an awful lot of people who are deeply dissatisfied with the way their lives are going. I think they have a vague feeling that there's something wrong, that their lives aren't very satisfying or fulfilling. I think we're going through a period where people are paying a very high price: giving away their lives to earn an income. I'm deeply concerned about the implications of this for the future of individuals and organizations. I feel this is one of the key issues OD practitioners should be addressing.

"I think we need to continue moving in the direction of person-centered values. It's not just the individual, but there are also social considerations in terms of the kind of world we want to create. The individual can't be fulfilled without also being part of relationships with others. Organizations provide a context for relationships. OD needs to address the needs of the individual within a larger context that considers interpersonal relationships, organizations, and society. We're all part of a larger whole; you can't consider one part without considering the others."

KH: What role should OD practitioners play in shaping organizational values?

BT: "They should first become better people themselves. Back in the 1950s, I suggested that the best way to become a better leader (or consultant) is to become a better person. I feel the same way today. Of course, there's no single path to becoming a better person—there are many processes available: honest and deep introspection, support groups, psychotherapy, and personal growth workshops are only illustrative of the many options. It's crucial for practitioners to invest time in their own personal development and to carve out their own path because their work impacts the lives of so many others. Becoming the best person we can be allows us to do the same for other individuals as well as organizations. Then we can help create a better world for all of us." ◀

The time I spent with Bob had a great impact on me. First, I was greatly impressed with his vitality and enthusiasm at age 85. While he has cut back on work to some extent in recent years to spend more time with his family, he is keenly aware of the issues that organizations confront in the global economy. Second, his impression that organizational change occurs largely in reaction to external pressures rather than internal convictions about values planted the seeds for some of the main ideas in this book. Specifically, it helped to shape my views about the limitations of defensive values and the benefits of growth values and my thinking about the importance of striving for balance among individual, team, and organizational values as a primary strategy for creating a healthy work environment and sustaining long-term financial success. These notions are central to the value positions advocated in the remainder of this chapter.

Growth Values and Behavior

Through a combination of my own experience, reading, and conversations with other OD practitioners, I've identified fifteen growth values that have special relevance today. Recall that growth values are standards of importance related to providing movement toward wholeness. They operate within the Motivational System Model (see Figure 2.1), which includes individuals, interpersonal relationships, teams, the overall organization, and their environment. All parts of the system are dynamically interrelated. To be effective, a growth value must meet whole system needs, not the whole at the expense of the parts, or one or two parts at the expense of others. Harmony must exist among growth values at all four levels in order for their full potential to be realized. The opposite of harmony is conflict. Conflict is good when it shakes up an entrenched system requiring change, but it can also limit growth. Growth is fostered by providing conditions that will allow individuals, teams, and the organization to develop their full potential and by identifying and removing barriers to progress at these different levels.

The fifteen values, depicted in Table 6.1, are presented in the same "away from/toward" format originally employed by Tannenbaum and Davis, and I will point out when the values I identify overlap with theirs as well as with Warner Burke's list of founding OD values. In addition, I have organized the list of values according to the specific competence or integrity need they address. In each case the value-oriented behavior to move away from is either a defensive or stabilizing value, and the behavior to move toward is based on a growth value.

Notice that there are more items in the social competence area than in any other. This is where the real payoff is in terms of aligning personal and organizational values.

Table 6.1. Toward Growth Values

	Away From	← →	Toward
Personal Competence	Being a dependent learner	← →	Being a self-directed learner
	Learning specific skills	← →	Learning to change and adapt
	Emphasizing compulsive productivity	← →	Emphasizing balance
	Seeking certainty	← →	Seeking opportunities in the midst of uncertainty
Social Competence	Defining narrow work roles	← →	Fully utilizing ability
	Distributing rewards unfairly	← →	Distributing rewards fairly
	Working only for external rewards	← →	Working for satisfaction from work itself
	Serving self-interest	← →	Serving mutual interests
	Working only as an employee	← →	Working as an owner
	Devaluing experience	← →	Prizing wisdom
Personal Integrity	Posturing	← →	Being authentic
	Concealing the truth	← →	Seeking truth
Social Integrity	Viewing differences as a negative	← →	Celebrating differences
	Judging people	← →	Accepting people
	Viewing people as means to an end	← →	Viewing people as ends in themselves

Personal Competence
Away from Being a Dependent Learner
Toward Being a Self-Directed Learner

The prevailing learning model in our society places the learner in the position of being a passive recipient of knowledge and skills; others are responsible. In this model, teachers decide what should be learned, how and when the learning will take place, and how students will prove they have learned what the teacher has taught. This model is pervasive in our formal educational system, from kindergarten through graduate school and continuing education. Peter Vaill, who refers to this as institutional learning, said, "Since it is adhered to in virtually all learning projects at all levels of society, there is a basic psychological state one enters as a learner—a state of felt inferiority; of tentativeness, cautiousness, and dependence on those in authority; and of suppression of here-and-now feelings in favor of anticipation of future comfort and success. These characteristics describe a person with a substantially diminished sense of self, a person who is not yet an authentic being but who is going to try to learn as a means to becoming an authentic being, a real person" (Vaill, 1996, p. 39).

In addition to its negative impact on self-esteem, the rapid pace of change has made the institutional model inadequate to satisfy people's growth needs. Instead of waiting for someone else to determine what he or she needs to learn and how, self-directed learners must now take responsibility for their own learning and look for creative ways to keep their knowledge and skills up-to-date. During the past decade, the concept of the learning organization has highlighted the importance of shifting from institutionalized to self-directed learning. In speaking about the learning organization, Vaill (1996, p. 53) said, "It is constituted to learn and grow and change—as opposed to traditional bureaucratic models constituted to be stable and predictable in their operation, to hold the line and not to change." Institutionalized learning and the underlying bureaucratic model sustaining it are based on stabilizing values, but what we need now is learning based on growth values.

While the concept of the learning organization has struck a responsive chord and more innovative approaches to learning are emerging (e-learning is opening up unprecedented access to self-directed learning opportunities), the vast majority of staff development sponsored by organizations is still done in the traditional manner, with a teacher (workshop leader, presenter) in the front of the room and students (participants, learners) in the role of passive recipients. For example, I've done a lot of workshops for government agencies that require employees to log a certain number of training hours per year. Although providing such opportunities represents an investment in staff development, employees pick and choose programs to fulfill their training hour requirements rather than to enhance job performance or personal growth. This also reinforces the view that people have to be forced to learn.

Burke (1998) challenged OD practitioners to emphasize a value for human development in their work. Encouraging self-directed learning means helping people overcome many years of conditioning, which takes considerable determination and effort. The payoff will be worth the effort, however, because people with an enhanced sense of self-esteem and a greater sense of empowerment will have more motivation to develop their full potential.

For more on becoming a learning organization, read the case example that follows.

▶ Learning as an Organizational Value: A Self-Help Approach to Creating a Learning Organization
MIKE MORRIS, PRESIDENT, THE CONTACT GROUP, INC.

Background

The organization is a significant but relatively small company of five hundred people. The corporate offices are in the dynamic but turbulent Witwatersrand area of South Africa. Their mission is to underwrite credit risks. They underwrite the risks—economic, political, and physical—that people in business, including exporters and importers, take when they extend credit to their customers.

The first time I met their likeable and sincere CEO, he explained that the company was at a crossroads. He believed that everyone in the company had to become highly effective learners if they and the company were to continue to thrive. He had been studying the characteristics of learning organizations and had recently shared a paper with his senior managers that contained these statements:

- "It doesn't take a rocket scientist to realize that in our high-tech, globally wired, and highly competitive world, knowledge workers are in high demand and have to be treated as volunteers."

- "It is intellectual capital that is the key currency in the world today."

- "Our culture must encourage our staff to learn, to develop themselves and through this our business."

He was seeking help in making this last statement a reality.

My Role

We agreed that the road ahead could not be clearly mapped at the outset and that a collaborative, open-ended approach was needed. I offered to contribute the following: (1) be available to his people online from my base in Pittsburgh for support and research, (2) spend time on-site conducting workshops for senior executives and members of staff, and (3) make various instruments and materials available for use throughout the organization. We knew that several members of his team were skeptical about the value of the learning organization. They considered, with some justification, that the ideas were vague and largely untried. They doubted the likely payoff.

I suggested three initial steps: (1) articulating a vision that would inspire people to pursue the goal of becoming a learning organization, (2) using focus groups or a survey to establish the factors within the culture that were either helping or hindering learning, and (3) the development of learning capability in the organization's people. The first question that needed an answer was where to begin.

The Executive Team

In the period between reaching agreement to go ahead and getting started, I learned that the executives were resisting working on a vision because they had recently articulated a general vision and didn't want to return to that issue after such a short time. Also, the HR group had already conducted various surveys. I didn't want to push the vision issue against an already skeptical outlook and felt that the surveys that had already been completed and reported to the staff gave 90 percent of the information needed to assess the learning climate. It was too early to start working with the people about self-directed learning when there was skepticism at the top.

I had established via the CEO that his people were open to a general workshop on the subject of the learning organization. I saw this as the starting point I needed and also as a way to move the executives beyond their concerns. I selected three books and proposed a workshop format based on each executive undertaking a moderate amount of pre-reading. They agreed to deliver a brief summary to their colleagues and then identify those parts of the reading that were a good fit for their company. I call those "glimpses" of a better future. Glimpses are contrasted with "agitations," which are those things that might get in the way of movement toward a better future.

I facilitated the workshop and, after all the presentations had been completed and discussions held, we had developed a long list of glimpses and a shorter list of agitations. We used these lists to craft a statement articulating what their organization would look like if the glimpses had already become reality and the agitation had been removed. This resulted in a vision statement that helped ground the rest of the work. The resulting statement was the vision of a better future that was needed to ground the remainder of the work. The shorthand version of the vision was "Growth Through Knowledge." Growth refers to the development of people as well as growth in clients and revenue.

After the first draft had been articulated and before a final commitment had been made, the CEO sought to establish whether there was consensus about proceeding. He asked the executives whether they believed the organization should aim to become a learning organization. There was unanimous agreement that they should be working toward such an organization. That change in outlook has since been borne out during their involvement in subsequent initiatives. They developed an action plan that called for (1) the creation of two pilot teams in which learning would be a strategic driving force, (2) a strategy to share the vision with everyone in the organization and get their input, and (3) promotion of the whole concept through newsletters and other communication vehicles. The longhand version of the vision was submitted to the Board and adopted and has since been communicated throughout the organization and was published in the Annual Report.

Pilot Teams

The pilot teams were introduced to the concepts and methods four weeks later. They were briefed on the history of the project and provided with background information on the learning organization. They have developed their own list of glimpses and agitations as they relate to their own team. They have worked through several learning modules that examine the difference between being taught and learning, provide insight into each person's learning style, and describe how engagement with learning can be increased. They have developed action plans that entrench learning as a growth strategy for each person and also for each team and that lead to performance improvements through the application of existing and new knowledge. These action plans take full advantage of all of the knowledge and resources that already exist within the teams.

Follow-Up

Six months later, follow-up meetings were held. I extracted statements from the longhand version of the vision that represented needed changes in day-to-day behavior. The senior managers used these statements to create a detailed action plan based on the Growth Through Knowledge vision designed to ensure that the vision becomes a reality. They also articulated the role they need to play in ensuring the vision was accomplished.

I provided the senior team with information on the relationship between change initiatives and bottom-line results, which led to agreement that the overall project would be measured by tracking the implementation of action plans and the results of follow-up surveys that would show the extent to which the learning climate was improving. Meetings with the pilot groups showed that the original action plans had been implemented and that team members had gained significant benefits in personal competence and work-related knowledge. In each case, new and ambitious learning plans were developed. In one team there was a belief that they were moving to a time when they could become self-managing.

In-House Capability

A senior member of the HR/Training Division who had experience in credit insurance operations and a deep interest in the learning organization was coached to continue to meet a growing series of requests for the initiation of additional learning teams. That person will also publicize the various initiatives through internal newsletters and will liaise with me online for any needed help. Although the company is only one-quarter of the way along the road to becoming a learning organization, my work is 90 percent completed. I will remain available to support the project.

An old cliché is appropriate to this story—becoming a learning organization is a journey and not a destination. In the early stages the journey requires an act of faith. My clients have shown enough faith to step onto a path that can lead to exciting places and significant rewards. Each milestone reached promises benefits for everyone involved. As individuals and teams reap those benefits, improvements will be seen in the traditional measures used to gauge organizational success. ◀

Away from Learning Specific Skills
Toward Learning to Change and Adapt

Most programs offered by organizational training departments focus on what might be called "how-to" skills—the legacy of our pragmatic society. This approach is appropriate when introducing new equipment, computer software, and so on, but many people still believe that such topics as leadership, building interpersonal relationships, and managing change can be reduced to a set of linear steps that can easily be mastered. Programs like these offer the illusion of simplicity, false security in today's increasingly complex and rapidly changing world. While learning specific skills will always have its place, facing many of the challenges in organizations today requires an ability to change and adapt that cannot be reduced to skills.

Kotter and Heskett (1992) concluded from their extensive research on corporate culture that organizations won't be able to sustain excellent performance over the long haul unless they have values allowing them to change and adapt. In describing the current learning environment, Peter Vaill (1996, pp. 135–136) said, "Organizational members are constantly on what might be called process frontiers, where they must find ways of doing something they have never done before, yet where there is little precedent or 'best practice' to guide them. . . . Institutional learning philosophy and practice have bred into many of us an obsession with 'how to do it.' This obsession amounts to a desire *not* to have a learning experience. We do not want to go through the creative learning that process frontiers require."

Functioning effectively on process frontiers means placing less emphasis on such stabilizing values as order and routine and more emphasis on such growth values as creativity and innovativeness. This means being open to our environment and recognizing that learning can occur in novel and unexpected ways. It also means shifting from analytic, cause-effect thinking to systems thinking. Instead of trying to break down complex issues into sequential steps, we must visualize the whole and look for the dynamic interconnections existing among its various parts. This will allow us to see things we never saw before, increasing our ability to change and adapt individually and as organizations.

Away from Emphasizing Compulsive Productivity
Toward Emphasizing Balance

When buying a house, the three most important things are location, location, and location. Similarly, it appears that the three most important things in organizations today are speed, speed, and speed. This has resulted in a pervasive pattern of compulsive productivity, people working longer and longer hours to complete their assignments. The origin of this pattern lies at the heart of our concept of work. Many people view work, the act of productivity, as an end in itself. In speaking about the meaning of work, theologian Paul Tillich (1963, p. 105) said, "It has become a religion itself, the religion of modern industrial society." Tillich wrote this in 1963. If people were fervent believers in work back then, they've become fanatics in the global economy.

When I go into an organization characterized by compulsive productivity, I can feel it instantly. People move and talk with a constant sense of urgency. They're unable to slow down. It feels like you're in a car and people are honking at you for driving too slowly. Nevertheless, compulsive productivity is so ingrained in most organizations that people generally take it for granted. Some employees like to be frantically busy, but others feel that they have to because that's what everyone else is doing, and they don't want to appear to be goofing off. People brag about how much work they do and believe that working constantly is the key to success. During workshops on job interviewing skills, people are coached to come across as perfectionists and to answer questions about weaknesses by confessing that sometimes they expect too much of themselves, and they can't sleep at night unless their jobs are done right.

Perhaps compulsive productivity would have some merit if it were a healthy process, but abundant evidence exists that it is not. In their book, *The Addictive Organization,* which focuses on workaholism in organizations, Schaef and Fassel (1988, p. 4) said:

> "We have begun to recognize that many of the behaviors considered 'normal' for individuals in organizations are actually a repertoire of behaviors of an active addict or a non-recovering co-dependent. . . . In addition, many of the organizational processes deemed 'acceptable' in companies are just more of the same addictive behavior masquerading as corporate structure and function."

Focusing on surface tasks and activities gives people an illusion of control and allows them to avoid facing deeper questions, such as, "Why am I doing this?"

and "What are the consequences of this behavior for me and others?" These dynamics get in the way of seeking the truth, one of the values discussed below in the section on personal integrity.

An emphasis on compulsive productivity is short-sighted, because people can only be in this mode for a period of time before they start breaking down. The behaviors associated with this pattern have led to a steady increase in the use of health care and employee assistance benefits, absenteeism due to illness, and workplace violence—even killing. Nevertheless, instead of examining the values driving this pattern of behavior, most organizations focus on symptom reduction. One way they do this is by sponsoring programs designed to increase employees' coping skills. The demand for workshops on stress management, anger management, and violence in the workplace continues to increase.

Another way organizations focus on symptoms is by striving to become more efficient. This is a dilemma because it's where a lot of the action in OD is nowadays. It's easy for OD practitioners to be co-opted by unhealthy, compulsive organizations, which will pay big bucks for interventions that improve performance and lower costs. Nicoll (1998) said that OD practitioners should be challenging dysfunctionalities in organizations, and in my view compulsive productivity is one of them. One of the questions all of us need to ask ourselves is, "Would I turn down work because I believe the project would lower the quality of life?"

I once interviewed for a job with a consulting firm that provided interpersonal skills training for new MBAs in a client organization. During the interview I was informed that the client culture was characterized by fourteen- to sixteen-hour days; it was their way of separating the goats from the sheep. I was told that I could facilitate interpersonal skill development, but I couldn't touch the culture. I knew I couldn't survive this pace myself, let alone stand by and watch others try, so I withdrew my application. I could have rationalized to get the work. I was tempted because I was under financial pressure at the time, but I didn't think I could live with myself if I reinforced unhealthy work practices. I also think it would have compromised the sense of personal integrity I've needed to write this book.

It's important to emphasize balance among people's physical, emotional, psychological, and spiritual needs. I have a friend who maintains that we have two choices: balance or insanity. Some organizations are encouraging balance by adding exercise facilities, child day care programs, flexible work schedules, and in-home offices. Most organizations still have a long way to go. Changing from a culture of compulsive productivity to balance requires strong leadership firmly grounded in a long-term regard for an organization's most important asset—its people.

Away from Seeking Certainty Toward
Seeking Opportunities in Uncertainty

This is similar to the behavior identified by Tannenbaum and Davis as *away from avoiding risks toward taking risks.* At the root of many organizational issues, including the emphasis on being a dependent learner, the narrow focus on specific skills, and the emphasis on compulsive productivity, is a perception that the unknown is dangerous, which leads to fear. Uncertainty is viewed as "bad," and we're always searching for someone to make us feel more secure. This is where the idea of the "hero leader" comes from. We crave a quick fix. We want someone to save us. We lack confidence in ourselves and want someone to ride in on a white horse and tell us that everything is going to be all right.

The fact is, however, that life has always been full of uncertainty, because the results of our efforts can't be determined in advance. The only difference is that with the increasing pace of change and the rapid obsolescence of knowledge, we're more aware of the uncertainty now. Nevertheless, wishing for more certainty—pining for the "good old days"—will lead to failure. We also need to face our existential condition squarely and find the inner courage to take risks in spite of uncertainty. We also need to stop interpreting uncertainty as "bad" and look at it as an opportunity. By definition, opportunities lie ahead of us, in the midst of the unknown, and exploring those opportunities can substantially improve the quality of our lives and the effectiveness of our organizations. Therefore, we need to move into it with a sense of anticipation, like digging for buried treasure.

Social Competence

Away from Defining Work Roles Narrowly
Toward Fully Utilizing Abilities

This is similar to the behavior on the Tannenbaum and Davis list *away from viewing people primarily as workers toward viewing them as whole persons.* Narrowly defined work roles are based on reductionistic, analytic thinking that tries to break things down into their component parts and fit them into boxes. Such thinking emphasizes the separateness of the components and de-emphasizes their interconnections. It reflects a view of an organization as machine, rather than organization as living system. When this type of logic is applied to jobs, the result is very tight job descriptions that place tight parameters around what a person may and may not do.

In addressing this subject, Argyris (1997, p. 58) concluded from a review of various studies that "organizational demands . . . tend to require individuals to experience dependence and submissiveness and to utilize few of their relative peripheral abilities." Using my terminology, such limiting work roles serve defensive and stabilizing values for order and control, which then often leads to turf protection and a silo mentality ("This is my job," "It's not your job to do that," "Why is your department trying to do our work?"). Many distinctions between jobs are arbitrary, however, and only serve to restrict creativity and innovativeness. Such restrictions widen the gap between what people are giving currently and what they're capable of giving, which represents a loss to the organization. It also limits the sense of contribution people can gain from their work, detracting from their satisfaction, pride of accomplishment, and ability to use their full potential.

In a tight labor market in which intellectual capital is at a premium, it's in the best interests of teams and organizations to remove the arbitrary distinctions that result in narrowly defined work roles. The ability of organizations to survive and grow depends on this. Many organizations have made efforts in recent years to break down the silo mentality and to more fully utilize their people by emphasizing empowerment, involvement, participation, and cross-functional teams. Kotter and Heskett's (1992) research makes it very clear that encouraging leadership throughout the management hierarchy results in vastly superior financial performance. I would add that, in my view, leadership need not be limited to the management hierarchy. Overall system needs are served much more effectively by the belief that good ideas can come from anyone, anywhere, any time.

Away from Distributing Rewards Unfairly
Toward Distributing Rewards Fairly

Rewards are both material and psychological. Some organizations have more flexibility to offer employees material rewards, but all organizations can increase a sense of ownership by offering psychological rewards. First, let's talk about organizations that have latitude in offering material rewards. W. Edwards Deming (1986) recommended that a CEO should make no more than twenty times what the lowest paid employee makes. Nevertheless, the pay gap between the top and bottom has only grown wider over the past two decades. To increase their competitive position, many large organizations now pay their CEO up to two hundred times what the lowest paid employee receives, primarily from stock and options (see Friedlander, 1998). When you couple this with the fact that many people in downsized and restructured organizations now make less than their predecessors and, at the same time, are also being expected to do more work, a widespread sense of unfairness or inequitable distribution of the fruits of organizational productivity exists in the workplace.

Burke (1998) included fairness in his list of values OD practitioners should be championing. In determining the one hundred best companies to work for, Levering and Moskowitz (2000) use fairness, which they define as equitable sharing of opportunities and rewards, as one of their criteria. They maintain that in a tight labor market, companies have to offer perks to employees that were previously reserved for managers. While this is encouraging, many organizations have a long way to go before employees will feel they're receiving a fair and equitable distribution of rewards.

Not all organizations have the flexibility to offer more material rewards. For example, government agencies, nonprofit organizations, and schools most likely don't have the resources to offer employees additional monetary rewards. Nevertheless, all organizations can offer such psychological rewards as praise, positive performance feedback, and recognition. Work represents an expression of one's worth as a person. It's a major arena in which self-esteem can either be validated or negated. People gain a sense of fulfillment when they believe their work makes a contribution to the team or organization. Feeling that their efforts are helping the team or organization achieve its objectives gives them a sense of pride and fulfillment. When people don't believe their efforts make a difference, however, they feel alienated, demoralized, and resentful.

Meaning is intrinsic in some work, but not so in many routine tasks. A surgeon, for example, can gain a sense of contribution by saving a person's life, but an assembly line worker might have trouble seeing how his or her contribution helps the whole. Even small acts, such as expressing appreciation and pointing out the connection between people's efforts and the success of the overall organization, can produce a greater sense of fulfillment. Encouraging people's participation and involvement in decision making does this as well. Many people make the point that these psychological rewards don't cost the organization anything; nevertheless, many leaders and managers miss opportunities to utilize them. Finding creative ways to increase people's sense of contribution will pay great dividends in terms of morale and productivity.

Away from Working Only for External Rewards
Toward Working for Satisfaction from Work Itself

In his classic 1968 *Harvard Business Review* article, "One More Time: How Do You Motivate Employees," Frederick Herzberg differentiated real motivation from KITA (for kick in the ass). So many people have found that difference meaningful that the article has sold 1.2 million copies, making it the largest selling reprint in *HBR*'s history.

The key idea is that working for external rewards (such as pay or other incentives) or to avoid threats of punishment (such as job loss) are both forms of KITA (positive and negative), in contrast to real motivation. With KITA, the person offering the rewards or threats may be motivated to get the work done, but *not* the person doing the work. With real motivation, the person doing the work does so for reasons that, in one way or another, come from the work itself (such as pleasure from the work, sense of achievement, recognition for a job well done, and satisfaction with growth resulting from having done the job). In all cases of real motivation, the motivation is intrinsic to the work itself and not external to it. Kenneth Thomas (2000) distinguished between intrinsic and extrinsic motivation, indicating that, while extrinsics are important, they're never enough to bring out people's best.

This value, away from working only for external rewards toward working for satisfaction from work itself, is consistent with Herzberg's distinction in that it explicitly acknowledges the value of moving away from KITA toward real motivation. As the world of business and the world of work move into increasing complexity and rapid waves of change, the need for people who are able and willing to adapt will be essential for organizational survival. Creating the conditions that enable organizations' members to motivate themselves based on the work itself will become more and more important. In fact, organizations that do not create such conditions may die. Paradoxically, the initial energy to make the shift away from KITA toward real motivation may come from KITA itself, based on fear triggered by perceived threats. However, the energy for change may also come from perceiving opportunities to make life better for everyone involved, thereby making it real motivation.

Away from Serving Self-Interest Toward Serving Mutual Interests

Because values must serve system needs and wants in order to be effective, an overemphasis on self-interest at the individual, team, or organizational level prevents mutual interests from being served. Thus, if individuals are only looking out for themselves, they will not be thinking about the best interests of their team or organization. If a team is only looking out for itself, it won't be keeping in mind the best interests of individuals or the overall organization. An organization that's only thinking of itself will not be considering the best interests of the individuals and teams who are its members, on the one hand, and others in its external environment (such as distributors, suppliers, and communities) on the other.

Organizations receive information and resources from the external environment, and their efforts also impact the outside world. An organization focusing on self-interest will not consider how it uses those resources or its impact on the outside world. Self-interest of this kind has far-reaching consequences for society and the world. Barrett (1998, pp. 25–26) said:

> "Self-interest and the single-minded pursuit of accumulation of wealth lie at the heart of our current crisis. Fueled by greed, businesses all over the world are engaged in the wholesale exploitation of the Earth and its people. . . . So many of us are focused on creating personal wealth that we are unwilling to admit that our personal ambitions are contributing to the pollution of the Earth, the exploitation of its peoples, and the disintegration of our communities."

Globalization, the Internet and Web, and instant communication have shown us just how interconnected we all are on this planet. With the worldwide increase in population and the increasing scarcity of resources, the only way we can ensure our planet's survival for future generations is by focusing on *mutual* interests and the common good. This mindset needs to start at the level of the individual and work its way up to teams, organizations, and the larger world. Thus, before acting, we need to ask ourselves, "What impact will this decision have on others?" If a decision or course of action would have a negative impact on others, we need to rethink what we're trying to accomplish and look for a better alternative.

One widely used way of thinking about shifting from self-interest to mutual interest is called "win-win thinking." Focusing only on your narrow self-interest is called "win-lose thinking," which means you care only about what you want. In contrast, "win-win thinking" involves caring about others' wants as well as what you want (both win). And when many people are involved, the orientation to mutual interests is called "all-win thinking." When the parties to a conflict think in win-lose ways, the likely results are lose-lose (no one gets what he or she wants). And when the parties think in win-win or all-win ways, they are often able to create solutions that satisfy everyone, without compromise (or at least with minimum compromise). For more on why it's difficult for some companies to move from self-interests to mutual interests, see Bill Gellermann's piece below.

▶ Values and the Purpose of Business: Are Stockholders or Stakeholders Primary?

BILL GELLERMANN

OD practitioners face a difficulty in championing growth values that many seem to be unaware of, namely that their client businesses are required by law (based on the charters that have incorporated them) to "maximize profits for stockholders" or "maximize shareholder value." Those purposes make "profit" and "shareholder value" primary values for corporations with such charters—and managers or boards that do not comply can get into difficulty.

The "stockholder-oriented" purpose is legally required by incorporation statutes in many states (twenty-one as of 1994), including Delaware, which has incorporated many of the Fortune 500 corporations (Kelly, 1994).

To question the stockholder-oriented purpose is often deemed heresy, but since the early 1980s more than half of the states (twenty-nine as of 1994, but it could be more now) have changed their incorporation statutes to what are called "constituency statutes." Those statutes vary widely: one kind requires boards to consider constituencies in addition to stockholders in making decisions; another allows boards to consider other constituencies generally; and still another allows such consideration only in case of consolidations and mergers. The point is that the prevailing world view is in process of change (a paradigm shift?) from a "stockholder orientation" (with its narrowly limited, money-oriented values) toward some degree of a "stakeholder orientation" (with its more energizing, people-oriented values). A stakeholder-orientation includes stockholders (such as customers, employees and their families, creditors, suppliers, communities, and the environment). Three examples help clarify the difference between "stockholder" and "stakeholder" orientations.

1. Many years ago an automobile company was reported to have discovered a flaw in its cars that was likely to cause accidents, injuries, and deaths. The company made a cost-benefit analysis, comparing costs of fixing the flaw and costs of lawsuits for damages, and decided to live with the cost of the lawsuits rather than fix the flaw, clearly a reflection of a stockholder-profit orientation. (The recent

news about death-causing SUV rollovers and tire separations suggest that some businesses are still valuing profit more than life.)

2. Several years ago, the board at Kodak fired its CEO because he
    would not downsize as fast as the board wanted him to, which
    sounds like a value conflict between a stockholder-oriented board
    and a stakeholder-oriented CEO. (Paradoxically, the CEO may in fact
    have been serving the longer run interests of stockholders for rea-
    sons suggested by the research summarized in Chapter 1.)

3. Johnson & Johnson acted promptly to recall one of its products,
    Tylenol, when it became known that some of it (an unknown
    amount) had been poisoned by someone, a poisoning for which J&J
    could not be held responsible. In contrast to the stockholder-ori-
    ented valuing by the auto company mentioned in the first example,
    J&J's stakeholder orientation (explicit in their well-known Credo)
    guided people throughout the corporation to make decisions that
    resulted in prompt, large-scale withdrawal of their product from the
    market. Over time, this decision served to enhance consumer con-
    fidence in both Tylenol and in J&J.

The primary force behind the shift to constituency (stakeholder-
oriented) statutes has been a political response to the harm done by
corporate takeovers that had a negative impact on local workers and
communities. Legislatures felt the need to protect boards from stockholder
suits based on boards not having obtained the best deal for stockholders.
A Pennsylvania case illustrates the discretion boards can be allowed under
a constituency statute. Commonwealth National Financial Corporation
merged with Mellon Bank rather than Meridian Bancorp in part because
employees would have a greater opportunity with Mellon, a decision supported by the court.

The trend from "stockholder" to "constituency" statutes suggests that
purposes that focus primarily on stockholders have been found wanting,
at least in the eyes of state legislatures. And to facilitate a shift from narrowly focused stockholder-oriented statutes, it is worth noting that several
studies (briefly described in Chapter 1) suggest that making profits primarily is *not* necessary for achieving outstanding financial performance
that increases shareholder value over time.

One contribution to thinking about values and business I find particularly helpful is Steven Covey's (1991) concept of a *universal mission statement,* the purpose of which is, "To improve the economic well-being and quality of life of all stakeholders" (p. 296). Covey says that such a statement is intended to, "encompass . . . the core values of the organization . . . [and to] . . . create a context that gives meaning, direction and coherence to everything else" (p. 295).

But there is an even broader view of business purpose. In a PBS panel discussion a few years ago—which included CEOs of both Hewlett-Packard and Sears Roebuck and a former Johnson & Johnson CEO—the question of "purpose" came up. After discussion by several of the participants, James Burke, former CEO of Johnson & Johnson, summarized by saying, in effect, "It seems to me that we are in substantial agreement. *The purpose of business is to serve society. In order to do that we need to serve the long-term interests of our stakeholders and, if we do that well, we will serve the long-term best interests of our shareholders*" [emphasis added]. As I understand those words, they avoid the trap of either-or thinking and, in its place, they engage the power of "and." They indicate the possibility of a "win-win" (or "all-win") solution to the problem of defining the purpose of business.

It seems clear to me that somehow we need to shift our prevailing view about the purpose of business from a stockholder-oriented paradigm, with its focus on maximizing profits or shareholder value, to a society-oriented paradigm, with its focus on serving the interests of all stakeholders. As I see it, any other view of purpose gives greater value to the interests of one group of stakeholders over those of others (a win-lose orientation) and, in the long run, harms us all, including the advantaged few. As I reflect further on "values and the purpose of business," the following thoughts occur to me:

1. Ideally there is a high degree of alignment among individual, organizational, communal, and societal purposes and visions.

2. If the vision of businesses generally is grounded in a stockholder-oriented purpose—namely "to maximize profit or shareholder value"—it is difficult, if not impossible, for most members of our society to align their personal values with the exclusively stockholder-oriented values on which such a vision is based.

3. In contrast, if the vision of businesses generally were grounded in a society-oriented purpose—namely, "to serve society by serving the long-term economic well-being and quality of life of all stakeholders"—it is much easier to conceive of all members of our society aligning themselves with such a vision. (The results of the Collins & Porras research, along with several of the other studies cited in Chapter 1, seem to support this view.)

I believe that if we can collectively shift our paradigm about the purpose of business, we will be making a major contribution to putting ourselves back on the path toward the vision we call the "American Dream." I also believe that OD professionals have a primary role in bringing that about. And if we do that, we will have contributed substantially to improving the economic well-being and quality of life for everyone, including stockholders. ◀

Away from Working Only as an Employee
Toward Working as an Owner

"Working only as an employee" is heavily oriented toward *working only for external rewards* (in exchange for pay, benefits, and other compensation), rather than for *satisfaction from work itself*. It is also heavily oriented toward *serving one's self-interest* rather than *serving mutual interests*. The shift in value orientation described here involves a relatively new mental model for thinking about work and motivation, a shift implicit in the increasing number of employee-owned organizations and corporations that are giving their employees stock options.

The value of "working as an owner" builds on the values of "working for satisfaction from work itself" and "serving mutual interests," but it is more than the sum of the two. When both of those values are operative, their motivational power can be enhanced by "working as an owner." It evokes a different kind of energy (motivation) than is evoked by "satisfaction from the work itself." And over and above "serving mutual interests," it evokes energy to contribute to the good of the whole. "Working as an owner" tends to sensitize everyone who shares the "good of the whole" orientation to serving the organization to a greater degree than "serving mutual interests." In particular, that holistic orientation sensitizes people to conditions—particularly opportunities and threats—that may affect the "whole," although not themselves specifically. When people have an "owner" sensitivity, they sense the need for response by the whole, even when it is "not their job." For example, people at Intel spotted the threat to that organization's "memory business" from the Japanese who were intruding on Intel's market well before Andy Grove (Intel's board chairman) did and, without his direction, did what needed to be done to shift the company into the microprocessor business. As Grove described it:

> "More and more of our production resources were directed to the micro-processor business not as a result of any strategic direction but as a result of daily decisions by middle managers. . . . People in the trenches are usually in touch with impending changes early. Sales people understand shifting customer demands before management does; financial analysts are the earliest to know when the fundamentals of a business change" (Grove, 1999, pp. 96–97).

Economic ownership can enhance people's sense of psychological ownership and the lack of it may diminish it. But economic ownership is not the most important condition for "working as an owner"; rather, it is the feeling that this place (the organization) is one's own. It is similar to the feeling of pride that many people have when they say, "I am an American." They don't own the country economically, but it is *theirs* and, in the event of war, many are even willing to die for it.

Away from Devaluing Experience Toward Prizing Wisdom

During the past decade, many organizations have replaced older, experienced managers with younger, less experienced people, primarily as a cost-cutting measure. In many instances, the inexperienced people are given more responsibility than they can handle and, at the same time, they are put in the position of learning the job they're expected to do. While such an approach has an immediate bottom-line impact, and the less experienced people see it as an advancement opportunity, it's based on the mistaken assumption that experience isn't necessary to be an effective manager.

The fact is, however, that people in responsible positions face many complex issues requiring considerable judgment. Some of them are business issues, while others are complicated people issues. Learning how to do a specific job is an inductive learning process, where one skill builds on another until skill mastery has been achieved. As people develop many skills over a period of years, they gain insight and perspective about what works and what does not. This is deductive reasoning. They may not remember where they learned what they know, but when issues emerge they can tap into their memory bank and bring their accumulated experience to bear. Deductive reasoning brings wisdom. Wisdom is the ability to synthesize experience and apply it to new situations. Wisdom cannot be taught and, like fine wine, it takes time to develop fully. Wisdom results from having been there.

When experienced OD practitioners are brought in for a consultation, they're accorded a certain amount of credibility simply because they have some gray hair. Younger practitioners have a harder time establishing credibility because they're perceived as still being "wet behind the ears." Although these perceptions are sometimes unwarranted, it demonstrates that people intuitively equate experience with wisdom. Wisdom isn't tangible like technical skills, but it's a crucial aspect of an organization's intellectual capital. As organizations confront the challenges that lie ahead, it's important to preserve and utilize this capital because most decisions require a combination of inductive and deductive reasoning. Wisdom is to an organization what health is to the body.

Personal Integrity
Away from Posturing Toward Being Authentic

This is similar to Tannenbaum and Davis's value *away from maskmanship and game-playing toward authentic behavior.* It is one of people's deepest desires to have authentic and genuine relationships. While people crave this kind of openness, fear of judgment or criticism makes it a rare experience. Much of what is thought and felt remains unsaid. My personal estimate is that about 80 percent of the interaction between people represents posturing—the dynamics are tainted by "hidden agendas"—while only about 20 percent is genuine. How many times have you sat through a meeting during which two people were having a very diplomatic exchange, only to have one of them tell you later what he/she *really* thinks. Even during these moments of candor, however, it's difficult to tell whether the person is being honest with you or has a hidden agenda. This sort of drama takes place every day in every organization.

People are often skeptical that others are being authentic with them, so they play their cards close to the vest, only being open and honest after determining that it's "safe." Because it's difficult to tell whether it really is safe, however, people tend to err on the side of posturing. They wait to see whether others are authentic before being authentic themselves, but this means a lot of time is wasted waiting around.

It takes courage to let your guard down when you are unsure how others will respond, but this is preferable to spending eight hours a day pretending to be someone you are not. Another good reason for doing this is that genuineness is infectious; if you take the risk of being yourself, it frees others up to be themselves. This helps to create a healthier interpersonal environment in the workplace.

Away from Concealing Truth Toward Seeking Truth

This is similar to Tannenbaum and Davis's values *away from the suppression of feelings toward making their expression appropriate and effective* and *away from avoiding facing others with relevant data toward making appropriate confrontation.* In his summary of OD values, Burke (1998) stressed the importance of encouraging openness. How much we value truth affects how honest we are with ourselves and with others. When the goal is to maintain and enhance our own self-esteem, we tend to be defensive, hiding from anything that might make us feel bad about ourselves. For such people, being honest with themselves and with others is a risk to self-esteem. The dilemma is that people cannot have high self-esteem without being honest. There's a huge tradeoff here because at some level people know when they are being dishonest—inwardly they feel like cowards—but they settle for the immediate relief that comes from getting themselves off the hot seat. They see life as a never-ending battle to protect their self-esteem from threat.

Peter Senge identified a commitment to the truth as one of his requirements for the discipline of personal mastery. He defined this as "a relentless willingness to root out the ways we limit or deceive ourselves from seeing what is, and to continually challenge our theories of why things are the way they are" (Senge, 1990, p. 159). It takes courage to face yourself honestly, but you won't be able to grow personally unless you do. People who aren't honest with themselves have trouble being honest with others. They prefer to avoid or escape tough situations rather than confront them directly. Consequently, they may not address issues critical to team and organizational success; however, truth and progress go hand in hand.

It's important for OD practitioners and managers to encourage people to move beyond their fears and become truth seekers. This means championing a work environment that values choice and a balance between autonomy and constraint (Burke, 1998). They must also model honesty and openness themselves and stress the benefits of emphasizing continuous improvement and learning rather than placing blame.

Social Integrity

Away from Viewing Differences as Negative
Toward Celebrating Differences

Through childhood conditioning, most of are taught either directly or by observing the behavior of significant others that similarities are "safe" and differences are dangerous. We learn to feel secure with the familiar, the known, the predictable, and insecure with the unfamiliar, the unknown, the unpredictable. When we go to school, we begin to encounter differences. There are people who look, talk, and act in ways that are unfamiliar. Our first inclination is to shy away from these people, seeking the security of those who are more like us. We remember mother's warning to be cautious.

Unless challenged, these narrow views carry over into our adult lives, affecting how we orient ourselves to others. Viewing differences as negative places severe limits on our psychological freedom to move and act around others. It limits our ability to form relationships and engage in collaborative partnering. This is especially problematic given the increasingly pluralistic nature of our society. Our ability to succeed in the global economy will be restricted unless we feel confident and self-assured in the midst of diversity.

The alternative to viewing differences as negative is to appreciate and celebrate differences. This requires us to confront any negative attitudes or stereotypes stemming from childhood, replacing them with more positive views. People with unconditional self-esteem are able to be more open to differences because they're less prone to dogmatic, black-and-white thinking. Instead of being defensive and suspicious, they show interest in people who are different. They realize that differences bring fresh perspectives that they can learn from, which not only enriches their lives but adds to the intellectual capital of teams and organizations.

Away from Judging People Toward Accepting People

This is similar to Tannenbaum and Davis's *away from avoidance or negative evaluation of people toward confirming them as human beings.* As humans we have the capacity to determine what does and does not have value, and just how much value something has. We're judging, evaluating beings. We not only assign value to objects, but also to ourselves, to other people, and to life itself. There's nothing that escapes our judgment. If we're aware of it, we judge it.

The capacity to assign worth—to weigh, judge, and evaluate—is both a blessing and a curse. On the one hand it's the doorway to personal choice. Instead of acting on instinct, responding automatically, we weigh options, alternatives. We can distinguish between the significant and the insignificant, the sublime and the ridiculous. We can embrace high callings and noble pursuits, fulfilling our destiny and improving the world. At the same time, the judgments we make are based on our perceptions. We're not completely rational beings relying on pure logic and reason to make assessments. There are limits to our understanding. We also have feelings, drives, urges, and desires that can distort our perceptions. We're capable of misinterpreting information and formulating irrational beliefs with disastrous consequences. Most psychological fears go back to some negative judgments about self, others, and the world, often based on inaccurate or distorted perceptions.

The belief that some people are worth more than others is deeply ingrained in our society. It would be hard for me to think of a belief that has had more destructive consequences. Consider, for example, the following beliefs, which have had a pervasive impact on human behavior throughout history and still exert a powerful influence:

- Males are worth more than females.

- Whites are worth more than Blacks or Hispanics or Asians, and so on.

- The young are worth more than the old.

- White-collar workers are worth more than blue-collar workers.

- The able-bodied are worth more than the handicapped.

- The healthy are worth more than the sick.

- Attractive people are worth more than unattractive people.

- The educated are worth more than the uneducated.

- The wealthy are worth more as persons than the poor.

Each of us needs to search ourselves and root out beliefs that lead to rejecting others. This is necessary to move toward wholeness. We also need a strong resolve to establish work environments that accept differences and in which discrimination is not tolerated, so others can move toward wholeness.

Away from Viewing People as Means to an End
Toward Viewing People as Ends in Themselves

I've noticed that a pervasive sense of expendability exists among people in the workplace. Although people don't usually discuss this, when I ask them, their underlying fear and insecurity come out in the open. I think a lot of the compulsive productivity discussed above is driven by people's perceptions that if they don't meet performance expectations, even if these demands are unrealistic, they'll be replaced with someone else. A major source of this perception is that people are viewed as "employees" (means to an end) rather than as "people" (ends in themselves). Organizations wield considerable power over their employees. They control whether or not employees can make a living, pay their bills, and support their families. Some organizations abuse this power by creating a hostile, threatening environment. Such an environment might meet an organization's productivity needs in the short term, but because it's done at employees' expense, it will undermine effectiveness over the long range.

People want to feel prized and valued as persons, not feel like expendable cogs in a machine. A work environment characterized by genuine regard and appreciation for people as human beings is much healthier than one in which people feel like a means to someone else's end. Such an orientation also makes good business sense because when people feel valued as persons and are given opportunities to express their best efforts, they want to do that.

What growth values are crucial to your success? How about the success of your team or organization? The Growth Values Exercise (Exhibit 6.1) is included to help individuals, teams, and organizations assess where they are now and where they want to go in relation to those values.

Exhibit 6.1. Growth Values Exercise

Purpose

The purpose of this exercise is to help individuals, teams, and organizations assess their current values and establish direction for value change. The exercise is designed to take two hours for individuals and four hours for a team or organization.

Procedures for Team Use

This exercise can be used with a team to assess its values and make decisions for team value change. The entire team should remain intact as the values are discussed. A facilitator can use the following procedures when working with a team:

1. **Cover** the following points (in whatever way feels right to you):
   - "A value can be defined as a standard of importance. Embracing any particular value (say honesty) means we prefer it over its opposite (dishonesty). It can also mean that we prefer it over other values, such as choosing quality of work life over employment in a job we do not like."
   - "Even though we can say we prefer one thing over its opposite, in actual practice values are not black and white choices. No one is 100 percent honest. Instead, values are ideals reflecting what we believe is important in life. They specify a direction—what we want to move away from and what we want to move toward. Regardless of age, opportunities exist to clarify and move toward fuller realization of our values."
   - "The Growth Values Exercise is intended to help you assess your actual and desired values and to develop action plans for moving from one toward the other."

2. **Hand out** a copy of the Growth Values Worksheet to each participant and tell the participants that they will be focusing on team values.

3. **Present** a brief overview of the fifteen values. (*Note:* Review the material on these values in Chapter 6 prior to the session.)

4. **Ask:** Are these ideas meaningful? If people raise questions at this point, explore them briefly enough so that they understand the values.

5. **Give** the following instructions:
   - "The Growth Values Worksheet identifies fifteen values that are important for growth in today's business climate. A growth value is one that allows for forward movement, that is, progress. The values are displayed as scales between two polar opposites. The pole at the left represents a limiting value— one that can hold you back—while the pole at the right represents a growth value. In each instance, the goal is to move away from the left pole and toward the right pole."

Exhibit 6.1. Growth Values Exercise, Cont'd

- "For each scale (1) place an X at the point along the arrow that reflects where you are currently, (2) place a check mark at the point that reflects where you would like to go, (3) describe action steps that will help you make progress, and (4) indicate how you will measure progress."

- "Individually, take fifteen minutes to place Xs and checks along the fifteen arrows and to respond to the questions about actions and progress."

6. **Ask** team members to share their individual work and then facilitate discussion to (1) clarify current team values, (2) establish direction for team value change, (3) agree on actions to be taken, and (4) agree on how progress toward value change will be determined.

Afterward, prepare a summary of the discussion and give each team member a copy. Additional sessions might be necessary to agree on changes and how they will be implemented and to follow up on progress.

Procedures for Organizational Use

This exercise can be used by a leadership team to assess organizational values and make decisions for organizational value change. When employed this way, the same procedures as for teams can be used, only the focus of attention is on organizational values instead of on team values.

It is also possible to use this exercise with several teams, such as all the teams within a department or division (or even a whole organization if total size does not become too unwieldy). In this case, a facilitator who is experienced in working with large groups is usually required. In addition to the special skills needed for large group work, another reason for using a facilitator is that it leaves senior managers free to participate without having to concern themselves with facilitating the process in ways that would distract from their contribution to the content of the group's discussion. If this option is selected, explain the purpose of the exercise and follow the first five steps in the procedures described for teams. Then follow these additional instructions:

1. **Divide** individuals into subgroups (normally individuals would meet with other members of their natural work team, but other groupings are also possible).

2. **Give** these directions to the subgroups:
   - "Appoint a recorder and briefly discuss each value: What does it mean to you? Where is the organization now? Where do you think the organization should go? How can we measure progress? What can we do to keep moving in the direction we want?"

Exhibit 6.1. Growth Values Exercise, Cont'd

- • "The recorder should take notes and prepare a composite report summarizing all relevant information for his or her subgroup. The people in each subgroup do not need to agree, although if they can reach agreement, that's desirable. If they do not, the recorder should be prepared to report the different views." (*Note:* Give each recorder an extra copy of the Growth Values Worksheet and/or sheets of easel paper for this purpose.)

3. **Debrief** key learning points with the full group by asking the subgroup recorders to address the following questions:

"What changes in values would you like to see?"

"How can you measure progress toward the changes?"

"What action steps did you identify for moving in the direction you want?"

Afterward, the facilitator should prepare a summary of the discussion and give a copy to each person in attendance. Additional sessions might be necessary to agree on changes and how they will be implemented and to follow up on progress.

Procedures for Personal Use

This exercise can also be used to help individuals assess their current values and make decisions for personal value change. If this option is selected, explain the purpose of the exercise and follow the first five steps in the procedures described for teams. (Be sure to explain that this evaluation is of personal values.) After that, you can either ask individuals to share their work in subgroups prior to large group discussion, or you can skip the subgroup discussions and ask individuals to share their work with the large group.

Procedures for Customized Use

This exercise can be customized so that an individual, team, or organization can choose its own values, instead of the fifteen identified here. To do this, an individual, team, or organization would (1) identify the values they want to work toward, either by using the Desired Values Form in the Values Identification Survey (Exhibit 5.2) or through some other method, and (2) develop scales by identifying the opposite of each desired value, asking, "What is the opposite of that value?" After doing this for all desired values, follow the procedures for individual, team, or organizational use provided above.

Exhibit 6.1. Growth Values Exercise, Cont'd

Growth Values Worksheet

Instructions: For each value continuum (1) place an X at the point along the arrow where you are currently, (2) place a check mark at the point to which you want to go, (3) describe what you can do to make progress, and (4) indicate how you will measure progress.

Note: Specify your focus of attention for this exercise:

☐ Yourself   ☐ Your team   ☐ Your organization

Being a dependent learner ←———————————————————→ **Being a self-directed learner**

· What actions can I take?

· How will I determine progress?

Learning specific skills ←———————————————————→ **Learning how to adapt and change**

· What actions can I take?

· How will I determine progress?

Compulsive productivity ←———————————————————→ **Balance**

· What actions can I take?

· How will I determine progress?

Exhibit 6.1. Growth Values Exercise, Cont'd

| **Seeking certainty** | | **Seeking opportunities in uncertainty** |

· What actions can I take?

· How will I determine progress?

| **Defining work roles narrowly** | | **Fully utilizing ability** |

· What actions can I take?

· How will I determine progress?

| **Distributing rewards unfairly** | | **Distributing rewards fairly** |

· What actions can I take?

· How will I determine progress?

| **Working only for external rewards** | | **Working for satisfaction from work itself** |

· What actions can I take?

· How will I determine progress?

Exhibit 6.1. Growth Values Exercise, Cont'd

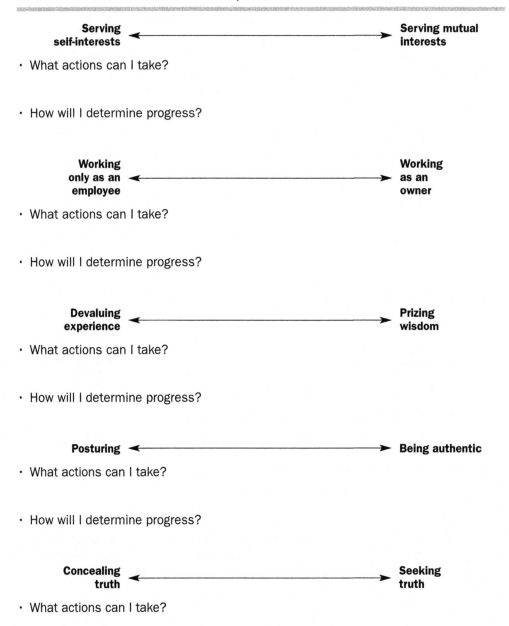

Serving   **Serving mutual**
self-interests ⟵⎯⎯⎯⎯⎯⎯⎯⎯⎯⎯⎯⟶ **interests**

· What actions can I take?

· How will I determine progress?

Working   **Working**
only as an ⟵⎯⎯⎯⎯⎯⎯⎯⎯⎯⎯⎯⟶ **as an**
employee   **owner**

· What actions can I take?

· How will I determine progress?

Devaluing   **Prizing**
experience ⟵⎯⎯⎯⎯⎯⎯⎯⎯⎯⎯⎯⟶ **wisdom**

· What actions can I take?

· How will I determine progress?

Posturing ⟵⎯⎯⎯⎯⎯⎯⎯⎯⎯⎯⎯⟶ **Being authentic**

· What actions can I take?

· How will I determine progress?

Concealing   **Seeking**
truth ⟵⎯⎯⎯⎯⎯⎯⎯⎯⎯⎯⎯⟶ **truth**

· What actions can I take?

· How will I determine progress?

Exhibit 6.1. Growth Values Exercise, Cont'd

Viewing differences as negative ←——————————→ **Celebrating differences**

· What actions can I take?

· How will I determine progress?

Judging people ←——————————→ **Accepting people**

· What actions can I take?

· How will I determine progress?

Viewing people as means to ends ←——————————→ **Viewing people as ends in themselves**

· What actions can I take?

· How will I determine progress?

Other (specify your own)

←——————————→

· What actions can I take?

· How will I determine progress?

In this chapter I presented fifteen growth values that hold special promise for creating healthier organizations and producing long-term financial success. Values exist within a larger Motivational System, which includes needs and wants, thinking, feeling, and doing. In the next chapter, I offer some guidelines for assessing and changing the Motivational System so that you can move toward growth values.

7

Enhancing the Motivational System

ⓋALUES DO NOT EXIST IN ISOLATION, but are part of a larger Motivational System, which includes needs and wants, thinking, feeling, and doing. Therefore, the entire system must be considered before changes are made. This chapter focuses on how to assess and bring about change within the Motivational System. Values are given special attention because of their role in decision making. Our exploration opens with some general guidelines for assessing motivation, followed by some tips for moving beyond symptoms of motivational problems to causes. Suggestions for helping individuals, teams, and organizations move toward greater integration and higher levels of motivation are then offered.

General Guidelines for Assessment and Change

In Chapter 2, I described the Motivational System Model (Figure 2.1), which is comprised of four loops or levels (personal, interpersonal, team, and organizational), with five variables within each loop (needing/wanting, thinking, feeling, valuing/deciding, and doing). Taken together, the four levels and five variables identify twenty potential focal points or targets for assessment and change. At the personal level, the five variables shape *personality*; at the interpersonal, team, and organizational level, they shape *culture*. Constant dynamic interaction takes place within each loop of the Motivational System, among the four loops, and between the Motivational System and its external environment (everything outside that affects or is affected by it); change in one level has ripple effects, some anticipated, others unexpected, impacting the whole.

A Motivational System that operates smoothly and satisfies needs will resist change. Sometimes change is initiated to enhance an already effective system or because the need for change is identified or anticipated within the system or between the system and its external environment. Problems, such as lack of alignment between the personal and organizational levels, produce conflict and fragmentation, resulting in ineffective functioning, unsatisfied needs, and failure. Assessment and change bring about greater integration or wholeness so that the system's potential can be fully realized, a purpose consistent with the "Organization and Human Systems Development Credo" (see the Appendix). The desired move, therefore, is from fragmentation toward wholeness.

Awareness of problems "unfreezes" the system, providing motivation for assessment. Schein (1992, p. 298) describes unfreezing as consisting of the following three processes: "(1) enough *disconfirming data* to cause serious discomfort and disequilibrium; (2) the connection of the disconfirming data to important goals and ideals causing *anxiety and/or guilt*; and (3) enough *psychological safety*, in the sense of seeing a possibility of solving the problems without loss of identity or integrity, thereby allowing members of the organization to admit the disconfirming data rather than defensively denying it."

Because beliefs about self are at the innermost core of the total belief system (Rokeach, 1973), one of the most important types of disconfirming data is a discrepancy between expected and actual performance, the gap between what we thought we could do versus what we did. Such discrepancies can occur at any level: individual, team, or organizational. When faced with disconfirming data, people have a number of choices. They can:

1. Rationalize the discrepancy;
2. Blame themselves and wallow in self-pity;
3. Strive compulsively to improve;
4. Minimize or play down problems;
5. Blame others;

6. Give up; or

7. Seek the truth in an effort to learn and improve.

Obviously the first six choices do not lead anywhere, even though they're used commonly; only the last choice allows for growth. However, finding the truth is often difficult. The apparent or "presenting" problem is almost never the *real* problem. Some potential problems relating to each of the five variables and possible approaches for dealing with them are offered in Table 7.1. Whether or not these turn out to be the real issues can only be determined by accurate and thorough assessment.

Table 7.1. Potential Problems

Variable	Presenting Problem	Possible Solution/Intervention
Need/Want	The external environment has changed Greater awareness of external circumstances is required Capabilities don't match requirements Regulatory changes have taken place New threats or opportunities have emerged	Needs analysis Cultural assessment Environmental scan Training Team intervention Large group and total system interventions
Think	Credibility of leadership is being questioned Rumors are pervasive Assumptions are blocking progress Alignment of thinking to strategies is needed Current thinking is outmoded Distortions and inaccurate information are impairing judgment	Needs analysis Cultural assessment Coaching Counseling Team intervention Personal growth groups
Feel	Differences in beliefs and/or values create conflict A crisis has occurred Some real or perceived loss has been experienced High levels of frustration, resentment, or anger exist Fear, anxiety are high A lack of trust exists A climate of uncertainty exists An unpopular decision has been made An atmosphere of cynicism exists	Coaching Counseling Needs analysis Team intervention Personal growth groups

Table 7.1. Potential Problems, Cont'd

Variable	Presenting Problem	Possible Solution/Intervention
Value/Decide	Change in priorities or strategy is needed Profound change is required A change in mission is needed A new vision is needed Alignment of goals to vision is necessary Organizational values need to be established Discrepancies exist between espoused and actual organizational values Discrepancies exist between actual and desired organizational values Alignment among individual, team, and organizational values is needed Current values are outmoded A change in leadership has taken place A long-range perspective is needed	Needs analysis Coaching Counseling Leadership team intervention Cultural assessment Strategic planning Large group and total system interventions
Do	Behaviors are not aligned to organizational values Skill deficiencies exist Performance improvement is required Performance is inconsistent Coordination is necessary Implementation planning is needed Follow through is necessary Tactical change is needed Current behaviors are outmoded New skills or behaviors are needed Immediate change is required Incremental change would be useful	Needs analysis Job redesign Competency assessment Performance feedback Coaching Counseling Skill-building workshops Management systems Project planning Process improvement Team intervention Large group and total system interventions

Once I was working with a virtual team in a major oil company that was geographically dispersed. They had the typical problems of communication and coordination that occur when members are separated by large distances, but the corporate manager was frustrated by a stalemate in new account development. He felt that the team members, who operated independently in field offices, lacked the imagination and creativity required to expand their businesses. He was constantly on their case with no tangible results. I interviewed the team members individually, and all of them said that the problem was with the manager's approach. They saw him as rigid, narrow-minded, and closed to feedback. They were also reluctant to be honest with him, fearing reprisals.

When I shared this information with the manager, he became very defensive. His perceptions and those of the team were totally different. After discussing ways he could change his approach, I facilitated a very productive meeting between the team and the manager wherein they discussed the issues openly for the first time. This established a new beginning to a more open and constructive working relationship.

People first must feel safe before looking at disconfirming data nondefensively and choosing to seek the truth; a facilitator can help that happen in situations such as the one I described when a manager cannot do it alone. There's more risk involved in owning up to some disconfirming data than to others. The most threatening disconfirming data is that which has negative implications for self-esteem (Harrison, 1970). Figure 7.1 depicts the risks to self-esteem of disconfirming data for each variable in the Motivational System Model.

Figure 7.1. Disconfirming Data and Potential Risk to Self-Esteem

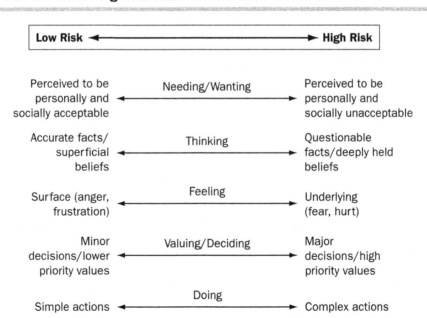

Assessment and response processes must function to decrease fear and foster understanding, so people will be willing to look at high-risk information honestly and directly without defensiveness. People immersed in a system are often blocked from understanding the real issues by biases, emotions, and distorted perceptions. A benefit of using outside OD facilitators is that they can offer an objective perspective on causes and solutions or, even better, help people clarify causes and solutions for themselves. To be effective, however, you must be able to establish credibility and trust very quickly. Clients must believe that you can help them pass through the swamp and cope with the alligators so that they will come out of it in a better place. This is enhanced if the emphasis is on learning and growth, rather than on attempting to solve problems by blaming, criticizing, and punishing those who are "at fault."

In addition to concentrating on low-risk information, people also tend to focus on symptoms and not causes. Feelings and behavior are usually *symptoms*; distorted beliefs and defensive values are usually *causes*. Symptoms are easily seen; causes are often hidden. The efforts of OD facilitators will be short-lived and ineffective unless they can get beyond symptoms—the crisis clamoring for immediate attention—to underlying causes.

The next section offers some general guidelines for bringing about greater alignment within the Motivational System Model, with a specific focus on working with individuals, with teams, and with organizations.

Guidelines for Working with Individuals

It's possible for a person to achieve a higher level of personal integration during team and organizational interventions, but the greatest potential for this is through one-on-one coaching and in personal growth groups.

Coaching

Coaching clients can be self-referred or referred by someone else, such as a supervisor or colleague. Often the presenting problem centers around the person's performance, and there's pressure on the person to improve in order to avoid a negative outcome, such as termination, transfer, or demotion. At other times, the person may be struggling with personal and/or career issues that are less clear. In either case, it's important to avoid accepting the presenting problem at face value and to seek a holistic understanding of the person's situation.

The most effective way for someone to achieve a higher level of personal integration is by moving away from conditional toward unconditional self-esteem. The reason for this is that people's beliefs about themselves are at the core of their total belief systems, followed by values, attitudes, and other types of beliefs (Rokeach, 1973). Movement toward unconditional self-esteem, therefore, can be expected to have a positive impact on these other variables. A coach can facilitate this process by helping people identify self-limiting beliefs and defensive values and by encouraging them to shift to more self-affirming beliefs and growth values.

Helping people alleviate discrepancies between beliefs about self and performance can be healthy or unhealthy, depending on the basis for a person's self-esteem. When people with conditional self-esteem have performance problems, it makes them feel less valuable as persons, and they strive defensively to feel better about themselves. Therefore helping them improve their performance is only a temporary solution, unless this gets at the conditional nature of their self-esteem.

Once I was coaching a vice president who was considering going into business for himself. He had the experience necessary to make such a move but, because he lacked formal education, he had self-doubt. He had allowed his lack of formal education to undermine his self-esteem, jeopardizing his ability to realize his dreams. After a number of discussions, however, he realized that his experience was the crucial factor, and not his education; and his self-esteem increased.

People with unconditional self-acceptance separate their self-esteem from their performance, making them freer to focus on learning and developing their potential. Helping them identify and engage in learning opportunities allows them to achieve an even higher level of personal integration. There's nothing wrong with trying to improve performance as a way of moving toward self-actualization, but linking performance and self-esteem together is a killer.

You can usually tell where people are at in terms of their self-acceptance by the way they respond to you during coaching. Those with conditional self-acceptance tend to be threatened by feedback and respond in a defensive manner; those with more unconditional self-acceptance are more open to feedback and even actively seek it. If I'm not sure where someone stands on this question, I will often ask him or her directly, "How do you feel about yourself?" This moves the discussion from the surface to underlying issues.

Helping people become more self-accepting allows them to be more accepting of others, often bringing about a greater integration among people who work together interpersonally and in teams. Leaders who become increasingly self-accepting can have a positive impact on a team or even an entire organization. People who lead from conditional self-acceptance evoke fear and defensiveness in others, increasing fragmentation; people who lead from self-acceptance inspire others to move beyond safety and embrace growth-fostering values.

To be an effective coach, you must genuinely want to help people, and you must also be self-accepting. If you don't really want to help people, you won't enjoy the process. If you aren't self-accepting, you won't be able to help anyone achieve a higher level of self-acceptance. You can't help people achieve a level of integration you haven't achieved yourself. For this reason, coaches should also have coaches to further their own development.

In my experience, the keys to effective coaching are listening, providing non-judgmental understanding, and fostering dialectical thinking.

Listening and Non-Judgmental Communication

Listening is necessary to identify needs and formulate responses, whereas nonjudgmental understanding is necessary to establish rapport and trust. Receiving nonjudgmental, unconditional acceptance from another person provides opportunities to move toward more unconditional self-esteem (see, for example, Rogers, 1961).

People have a deep need to be heard, understood, and accepted. Feeling understood allows people to feel less isolated and evokes within them a sense of hope when discouraged. Unfortunately, people seldom believe that others are willing to listen. Today's fast-paced work environment is characterized by *techno-relationships* and pervasive computing, where people communicate electronically rather than personally because it's faster. They send e-mail messages to people in nearby offices, rather than opting for face-to-face dialogue. These messages are usually superficial and business-related, seldom getting below the surface to what's *really* going on with people.

It's commonplace to hear people say, "No one listens to me," "No one understands me," or "No one cares what I think." This is why expressing nonjudgmental understanding is so important, especially at the beginning of a relationship. Here are some ways this can be done:

"What you're saying is. . . ."

"If I heard you correctly, it sounds like. . . ."

"So far I think you've said three things. Let me summarize. . . . Is that right?"

"I want to make sure I got it right. Are you saying. . . ?"

"One of the things that troubles you is. . . ."

"You're concerned about what happened because. . . ."

Listening and expressing understanding are beneficial in and of themselves. In fact, sometimes this is all a coach needs to do. Over the years, people have frequently said to me such things as, "I don't feel as overwhelmed as I did an hour ago," "Thanks for letting me put my thoughts into words," or "The issues seem much clearer to me now."

Dialectical Thinking

Often problems cause people to feel isolated and they box themselves in a corner with their own swirling beliefs. Experiencing acceptance allows them to gain perspective and move away from dogmatic, black-and-white thinking. Dogmatic thinking, usually driven by fear and defensive values, blocks self-acceptance and the ability to accept others. It is a closed system, but beliefs and values can only be understood within the framework of an open system. Weisskopf (1959) said black-and-white distinctions lead to *repressive value systems,* while dialectical thinking leads to *integrative value systems.*

Many problems can only be understood and resolved by helping people shift from dogmatic to dialectical thinking. A *dialectic* is a process of change whereby a thesis and its antithesis are combined to form a synthesis. Viewing performance problems from the perspective of learning instead of from the perspective of success and failure represents a value synthesis that allows movement toward growth. Shifting from dogmatic to dialectical thinking is a powerful way to bring about greater integration and wholeness, not only for individuals, but also for teams and organizations.

Dialectical thinking is related to the system concept of *equifinality.* Morgan (1986, p. 47) described equifinality this way: "Living systems have flexible patterns of organization that allow the achievement of specific results from different starting points with different resources in different ways." If everything were black and white, people might not see a way out of their situations, causing them to feel trapped and desperate. But most human problems can be looked at from more than one perspective and have more than one solution. Open systems accommodate creativity, whereas closed systems do not. Helping people understand this can restore their sense of hope and lead them into a creative search for causes and alternative solutions.

The state director of a nonprofit agency came to me for coaching. He had been with the agency for over twenty years and was instrumental in its continuing growth. Gradually, however, his interest in fund-raising activities waned and he lost his effectiveness. When he was asked to resign, he felt as though his world was collapsing around him. Fearful of the future, he asked, "What will happen to me? I don't even have a resume." After several meetings, he began to see that over the years he had developed a wide range of transferable skills. Less desperate, he mounted a job search with the help of an employment agency and found another position within a month.

If people seek coaching, usually their distress is great enough that they'll relax their defenses and be open to help, particularly help in helping themselves, unless they've been "sent" to coaching as some kind of ultimatum. I don't work with someone unless he or she is a willing participant. If not, the person will try to placate me—I become a hurdle to get over—making the situation untenable and ultimately a waste of time. It is possible to help a person who has been "sent" become a willing participant in coaching, but without that shift coaching is ineffective. Honesty is a key to coaching effectiveness and a prerequisite to self-acceptance.

You can't help someone who doesn't want to be helped. As a coach, you can provide the conditions necessary for personal growth, but people may not make healthy choices. Sometimes, for example, people will hold on to low self-esteem in order to avoid the anxieties of growth. This is called *secondary gain.* In addition, people often bring issues with them that even a very healthy workplace cannot overcome. They may need more help than you can provide. It's crucial, therefore, to know your own limits and to make referrals when indicated.

After an effective coach-client relationship has been established, the next step is to clarify expectations. Sometimes the client just needs a sounding board; at other times the person needs feedback, opportunities to develop specific skills, or other interventions. Deep down I believe most people are aware of their shortcomings and limitations, and what they need is a relationship that's safe enough for them to be honest. If it's determined that feedback would be helpful, I encourage clients to ask others for it directly. This helps the clients feel more in control of the process, and it often increases the degree to which they trust others. In today's fast-paced work world, there's pressure on OD practitioners to give advice. This is short-sighted, however, because it doesn't help people learn how to help themselves.

Personal Growth Groups

As we noted earlier, along with coaching, personal growth groups hold the greatest potential for supporting personal growth. In essence, a personal growth group involves approximately eight to fifteen people who have come together to support one another's personal growth. Such groups have a variety of names, including "sensitivity training" and "encounter" as well as "personal growth."

Using a group to support personal growth emerged out of the T-group (T for training) experience, an approach to learning discovered more than fifty years ago. During informal conversations among participants in a formal training program, it was accidentally discovered that significant learning occurred when a group focused on its own process; for example, exploring group member perceptions of who said what to whom in what way, with what effects, and for what reasons. T-groups were groups of people who learned from their own experience. "Sensitivity training" focused the use of such groups on helping people learn about themselves and the dynamics of *their* interactions in a group, not just about group dynamics in general, but about the dynamics underlying *their* behavior. And, because high mutual trust was established, it was possible for individuals to explore important aspects of their own internal personal dynamics.

Often the learnings from groups focused on helping people learn about themselves were deeply personal, intangible, very real, and very important to the individuals who experienced them. For example, Bill Gellermann remembers one man who had become a father for the second time. He spoke during a group Bill was facilitating as part of an "Executive Effectiveness Course" for the American Management Association. On the fourth day of a five-day program, he said with deep conviction, "My first child grew up without me and I'm not going to let that happen again." He wasn't specifically saying what had happened within him, but it was clear to those who were there that he had made a fundamental shift in the priorities (values) by which he had been guiding his life. Bill said his hunch is that, without their saying anything, others in the group considered making similar shifts themselves.

Many of the personal growth issues that are dealt with during coaching are also dealt with as a result of a personal growth group experience. In general, these groups involve achieving higher levels of personal integration by moving away from conditional toward unconditional self-esteem. More specifically, they involve such experiences as identifying self-limiting beliefs and defensive values and shifting toward more self-affirming beliefs and growth values; moving beyond need for other-esteem toward unconditional self-esteem; and differentiating self from position, performance, and all the other attributes (such as age, ethnicity, gender, and race) that people confuse with "self."

In the same way that listening and nonjudgmental communication are important in coaching, they are important for the dynamics of a personal growth group. In fact, a major part of the role of group facilitator is to encourage such behavior by all participants by modeling it and nonjudgmentally confronting dysfunctional behavior in others. In its essence, nonjudgmental confrontation involves describing and exploring perceptions of why things are going on as they are. For example, "This is what I saw Dick do and this is how I saw Jane react. How did others see what went on?" "Why do you think it went on as it did?" "Did that help our process or hinder it?" "In what ways?"

As a personal growth group lives together (for a day or a week or more), the group's members learn to handle nonjudgmental confrontations themselves, and the facilitator can become less active. In fact, there is evidence that it is possible for personal growth groups to function effectively without a facilitator. The keys to that, I think, are the intensity of the group members' motivation to use the group experience to serve their own and others' growth; their willingness to be open about themselves (self-disclosing); and their ability to communicate nonjudgmentally.

As noted above, listening is important for personal growth groups as well as for coaching. Basically, it is listening for *understanding.* The examples given in the section above on listening also apply here, including "What you're saying is. . . ." "I want to make sure I got it right. Are you saying. . . ?" and "You're concerned about what happened because. . . ." It is important to note that understanding does not require agreement. As group members become aware of that fact, they are better able to understand others, in spite of differences in their points of view. It is also important to note that, as members learn to differentiate understanding from agreement, they are better able to accept others as they are and to suspend judgment about the goodness-badness or rightness-wrongness of others' views. And with that come greater mutual respect and trust that enable group participants to explore within themselves in ways that they seldom, if ever, are able to do in their regular lives. And out of that exploration can come significant personal growth.

One of the sources of personal growth in personal growth groups is the group's ability to help people shift from dogmatic to dialectical thinking. People often come into a group experience with the perspective that their point of view is "right" and from this flows what we referred to earlier as "dogmatic thinking." One of the extraordinary things about being in a group whose members have developed a high level of mutual respect and trust is that people, in the process of listening to others' views with understanding and acceptance, open themselves to other ways of thinking and, without consciously choosing to do so, move into the realm of dialectical thinking that can enable them to change their own minds. In other words, they are in a position to help themselves.

In this connection, two points in particular are worth noting. First, the role of "facilitator" is different from the role of "trainer." Personal growth groups are not about "training," but rather about helping people help themselves by facilitating their growth. And, as with plants, that growth comes from within under the influence of favorable conditions that the facilitator helps to make easier (facilitate). Second, a significant number of people in the so-called "helping professions," including OD, tend to see their role as helping their clients, rather than helping to create the conditions under which their clients can help themselves. Paradoxically, this often inhibits our ability to be fully helpful, because helping alone tends to increase dependency. Some of them appear to be doing this in order to build their self-esteem. For those of us for whom this is true, we need to be honest with ourselves, and on the far side of that honesty we may discover that it is possible to grow beyond our own conditional self-esteem.

Guidelines for Working with Teams

Teams are the primary context within which an organization's values are lived out, and this will become increasingly true in the years ahead. With the advent of global competition and instant communication, to a large extent an organization's success depends on how effectively it cultivates emotional intelligence and values encouraging the imaginative and innovative use of teams and networks. Organizations failing to nurture such team values as self-direction and collaboration will have trouble surviving because they'll lack the capacity to adapt. Elinor and Gerard (1998, p. 53) said, "Work has become increasingly specialized and complex. This in turn creates increasing pressure on teamwork for desired results. Where we used to only develop individuals and called it self-mastery, we are now in need of developing whole teams and can call it collective mastery. Integration of tasks and seeing how everything fits together is key. Specialization alone without integration doesn't get us very far. Collective mastery builds on self-mastery."

As with individuals, teams can experience a discrepancy between expected and actual performance, opening the door to assessment and possible change. Team performance encompasses both competence and integrity. These go hand in hand because teams struggling with interpersonal issues have trouble meeting performance goals. Acceptance and trust are especially important at the team level because this is the context wherein people work together most closely. When people feel marginalized or rejected for one reason or another, it has a detrimental impact on their team participation. Similarly, subgroups, cliques, and camps within teams compromise team cohesiveness, alignment, performance, and effectiveness.

Trust is never automatic, but must be developed. Teams go through three stages of development, what I call the three C's: *courtesy, conflict,* and *cohesiveness* (see Hultman, 1998b). In the "courtesy" stage, people are polite and guarded, checking each other out. In the "conflict" stage, differing views surface, triggering friction and polarization. Achieving the "cohesiveness" stage of interpersonal integration depends on how members handle conflict. Teams handling it poorly remain defensive and guarded, while teams handling it well move toward greater levels of trust, openness, and mutual acceptance, which will ultimately make them more successful.

Mistrust is often an invisible barrier to such cohesiveness. A whole infrastructure can build up to accommodate mistrust. In such a climate, people don't deal with their trust issues directly, but spend lots of time trying to second-guess one another's intentions. They often draw wrong conclusions, never checking out each other's intentions for accuracy, simply assuming them to be true. The assumptions then function as self-fulfilling prophesies; false beliefs produce true reality. Mistrust becomes self-perpetuating. Although you can sometimes infer other people's intentions from how their behavior makes you feel—it's important to trust your intuition—one always should corroborate by using other sources of information.

I once worked with a human resources team bitterly divided into two camps: the old-timers and the young professionals. At times the conflict was so intense that members refused to talk with one another. Disagreements were viewed as personal attacks. I used the Myers-Briggs Type Indicator® (MBTI) to help team members understand their similarities and differences more fully. The MBTI identifies people's preferences along four scales: introversion-extroversion, sensing-intuition, thinking-feeling, and judging-perception. They learned that many disagreements were the result of differences in type; understanding enabled them to stop making their differences so "personal." This allowed them to come out from their defensive positions and develop more constructive relationships based on mutual understanding.

In some teams, people develop a vested interest in mistrust. In other words, they have something to gain from a climate of mistrust. Unions, for example, often develop a vested interest in mistrusting management because their ability to gain and keep members is enhanced by an adversarial relationship. Similarly, management can develop a vested interest in mistrust in order to maintain its power base. In situations like these, people resist trusting, equating it as a loss of power and control.

Organization development facilitators can play a key role by bringing unspoken issues regarding lack of acceptance and mistrust out in the open for discussion. They can give the team permission to "discuss the undiscussables." To be effective, team members must feel safe enough to express themselves openly and honestly. I often start by asking, "How would things be different if you trusted each other?" This allows members to recognize the benefits of trust and the consequences of mistrust and to explore their current level of trust or mistrust.

The same interpersonal skills described in the section on working with individuals are useful when working with teams. Additional skills needed are the ability to manage team interaction and the ability to be perceived as neutral. If team members think you're aligned with an individual or subgroup, your effectiveness will be compromised. With these conditions in place, it's not uncommon to see dramatic improvements quickly. Once distorted beliefs and defensive values that have limited team interaction are exposed, they can be replaced with more reality-based beliefs and performance-enhancing values.

Guidelines for Working with Organizations

Essentially, the purpose of leadership is to ensure that an organization becomes all that it is capable of becoming. As Jaworski (1996, p. 66) said, "Leadership is all about the release of human possibilities." This can best be accomplished by establishing a vision and creating conditions whereby people can move toward that vision in healthy and positive ways. Essentially, this means providing them with opportunities to use their skills and learn (personal competence) and make a contribution (social competence) within an atmosphere conducive to self-respect (personal integrity) and acceptance/mutual respect (social integrity). If you want to get a quick read on the effectiveness of leadership, ask employees these questions:

- "Are your knowledge and skills being fully utilized?"
- "Do you have opportunities to further develop your skills?"
- "Do you believe your work makes a difference?"
- "Are your ethical and moral standards respected?"
- "Do you feel accepted and valued as a person?"

A *no* answer to any of these questions indicates limited organizational success.

Some charismatic leaders are able to formulate a vision with which others can freely align and then to gain widespread commitment through the sheer force of their personality, such as Martin Luther King and his "dream." More commonly, however, visions evolve during interaction among people within the organization. Broholm (1990, p. 4) said, "While these solitary visionaries will continue to provide leadership for some organizations, we are also discovering evidence of a type of leader who, rather than creating a single vision and then *selling* it to others, has the ability to *listen* to others and help them articulate a shared vision which reflects their deeply-held values."

Previously I talked about the power of listening to facilitate movement toward more unconditional self-esteem, but listening also has the power to produce *shared* vision. Although it's important for leaders to articulate their vision clearly, dialogue with others is necessary for it to become shared. This is a process, not an event. Over time, the patient leader can help people integrate their dreams into the organizational vision.

Such dialogue focuses on a fundamental question: "What kind of an organization do we want to become?" This can be a creative process if leaders are open to input and if people feel safe enough to speak frankly. In addition to producing a greater integration, such discussions can serve the purpose of clarifying needs and facts and correcting inaccurate beliefs. Leaders who are self-accepting and accepting of others will be more effective at this than others. Like any change agent, leaders cannot take anyone to a higher level of functioning than they have achieved. People leading from strength can encourage others to do their best. You see this in sports when athletes competing against the best are inspired to elevate their game. Those defensively striving to prove their worth have trouble inspiring anyone.

Moving toward greater integration must be a continuous leadership priority. In every organization, there are forces pulling toward both fragmentation and integration. Leaders must be alert to these forces, discouraging the former and encouraging the latter. This requires determination because forces pulling toward defensiveness can be strong and frustrating. When a gap appears between an organization's expected and actual performance, the need for a cultural reassessment will be more obvious than at more placid times.

During a reassessment, an organization must decide what to keep and what to change. Collins and Porras (1994) boiled the success of visionary companies down to one key principle: preserving the core ideology (values and purpose) and stimulating progress. Bellman (2000) emphasized the importance of keeping what has worked in the past when he said:

"Here lies the dilemma you face in each moment of an organizational renewal effort: respecting what has gone before while discovering what might happen next. Live in that dilemma. Don't put yourself on one side or the other, but keep the dilemma alive in yourself and in the people around you. The dilemma lives in the discussions held, the future imagined, and the past respected—assuring a deeper consideration of how to best renew the organization. Here are some questions for that dynamic:

- What are the essential values and purposes that made us what we are, without which we would cease to be?
- Which of those are most important to our future?
- How are we supporting their continuity from the past to the future?" (pp. 71–72)

In this chapter, I presented some general guidelines for enhancing the Motivational System and discussed their relevance to individuals, teams, and organizations. Motivational System Mapping™ (MSM) is a systematic process that can be used to assess and change the Motivational System. Motivational System Mapping™ will be discussed in the next chapter.

(8)

Motivational System Mapping™

THE MOTIVATIONAL SYSTEM INCLUDES needing/wanting, thinking, feeling, valuing/deciding, and doing. Because a dynamic relationship exists among the variables, they must all be considered in efforts to bring about greater integration within the Motivational System. Motivational System Mapping™ (MSM) is a systematic process that can be used for this purpose. In this chapter, MSM is described and guidelines for using it with individuals, teams, and organizations are given. Finally, suggestions are offered for embedding growth values in management systems and for renewing values.

Introduction to Motivational System Mapping™

Warner Burke (1982) has argued that facilitating values clarification is one of the most important functions of the OD practitioner. He said:

"A primary role of the practitioner is to help the manager or executive (1) to clarify his or her personal values and how they are congruent or incongruent with the organization's values; (2) to examine his or her stated values and how certain ones may be incongruent with behavior; and (3) to incorporate stated or implied organizational values within the fabric of the system, as manifested in the structure, reward system, control system, and political process." (1982, p. 373)

The concepts and tools presented in this book are intended to better equip OD practitioners so that they can facilitate these three processes more effectively. In Chapter 5, I presented two assessment tools that focus specifically on values, the Values Assessment Inventory (Exhibit 5.1) and the Values Identification Survey (Exhibit 5.2). Motivational System Mapping™ is intended to generate a holistic picture of the relevant factors in a system and their interrelationships so that appropriate actions can be developed and implemented. Motivational System Mapping is more comprehensive than the other tools because it gets at all the components within the Motivational System Model (needing/wanting, thinking, feeling, valuing/deciding, and doing).

Motivational System Mapping is based on the premise that people sometimes can benefit from help in identifying, organizing, and using information about themselves and their problems. The facilitator does this by asking questions to foster self-discovery. This allows people to retain responsibility for themselves, establishing clarity about their vision and ownership in both the causes of and solutions to their problems.

Theoretical Foundations

The theoretical foundation for MSM has been laid in a variety of disciplines. For example, in describing his theory of cognitive and behavioral change, Rokeach (1973, pp. 233–234) said, "A . . . method for inducing change is to expose a person to information about his own belief system, or to selected features of it, in order to make him consciously aware of certain contradictions that chronically exist within it below the level of awareness. . . . information about contradictions within one's belief system that are perceived to be incompatible with self-conceptions should motivate cognitive and behavioral change that will remove or reduce incompetent or immoral self-conceptions."

Consistent with this, Senge (1990, p. 164) said, "A useful starting exercise for learning how to focus more clearly on desired results is to take any particular goal or aspect of your vision. First imagine that the goal is fully realized. Then ask yourself the question, 'If I actually had this, what would it get me?' What people often discover is that the answer to that question reveals 'deeper' desires lying behind the goal." The questions asked during MSM often tap into deeper meanings that increase self-understanding. For example, asking someone, "What's the most important thing in your life?" and following it up with, "Why is that important?" helps the person get at something deeper. This allows the person to see what's driving what and to focus more intently on deeper meanings and motives.

There's also some overlap between methods suggested by MSM and personal construct psychology, which focuses on identifying the constructs (beliefs and values) people use to understand themselves and their world. One approach is called *laddering*, which uses facilitative questions to help people process the meaning of their responses. A variation of this, called *dialectical laddering*, relies on a series of questions to help people identify and resolve value conflicts. Neimeyer (1993, p. 63) described a dialectical ladder as, "a ladder whose antithetical construct poles are reconciled in a higher order integration or synthesis. When such integration is successful, dialectical laddering provides not only an assessment of the structure of the client's current system, but also a series of guideposts pointing toward new potentials to be explored in therapy and in daily life."

Such a method can be useful when someone is experiencing a basic dilemma between two alternatives that both seem bad. In situations like these, it can be helpful to ask:

- "Can you find an alternative that would reconcile these two poles?" and

- "How would that differ from the two polar extremes?"

Such questions not only help people to identify and resolve intrapersonal value conflicts, but also to value conflicts with others. I will have more to say about this in the section below on working with teams.

Similarities also exist between MSM and cognitive therapy (see, for example, Beck, 1976; Ellis, 1973). Cognitive therapists take the position that it's our interpretations of events that elicit emotional and behavioral responses. Emotional and behavioral problems are dealt with by challenging irrational beliefs because they can distort our interpretations. A cognitive therapist plays an active role in challenging irrational beliefs and cognitive restructuring, skills requiring specialized training. In contrast, the MSM coach facilitates client self-assessment. Although MSM can have some therapeutic outcomes, its purpose is developmental and educational.

MSM and Appreciative Inquiry

A brief comparison between MSM and Appreciative Inquiry (AI) is in order, because the latter approach to OD is growing in popularity and influence. Instead of focusing on traditional problem solving, AI seeks to find what's *right* in organizations.

Watkins and Cooperrider (2000, p. 6) described AI as "an articulated theory that rationalizes and reinforces the habit of mind that moves through the world in a generative frame, seeking and finding images of the possible rather than scenes of disaster and despair." Appreciative Inquiry practitioners help organizations to articulate key ingredients in past successes and then to use those as the basis for creating a positive future.

Appreciative Inquiry is a new movement in OD based on a philosophy of practicing the positive (see, for example, Cooperrider, et al., 2000; Watkins & Mohr, 2001), while MSM is a specific methodology for identifying and dealing with system issues. Whereas AI leads organizations to a focus on the positive, MSM is a balanced model that looks at both driving and restraining forces in the tradition of Kurt Lewin's force-field analysis (Lewin, 1947). My experience indicates that personal, interpersonal, team, and organizational problems usually stem from underlying issues that cannot be identified or resolved by focusing on the positive alone (for more on this subject, see Golembiewski, 2000).

Motivational System Mapping is based on the belief that under favorable conditions—those encouraging self-acceptance and trust—people will naturally move toward growth; therefore, the process starts wherever the client is ready to work and builds from there. The goal is to construct a map of the relevant factors in a situation so that patterns and relationships can be identified. These patterns and relationships then help to focus development.

It can distort understanding to guide a client toward either the positive or the negative. Motivational System Mapping attempts to minimize distortion by having clients decide what direction to take. If clients want to talk about the positive or the negative, MSM accommodates them either way. Thomas Head (2000) makes the point that AI eliminates resistance to change because of the positive focus. Motivational System Mapping lowers resistance because the client decides the direction.

This does not mean that MSM is value-free. I don't think any OD methodology can be totally value-free, nor do I think this is desirable. Even if you only ask questions and refrain from offering recommendations, you steer the process, consciously or unconsciously, by the questions you choose. When I use MSM, my underlying value biases are toward:

- Seeking balance within the Motivational System;
- Moving the Motivational System away from defensive values and toward growth values;
- Separating causes from symptoms of problems; and
- Focusing remedies on causes.

Also, while it is theoretically possible to use MSM by *only* asking questions, in actual practice I've never employed it this way. As I listen to a client, I gain insights into symptoms, causes, patterns and themes, consequences, and actions. I offer these insights when I think it's appropriate, although my bias is toward being patient, giving the client time to gain insights on his or her own. I will also offer my own recommendations, based on my biases toward balance, growth, and remedies that deal with causes.

One final point is that a thin line exists between assessment and development (Argyris, 1970; Burke, 1982). Motivational System Mapping is essentially an assessment method, but people gain insights during the process that change them, and anything producing positive change is developmental. Change in one belief or value has an impact on other beliefs and values because they are structurally and functionally related. Regarding this, Harrison (1969, p. 66) said, "Concepts are too closely and complexly linked to change one or two relationships in isolation. One change leads to another, pretty soon a major reorganization is going on." While MSM produces insight, its overall goal is to encourage change that helps people and organizations actualize their potential more fully.

Motivational System Mapping™ with Individuals

Motivational System Mapping can help a person gain in self-understanding, clarify personal/professional mission and vision, locate driving and constraining forces, and develop a strategy for serving mission and bringing vision into being. Specifically, individuals can:

1. Clarify their purpose (mission) and their dream for the future (vision);

2. Establish goals for serving purpose and actualizing vision;

3. Identify their current needs/wants, facts, beliefs, feelings, values, and behaviors;

4. Identify patterns and themes among current needs/wants, facts, beliefs, feelings, values, and behaviors;

5. Assess positive and negative consequences of current needs/wants, facts, beliefs, feelings, values, and behaviors;

6. Identify changes needed to build on the positive and deal with the negative;

7. Develop a plan for personal development; and

8. Monitor results and make necessary adjustments.

The key skills in MSM are (1) knowing what questions to ask and (2) understanding responses according to the variables in the Motivational System Model. Purpose and vision establish a frame of reference within which the Motivational System (as described in the Model, Figure 2.1) functions. Helping individuals clarify their purpose and vision before focusing on the variables within the model is generally desirable because, with a clearer frame of reference, their thinking about motivation is more meaningful. Questions for clarifying purpose and vision include the following:

Purpose (Personal Mission)

- "What is your reason for living?"
- "What is most important in your life?"
- "Why is that important?"
- "What values does that reflect?"
- "To what are you truly committed/dedicated?"
- "What do you truly care about?"
- "What will that give you?"
- "What needs or wants will that serve?"

Dream (Personal Vision)

- "What would your life be like if it were exactly the way you would like it to be?"
- "How would your dream allow you to fulfill your purposes?"
- "What would give you a sense of fulfillment?"
- "What do you want to accomplish?"
- "What will that allow you to accomplish?"
- "What do you see yourself doing?"
- "What would you do if money were no object?"
- "What do you do when nobody's telling you what to do?"
- "What would you regret not doing?"
- "Is there something you really want to do?"
- "What needs or wants will bringing your vision into being serve?"

As the client responds, the coach writes down notes about the responses in the Mission/Vision Worksheet, Exhibit 8.1.

Exhibit 8.1. Mission/Vision Worksheet

Mission (Purpose)

Vision (Dreams, Images of Desired Future)

The same kind of process can be used to generate information about the variables within the Motivational System Model. For example, a question such as, "What options do you see?" gets at beliefs and perceived facts. Following up with "What do you want to do?" moves the discussion to values. Table 8.1, Navigating the Motivational System, provides examples of questions relating to the five variables: need/want, think, feel, value/decide, and do.

Table 8.1. Navigating the Motivational System

Get From \ To	Need/Want	Think	Feel	Value/Decide	Do
Need/Want	What are your needs/wants? What needs/wants are/are not being satisfied? What are some of your other needs/wants? How have your needs/wants changed?	How could you satisfy your needs/wants? Are there better ways to satisfy your needs/wants? How will these changes in needs/wants impact your thinking?	How would you feel if you could not satisfy that need/want?	How do you decide the best ways to satisfy your needs/wants? How will these changes in needs/wants impact your decisions?	Does that satisfy your needs/wants? What do you get by doing that? How will these changes in needs/wants impact your actions?
Think	How does that thinking allow you to meet your needs? Does that thinking keep you from meeting your needs? Would changing those thoughts allow you to meet your needs? What impact does your thinking have on others' needs?	What do you think about yourself/others/the organization? What are your beliefs about that? What's another way of looking at this? What keeps you from changing your thinking? What do you think is going to happen? How do you know that's true? What would happen if you changed your thinking? What would happen if you did not change your thinking?	How do those thoughts make you feel? How would you feel if that happened? How would others feel if that happened?	What factors do you consider when making a decision? What other input will you need before making a decision? What thinking went into this decision? Who else should be involved in making this decision? Do some people's ideas carry more weight than others'? How could you change that decision? How do you evaluate your decisions?	How could you put those thoughts into action? What keeps you from doing that? How could you improve your actions? What would you gain if you changed your behavior? What would you lose if you do not change your behavior? What impact do your thoughts have on others' actions? How do you evaluate your actions?

Feel	How strongly do you feel about satisfying that need/want?	How do your feelings affect your thoughts?	What are your feelings? What other feelings do you have?	How do those feelings affect your decisions?	How do those feelings affect your actions?
Value/Decide	How would that decision allow you to satisfy your needs/wants? What impact does that decision have on others' needs/wants? How do you decide what needs/wants to focus on?	What thoughts led to that decision? What are the pros and cons? What would the costs/benefits be of that decision? What are the potential consequences of that decision? What are the trade-offs? Are they acceptable? What do you think will happen if you decide to do that? What do others think about your decisions?	How do you feel about your decision? How would that decision make you feel? How will you feel if your decision does not work out? How do others feel about the decision? What concerns do you have about the decision?	What is your mission/vision? What values do you consider in working toward your mission/vision? How do you determine your values? What criteria do you use in making decisions? What are your priorities? How could you improve your decisions? Who makes those decisions?	How could you put those decisions into action? What do you want to do? What impact do your decisions have on what others do? What are the most important things you can do?
Do	How does this action allow you to satisfy your needs/wants? What other actions could you take to satisfy your needs/wants?	What's the thinking behind those actions? How well do the actions work? What else do you think you could do? How could you change your thinking?	How did you feel about doing that? How would you feel if those actions did not work?	What impact do your actions have on your decisions? What impact do other people's actions have on your decisions?	What behaviors have you tried? What else could you do? What behaviors do you want to keep? What behaviors do you want to change? What new behaviors do you want to add?

As the client responds to questions, the coach writes down all responses in the appropriate category on an MSM Worksheet (Individual Version). A copy of the worksheet is included as Exhibit 8.2. The purpose of the worksheet is to show how responses are categorized. In actual practice, you will need much more space than is provided here. I suggest you place the headings on pieces of note paper or sheets of easel paper.

Exhibit 8.2. Motivational System Mapping™ Worksheet (Individual Version)

Needing/Wanting:
Thinking: 　Facts
Beliefs about self
Beliefs about others
Beliefs about the external environment
Feeling:
Valuing/Deciding: 　Terminal values
Instrumental values
Doing (behaviors):

Patterns/Themes:
Consequences:
Actions:

You can start your questioning anyplace. Start where the person is motivated to work; the process belongs to him or her. The Statement Categorization Exercise is included as Exhibit 8.3 to give you practice in categorizing responses. As the process progresses, the worksheet begins to fill in and the client sees patterns and relationships between bits of information—the "map" becomes clearer to understand. Clients often have many "ah-hahs" during this experience, discovering relationships among beliefs, feelings, values, and behaviors. They start synthesizing seemingly unrelated pieces of information, allowing them to work toward a deeper level of personal integration.

Exhibit 8.3. Statement Categorization Exercise

The Statement Categorization Exercise is designed to check your understanding of the key variables in Motivational Systems Mapping: facts, beliefs, feelings, terminal values, instrumental values, and behaviors. The answers can be found at the bottom of the page.

Instructions: Read each statement and, in the space to the right, indicate whether you think it reflects a fact, belief, feeling, terminal value, instrumental value, or behavior.

1. "It's important for us to be honest with one another." _____

2. "Our analysts tell us our market share dropped
   5 percent during the last quarter." _____

3. "That will never work here." _____

4. "We exist for our customers." _____

5. "Fear of making mistakes keeps us from taking risks." _____

6. "I just want to be treated fairly." _____

7. "These cutbacks will ruin us in the long run." _____

8. "One way would be to place more emphasis on diversity." _____

9. "In this company it's who you know that counts." _____

10. "We just pretend the problem doesn't exist." _____

11. "Everyone affected by the change should be involved." _____

12. "If you speak your mind, you won't last long around here." _____

13. "We're frustrated with these new procedures." _____

14. "I've heard rumors that more layoffs are expected." _____

15. "They don't care what happens to us." _____

16. "They're going about this all wrong." _____

17. "I want my work to enhance the quality of my life." _____

18. "We never received the training they promised." _____

19. "I bet they go back to the old system within six months." _____

20. "We complain but don't do anything about it." _____

Answers:

1. Instrumental value	6. Instrumental value	11. Instrumental value	16. Belief
2. Fact	7. Belief	12. Belief	17. Terminal value
3. Belief	8. Instrumental value	13. Feeling	18. Fact
4. Terminal value	9. Belief	14. Fact	19. Belief
5. Feeling	10. Behavior	15. Belief	20. Behavior

Change can be facilitated by asking questions about patterns/themes, positive and negative consequences, and possible actions. Some questions relating to these areas follow:

Patterns/Themes

- "What are the symptoms/causes?"
- "What patterns or themes do you see emerging?"
- "What connections do you see between these responses?"
- "What relationships do you see between your values and feelings, feelings and beliefs, beliefs and values, values and behaviors?"

Consequences

- "What positive consequences do you see?"
- "How can you capitalize on these consequences more fully?"
- "What barriers exist?"
- "How can you overcome or minimize these barriers?"

Actions

- "What actions can you take?"
- "How would those actions allow you to fulfill your purposes/dreams?"
- "What specifically are you prepared to do and by when?"
- "What resources do you have?"
- "What additional resources do you need?"
- "How can you get these resources?"

How long MSM will take depends on the situation and the degree of insight people have about the issues. If someone is upset emotionally, he or she will need to vent feelings before getting into the questions. Answering the questions is a more analytical process, so emotional issues must be dealt with before the person can focus on MSM.

It will take people capable of more insight less time to go through the process than it will take others. Also, it's easier for some people to be open and talk about feelings. I've worked with people who moved through the process in a few hours, while others took many meetings over a period of time. On one occasion, a CEO looked at his worksheet after about thirty minutes and said, "I know what I need to do. It's obvious that I'm unhappy in this job. I'm sick of the constant pressure about money. I'm going to do something that lets me enjoy myself more." I prefer a marathon session away from the workplace, where the person can focus intently on the situation without interruptions. If you have an entire day set aside for this, you get a sense for whether or not the session continues to be productive. If you reach a point of diminishing returns, quit for the day and pick it up later.

At other times, long sessions are not feasible due to time constraints. At the end of a session, I leave the worksheet with the person to ponder until our next meeting. Often he or she gains insights between sessions that become departure points for the next meeting. I tell people that the data are theirs, not mine, and that the information is confidential. When coaching concludes, I leave all my notes and worksheets with the client. Clients sometimes refer back to their notes months or even years later, gauging progress and gaining additional insights. This builds their self-confidence and helps them deal with new issues more effectively.

In my opinion, a lot of coaching based on 360-degree feedback assumes that people are generally unaware of their weaknesses and need to be confronted with outside data. The danger here is that acting on that assumption can inadvertently diminish self-esteem ("I can't even understand myself") and intensify mistrust ("They'll just get even with me"). However, there are times when people simply don't see their negative impact on others. For example, Ryan and Oestreich (1998) found that many managers were oblivious to the fact that their actions instilled fear in employees. In such instances, a more directive approach and outside feedback can be helpful. Both the Values Assessment Inventory (Exhibit 5.1) and Values Identification Survey (Exhibit 5.2) contain a 360-degree feedback option. These instruments also have a variety of applications for individuals, teams, and organizations, which were summarized in Chapter 5. In addition, the Value-Centered Planning Worksheet (Exhibit 4.1) can also be used with all three levels.

The VAI and VIS 360-degree feedback processes can be used as a one-time values assessment or as a pre/post measure to gauge progress. If a pre/post administration is used, the person should be allowed the time and resources necessary to make the agreed-on changes. When providing 360-degree feedback, it's important to present the data in a manner that supports the person's self-esteem. This is especially true if the person's self-perceptions vary considerably from supervisor, peer, and/or subordinate perceptions. After reviewing the data and answering any questions, listen, encourage nonjudgmental understanding, and keep the focus on learning.

Another approach that can be used by individuals to identify issues is self-confrontation. Self-confrontation means asking yourself before acting, "What's the *real* reason I want to do this?" or "What am I *really* trying to accomplish here?" These questions help people who want to become more honest with themselves and others to do so. Continuing self-confrontation can help them keep from slipping into self-deception and defensiveness. The limitation of self-confrontation is that it's difficult, if not impossible, for people to be completely objective about their experience as they're going through it (Kegan, 1982). A coach can help a person become more objective by serving as an external, relatively objective reference point for insights gained through self-confrontation and introspection.

Motivational System Mapping™ with Teams and Organizations

Motivational System Mapping can also be used with teams and organizations. The nondirective process allows a team to gain greater ownership of its issues and solutions. Motivational System Mapping has the added benefit of fostering greater trust and cohesiveness because everyone is participating in the process. It also tends to increase the integration or alignment among individual, team, and organizational values and enhances the team's confidence and skill in identifying and dealing with its issues. Specifically, MSM can help a team or organization do the following:

1. Define or redefine its mission and vision;
2. Establish goals for serving its mission and bringing its vision into being;
3. Identify current needs/wants, facts, beliefs, feelings, values, and behaviors;
4. Identify patterns and themes among current needs/wants, facts, beliefs, feelings, values, and behaviors;
5. Assess positive and negative consequences of current needs/wants, facts, beliefs, feelings, values, and behaviors;
6. Identify changes needed to build on the positive and overcome the negative;
7. Develop a plan for development and building alignment; and
8. Monitor results and make necessary adjustments.

As with individuals, mission and vision provide a frame of reference within which teams and organizations function. With appropriate modification, the questions relating to purpose and vision in the section on MSM with Individuals can be used with teams and organizations, along with the Mission/Vision Worksheet (Exhibit 8.1).

MSM with Teams

If a team already has a mission and vision, MSM can be used with teams to focus on the five motivational variables. An MSM Worksheet (Team/Organizational Version) is provided as Exhibit 8.4. This worksheet varies slightly from the one for individuals.

Exhibit 8.4. Motivational System Mapping™ Worksheet (Team/Organizational Version)

Needing/Wanting:
Thinking: Facts
Beliefs about self
Beliefs about others
Beliefs about the organization
Beliefs about the external environment
Feeling:
Valuing/Deciding: Terminal values
Instrumental values
Doing (behaviors):

Patterns/Themes:
Consequences:
Actions:

The process of using the worksheet with a team is much the same as the process with an individual. The major difference is that the focus of attention is on the team instead of on a person. After clarifying expectations, I start the session by defining mission and vision and describing how they establish a frame of reference for the Motivational System. Then I define the variables in the Motivational System Model (need/want, think, feel, value/decide, do). I write "mission" and "vision" and the name of each variable at the top of a separate sheet of easel paper and post them conspicuously around the room. Then I ask questions about mission and vision and record member responses. After enough responses have been recorded to gain a general sense for how these factors provide a frame of reference, I shift the focus to the five motivational variables.

Whenever someone makes a comment, I write it on the appropriate sheet of paper. As the sheets begin to fill up, members spot patterns and relationships among responses (sometimes I divide team members into subgroups and they generate this information on their own). Once their issues become clearer, members are then able to generate potential actions. At the end of the session, I compile all the information and distribute it to team members.

It's common for information raised by different team members to be contradictory. In fact, one of the goals of MSM is to bring such differences out in the open. For example, during one team session, two members saw their situation in entirely different ways. One was optimistic, while the other was pessimistic. They began arguing, and I called a time out. I suggested that they focus on getting their views out and each try to understand where the other was coming from. This allowed them to deal with the situation in a more open manner, leading to an increase in mutual understanding. The discussions that occur during MSM are more constructive if people avoid arguing about the validity of each other's perceptions and simply see their different views as data.

Many value conflicts between people or among members of a team occur because people become polarized in their positions. Such conflicts can often be resolved by moving from dualistic to dialectical thinking, including using win-win thinking, seeking a synthesis of the different positions (finding common ground), or looking beneath the values causing conflict to locate deeper shared values. I was working with one team in which members were entrenched in their positions, unwilling to budge. I asked them, "How do you think your clients perceive you as a team?" After pondering this for several minutes, one member said, "They probably see us as stubborn kids." Another member chimed in, "We'd better do a better job of working together before we lose our credibility." This exchange, based on the shared value of being looked on favorably by clients, enabled them to transform conflict into synthesis.

MSM with Organizations

When MSM is used with organizations, it has the power to transform large systems. Schein (1992, p. 307) said, "Members of the organization can collectively achieve insight if they . . . examine their culture and redefine some of the cognitive elements. Such redefinition involves either changing some of the priorities within the core set of assumptions or abandoning one assumption that is a barrier by subordinating it to a higher-order assumption."

I meet with the leadership team and take them through the process, much as described in the section on working with teams. The difference is that they are focusing on the whole organization, not on the leadership team itself. There's often a lot at stake in these sessions because everyone is affected by the outcome. Dialogue among leaders regarding the state of the organization and its future can be very intense and meaningful. The process serves as a reality check on the viability of an organization's culture, helping leaders spot distorted or outmoded assumptions and defensive values that are undermining performance and results.

Sometimes the team sees a need to clarify or even change the mission or vision of the business or a need for radical cultural changes. For example, I worked with a leadership team that identified a need to change from a product to a customer focus because they were losing market share to competitors stressing customer success. In addition to identifying new operating methods, they also had to completely overhaul their reward structure. Two top managers disagreed with the changes and decided to leave, but after the transition the company began regaining its competitive position.

In another company, MSM was used following a product recall. Leadership team members realized that they needed to restore consumer confidence, but the process revealed that they had compromised quality for speed and long-range objectives for short-term profits. These realizations led to changes in priorities, impacting many management and production methods.

Embedding Growth Values in Management Systems

In order for values to be "real," they must be integrated into key management practices, especially the selection and performance evaluation systems. Collins and Porras (1994) found that visionary companies work to make their core ideology pervasive throughout the organization. Barrett (1998, p. 105) said, "A strong positive culture can be established only if the values and concomitant behaviors are structurally integrated into the human resource system, particularly the personnel evaluation processes. A values-based performance evaluation process and hiring policy are essential for developing a strong, positive culture." Once guidelines consistent with organizational values have been established, everyone from top down must be held accountable for acting on the values in a consistent manner—that is "walking the talk." The key thing is to translate values into specific, behavioral terms ("When we say we value quality, it means that we follow Six Sigma criteria," "When we say we value honesty, it means we say the same things in private that we say in public").

At Menno Haven, Inc., after facilitating meetings with the leadership team to establish organizational values, I redesigned the selection and performance evaluation systems around those values. At Messiah Village, I designed a competency-based performance evaluation system that was tied to their values. The behaviors expected of every position were identified and classified under their values. This ensured that an organization's value system was complete. When supervisors gave performance feedback, they explained how an employee's work related to the organizational values, highlighting their contribution to the overall organization. For some other examples of how to embed values in management systems, see *Managing by Values* by Blanchard and O'Connor (1997).

Renewing Values

I've talked with leaders who said, "We did the values thing," as if this were a one-time experience like buying a factory. However, organizational values are always "works in progress." Renewing values is part of the discipline of personal mastery—and team and organizational mastery. Senge (1990, p. 141) said, "When personal mastery becomes a discipline—an activity we integrate into our lives—it embodies two underlying movements. The first is continually clarifying what is important to us. . . . The second is continually learning how to see the current reality more clearly."

Ongoing review is imperative to keep the values viable and up-to-date. The risks involved in not doing this are far-reaching. In their research on corporate culture, Kotter and Heskett (1992, p. 41) found that "(1) a culture can blind people to facts that don't match its assumptions, even very smart, experienced, and successful executives, and (2) an entrenched culture can make implementing new and different strategies very difficult." They concluded that organizations will not be able to sustain excellent performance over the long haul unless they have values and norms that allow them to adapt to a changing environment.

Life moves on. Values that promoted growth at one point can prevent growth at another; and in these days of rapidly changing business conditions, values that inhibit flexibility can lead to an organization's death. To prevent this from happening, leaders must nurture a climate that anticipates the need for value change and development. Motivational System Mapping can be used to reassess values and as an environmental scan. In addition, the Values Assessment Inventory and the Values Identification Survey can be used on a pre/post basis to assess the effectiveness of team and organizational values.

In conclusion, the quality of work life and organizational success depends on the degree of balance that exists within the Motivational System. Facilitating balance among individuals, teams, and the overall organization is one of the primary functions of OD practitioners and managers. The concepts and tools presented in this book are intended to help you in this important endeavor. The work can be difficult and requires a deep commitment to values fostering growth. The effort is well worth it, however, because self-actualizing individuals and effective interpersonal relationships and teams will enable organizations to achieve their full potential.

Appendix

ON 1981, WE BEGAN A PARTICIPATIVE PROCESS (involving more than six hundred people from more than twenty-five countries) for co-creating "A Statement of Values and Ethics by Professionals in Organization and Human Systems Development," along with an "Annotated Statement" and a summary Credo. The Credo and Annotated Statement have been endorsed as working statements by several leaders in our profession, including Dick Beckhard and Bob Tannenbaum. The latest version of the Credo is presented below. For more information and to join in the co-creation process, write for the Statement Development Package at this address:

Clearinghouse for Information about Values and Ethics in OD-HSD

P.O. Box 6, 400 Corporate Pointe

Culver City, CA 90230

Attention: David Jamieson and Terri Egan

Organization and Human Systems Development Credo (July 1996)*

Our purpose as professionals is to facilitate processes by which human beings and human systems live and work together for their mutual benefit and mutual well-being. Our practice is based on a widely shared learning and discovery process dedicated to a vision of people living meaningful, productive, good lives in ways that simultaneously serve them, their organizations, their communities, their societies, and the world.

We are an interdependent community of professionals whose practice is based on the applied behavioral sciences and other related sciences, a human systems perspective, and both human and organizational values. We serve people at all system levels, ranging from individuals and groups to organizations, communities, and ultimately the global community.**

We believe that human beings and human systems are interdependent economically, politically, socially, culturally, and spiritually, and that their mutual effectiveness is grounded in fundamental principles that are reflected in the primary values that guide our practice. Among these values are respect for human dignity, integrity, and worth; freedom, choice, and responsibility; justice and fundamental human rights; compassion; authenticity, openness, and honesty; learning, growth, and empowerment; understanding and respecting differences; cooperation, collaboration, trust, diversity, and community; excellence, alignment, effectiveness, and efficiency; democracy, meaningful participation, and appropriate decision making; and synergy, harmony, and peace.

We believe further that our effectiveness as a profession, over and above our effectiveness as individual professionals, requires a widely shared commitment to and behavior in accordance with certain moral-ethical guidelines. Among them are the following: Responsibility to Self—acting with integrity and being true to ourselves; striving continually for self-knowledge and personal growth; Responsibility for Professional Development and Competence—developing and maintaining our

---

*The moral-ethical position on which the OD-HSD profession is based, along with the beliefs and values underlying that position, are more fully described in "An Annotated Statement of Values and Ethics by Professionals in Organization and Human Systems Development." This Credo is based on the Annotated Statement.

**The global perspective does not mean changing the focus of our practice, but only the context within which we view our collective practice. And by shifting our paradigm of who "we" are, we can become a global professional community whose collective action will have global significance based on both our practice and ways in which we "walk our talk."

individual competence and establishing cooperative relations with other professionals to expand our competence; practicing within the limits of our competence, culture, and experience in providing services and using techniques; Responsibility to Clients and Significant Others—serving the long-term well-being of our client systems and their stakeholders; conducting any professional activity, program or relationship in ways that are honest, responsible, and appropriately open; Responsibility to the OD-HSD Profession—contributing to the continuing professional development of other practitioners and of the profession as a whole; promoting the sharing of professional knowledge and skills; Social Responsibility—accepting responsibility for and acting with sensitivity to the fact that our recommendations and actions may alter the lives and well-being of people within our client systems and within the larger systems of which they are subsystems.

Follow-Up Notes

So far, those who have endorsed the Credo and Annotated Statement as working statements include Richard Beckhard, John C. Bryan (Canada), Ezequiel Nieto Cardoso (Mexico), Jeanne Cherbeneau, Donald W. Cole, A. W. Cragg (Canada), Elsie Cross, Karen Davis, Nancy Davis, Chris Edgelow, Joey Finlay, Frank Friedlander, William Gellermann, Robert T. Golembiewski, Roger Harrison, Judy Heinrich, Judith C. Hoy, Ken Hultman, David W. Jamieson, Guadalupe Martinez De Leon (Mexico), Harry Levinson, Frederick A. Miller, Matjaz Mulej (Slovenia), Larry Polsky, Arkady Prigozhin (Russia), Joanne C. Preston, Anthony P. Raia, Robin Reid, Ed Schein, Charles Seashore, Beverly Scott, Peter C. Shepard (Malaysia), John J. Sherwood, Marc H. Silverman, Oron South, Perla R. Tayko (Philippines), George C. Thornton, Robert Tannenbaum, Lorraine R. Walsh, and Marv Weisbord.

In reading the Credo (as well as the Statement and the Annotated Statement), keep in mind that it is a working statement. For example, some issues currently under discussion are whether or not it is appropriate to becoming a "global professional community" or to say that we aspire to serve "the global community." These issues are raised in the footnote to the second paragraph of the Credo and the last sentence of that paragraph.

Bibliography

Abrams, J. (1999). *The mission statement book: 301 corporate mission statements from America's top companies.* Berkeley, CA: Ten Speed Press.

Adorno, T.W., Frenkel-Brunswik, E., Levinson, D.J., & Sanford, R.N. (1950). *The authoritarian personality.* New York: Harper.

Anderson, D., & Ackerman Anderson, L. (2001). *Beyond change management: Advanced strategies for today's transformational leaders.* San Francisco: Jossey-Bass/Pfeiffer.

Argyris, C. (1962). *Interpersonal competence and organizational development.* Homewood, IL: Dorsey Press.

Argyris, C. (1970) *Intervention theory and method.* Reading, MA: Addison-Wesley.

Argyris, C. (1997). *Integrating the individual and the organization.* New Brunswick, NJ: Transaction Publisher.

Badaracco, J.L., Jr., & Ellsworth, R.R. (1989). *Leadership and the quest for integrity.* Boston, MA: Harvard Business School Press.

Barrett, R. (1998). *Liberating the corporate soul: Building a visionary organization.* Boston, MA: Butterworth-Heinemann.

Beck, A. (1976). *Cognitive therapy and emotional disorders.* Madison, CT: International Universities Press.

Bellman, G.M. (2000). Discovering the beauty of the organizational beast. *Training & Development, 54*(5), 67–73.

Bennis, W.G. (1969). *Organization development: Its nature, origins, and prospects.* Reading, MA: Addison-Wesley.

Bilodeau, L. (1992). *The anger workbook.* Center City, MN: Hazeldon.

Blake, R.R., & Mouton, J.S. (1978). *The new managerial grid.* Houston, TX: Gulf.

Blanchard, K., & O'Connor, M. (1997). *Managing by values.* San Francisco: Berrett-Koehler.

Bramel, D. (1968). Dissonance, expectation, and the self. In R.P. Abelson, et al. (Eds.), *Theories of cognitive consistency: A sourcebook.* Chicago: Rand-McNally.

Broholm, R.R. (1990). *The power and purpose of vision.* Indianapolis, IN: Author.

Burke, W.W. (1982) *Organization development: Principles and practices.* Boston, MA: Little, Brown and Company.

Burke, W.W. (1997, Summer). The new agenda for organization development. *Organizational Dynamics,* pp. 7–20.

Burke, W.W. (1998). Living OD values in today's changing world of organizational consulting. *Vision/Action, 17*(1), 3–7.

Cameron, K.S., & Quinn, R.E. (1999). *Diagnosing and changing organizational culture: Based on the competing values framework.* Reading, MA: Addison-Wesley.

Church, A., Burke, W., & Van Eynde, D. (1994). Values, motives, and interventions of organization development practitioners. *Group & Organization Management, 19*(1), 5–50.

Collins, J.C., & Porras, J.I. (1994). *Built to last: Successful habits of visionary companies.* New York: The Free Press/HarperBusiness.

Cooperrider, D., Sorensen, P., Whitney, D., & Yeager, T. (2000). *Appreciative inquiry.* Champaign, IL: Stipes Publishing.

Covey, S.R. (1991). *Principle-centered leadership.* New York: Summit Books.

Cummings, T., & Worley, C. (2000). *Organizational development and change* (7th ed.). Cincinnati, OH: Southwestern.

Deal, T.E., & Kennedy, A.A. (1982). *Corporate culture.* Reading MA: Addison-Wesley.

Deming, W.E. (1986). *Out of the crisis.* Cambridge, MA: MIT Center for Advanced Engineering Studies.

Dyer, W.G. (1976). *Insight to impact: Strategies for interpersonal and organizational change.* Provo, UT: Brigham Young University Press.

Ellinor, L., & Gerard, G. (1998). *Dialogue: Rediscover the transforming power of conversation.* New York: John Wiley & Sons.

Ellis, A. (1973). *Humanistic psychology: The rational-emotive approach.* New York: Julian Press.

Erikson, E.H. (1959). *Identity and the life cycle.* New York: International Universities Press.

Feather, N.T. (1971). Value differences in relation to ethnocentrism, intolerance of ambiguity, and dogmatism. *Personality, 2,* 349–366.

Frankl, V.E. (1963). *Man's search for meaning.* New York: Washington Square Press.

French, W.L., & Bell, C.H., Jr. (1999). *Organizational development* (6th ed.). Upper Saddle River, NJ: Prentice Hall.

Friedlander, F. (1998). The evolution of organization development: 1960s to 1990s. *Vision/Action, 17*(1), 10–12.

Fromm, E. (1963). *The art of loving.* New York: Bantam Books.

Gelinas, M.V., & James, R.G. (1998). Living OD values in today's changing world of organizational consulting: Response II. *Vision/Action, 17*(1), 9.

Gellermann, W., Frankel, M.S., & Ladenson, R.F. (1990). *Values and ethics in organization and human systems development: Responding to dilemmas in professional life.* San Francisco: Jossey-Bass.

Gibb, J.R. (1961). Defensive communication. *The Journal of Communication, 11*(3), 141–148.

Gibb, J.R. (1978). *Trust.* Los Angeles, CA: Guild of Tutors Press.

Golembiewski, R. (2000). Three perspectives on appreciative inquiry. *OD Practitioner, 32*(1), 53–58.

Grant, L. (1998, January). Happy workers, high returns. *Fortune.*

Greenleaf, R. (1977). *Servant leadership: A journey into the nature of legitimate power and greatness.* New York: Paulist Press.

Grove, A.S. (1999). *Only the paranoid survive: How to exploit the crisis points that challenge every company.* New York: Bantam Books.

Hackman, J.R., & Oldham, G.R. (1975). Development of the job diagnostic survey. *Journal of Applied Psychology, 60,* 159–170.

Harrison, R. (1969). Defenses and the need to know. In W.B. Eddy, et al. (Eds.), *Behavioral science and the manager's role.* Washington, DC: NTL Learning Resources Corporation.

Harrison, R. (1970). Choosing the depth of organizational intervention. *Journal of Applied Behavioral Science, 6,* 181–202.

Harvey, J.B. (1988). *The Abilene paradox and other meditations on management.* San Francisco: Jossey-Bass.

Head, T.C. (2000). Appreciative inquiry: Debunking the mythology behind resistance to change. *OD Practitioner, 32*(1), 27–35.

Helmstetter, S. (1990). *What to say when you talk to your self.* New York: Pocket Books.

Helmstetter, S. (1998). *The self-talk solution.* New York: Pocket Books.

Herzberg, F. (1966). *Work and the nature of man.* Orlando, FL: Harcourt Brace.

Herzberg, F. (1968). One more time: How do you motivate employees. *Harvard Business Review, 46*(1), 53–62.

Hultman, K.E. (1976). Values as defenses. *Personnel and Guidance Journal, 54*(5), 269–271.

Hultman, K.E. (1979). *The path of least resistance: Preparing employees for change.* Austin, TX: Learning Concepts.

Hultman, K.E. (1998a). *Making change irresistible: Overcoming resistance to change in your organization.* Palo Alto, CA: Davies-Black.

Hultman, K.E. (1998b). Ten commandments of team leadership. *Training & Development, 52*(2), 12–13.

Jaworski, J. (1996). *Synchronicity: The inner path of leadership.* San Francisco: Berrett-Koehler.

Kanter, R.M. (1977). *Men and women of the corporation.* New York: Basic Books.

Kegan, R. (1982). *The evolving self: Problems and process in human development.* Cambridge, MA: Harvard University Press.

Kelly, M. (1994, March-April). A Copernican revolution in corporate governance. *Business Ethics,* p. 6.

Kets de Vries, M.F.R., & Miller, D. (1984). *The neurotic organization.* San Francisco: Jossey-Bass.

Korten, D.C. (1995). *When organizations rule the world.* West Hartford, CT: Kumarian Press/San Francisco: Berrett-Koehler.

Kotter, J.P. (1990). *A force for change: How leadership differs from management.* New York: The Free Press.

Kotter, J.P., & Heskett, J.L. (1992). *Corporate culture and performance.* New York: The Free Press.

Lausanne Institute. (1998). *Evaluating the team process in government.* Kennett Square, PA: Author.

Leimbach, M. (1994). *Business performance, employee satisfaction, and leadership practices.* Eden Prairie, MN: Wilson Learning Corporation.

Levering, R., & Moskowitz, M. (2000, January 10). 100 best companies to work for. *Fortune, 141*(1).

Lewin, K. (1947). Group decision and social change. In T.N. Newcomb & E.L. Hartley (Eds.), *Readings in social psychology.* Troy, MO: Holt, Rinehart & Winston.

Margenau, H. (1959). The scientific basis of value theory. In A.H. Maslow (Ed.), *New knowledge in human values.* New York: Harper & Brothers.

Maslow, A.H. (1954). *Motivation and personality.* New York: Harper & Row.

Maslow, A.H. (1968). *Toward a psychology of being* (2nd ed.). Princeton, NJ: D. Van Nostrand.

Maslow, A.H. (1970). *Religion, values, and peak-experiences.* New York: Viking Press.

Maslow, A.H. (1976). *The farther reaches of human nature.* New York: Penguin.

May, R. (1976). *Man's search for himself.* New York: New American Library.

McAniff, R. (1999). *The outrageous manager.* Polson, MT: McBliss & Associates.

McClelland, D.C., Atkinson, J.W., Clark, R.A., & Lowell, E.L. (1953). *The achievement motive.* Englewood Cliffs, NJ: Appleton-Century-Crofts.

McClelland, D.C., & Burnham, D.H. (1976). Power is the great motivator. *Harvard Business Review, 54*(2), 100–110.

McGregor, D.M. (1960). *The human side of enterprise,* New York: McGraw-Hill.

Morgan, G. (1986). *Images of organizations.* Thousand Oaks, CA: Sage.

Nadler, L. (1985). The organization as a micro-culture. In C.R. Bell & L. Nadler (Eds.), *Clients and consultants* (2nd ed.). Houston, TX: Gulf.

Neimeyer, R.A. (1993). Constructivist approaches to the measurement of meaning. In G.J. Neimeyer (Ed.), *Constructivist assessment: A casebook.* Thousand Oaks, CA: Sage.

Nicoll, D. (1998). Is OD meant to be relevant? Part III. *OD Practitioner, 30*(4), 3–8.

OD Network. *Mission, vision, values, responsibilities.* [www.odnetwork.org/mission values.html].

OD Network. *Organization and human systems development credo.* [www.odnet work.org/credo.html].

Pollard, C.W. (1996). *The soul of the firm.* Grand Rapids, MI: Zondervan.

Rim, Y. (1970). Values and attitudes. *Personality, 1,* 243–250.

Rogers, C.R. (1961). *On becoming a person.* Boston, MA: Houghton Mifflin.

Rokeach, M. (1964). *The three christs of Ypsilanti.* New York: Kroft.

Rokeach, M. (1968). *Beliefs, attitudes and values.* San Francisco: Jossey-Bass.

Rokeach, M. (1973). *The nature of human values.* New York: The Free Press.

Ryan, K.D., & Oestreich, D.K. (1998). *Driving fear out of the workplace: Creating a high-trust, high-performance organization* (2nd ed.). San Francisco: Jossey-Bass.

Schaef, A.W., & Fassel, D. (1988). *The addictive organization.* San Francisco: Harper & Row.

Schein, E.H. (1992). *Organizational culture and leadership* (2nd ed.). San Francisco: Jossey-Bass.

Schein, E.H., & Bennis, W.G. (1965). *Personal and organizational change through group methods: The laboratory approach.* New York: John Wiley & Sons.

Senge, P.M. (1990). *The fifth discipline: The art & practice of the learning organization.* New York: Doubleday.

Senge, P.M., Kleiner, A., Roberts, C., Roth, G., Ross, R., & Smith, B. (1999). *The dance of change.* New York: Doubleday.

Sherwood, W. (1998, November/December). The cat's in the cradle. *Across the Board.*

Tannenbaum, R., & Davis, S.A. (1969). Values, man, and organizations. In W.B. Eddy, et al. (Eds.), *Behavioral science and the manager's role.* Washington, DC: NTL Learning Resources Corporation.

Tillich, P. (1952). *The courage to be.* New Haven, CT: Yale University Press.

Tillich, P. (1963). *The eternal now.* New York: Charles Scribner's Sons.

Thomas, K.W. (2000). *Intrinsic motivation at work: Building energy and commitment.* San Francisco: Berrett-Koehler.

Vaill, P.B. (1996). *Learning as a way of being.* San Francisco: Jossey-Bass.

Vierling-Huang, J. (1999). Culture change at GE. In P. Senge, et al., *The dance of change.* New York: Doubleday.

Watkins, J.M., & Cooperrider, D. (2000). Appreciative inquiry: A transformative paradigm. *OD Practitioner, 32*(1), 6–12.

Watkins, J.M., & Mohr, B.J. (2001). *Appreciative inquiry: Change at the speed of imagination.* San Francisco: Jossey-Bass/Pfeiffer.

Weisskopt, W.A. (1959). Existence and values. In A.H. Maslow (Ed.), *New knowledge in human values.* New York: Harper & Brothers.

Williams, R.M. (1968). Values. In E. Sills (Ed.), *International encyclopedia of the social sciences.* New York: Macmillan.

About the Authors

Ken **Hultman** has over twenty-five years of experience as a consultant, trainer, and clinical counselor, with an emphasis on helping individuals, teams, and organizations remove barriers to achieving their full potential. He has written two books on change management: *The Path of Least Resistance: Preparing Employees for Change* (Learning Concepts, 1979) and *Making Change Irresistible: Overcoming Resistance to Change in Your Organization* (Davies-Black, 1998). In addition, he has published many articles on team leadership, performance improvement, values, and training methods, several of which have been reprinted in books and professional association newsletters.

Over the course of his career, Dr. Hultman has worked in a variety of roles, including therapist, staff manager, line manager, business owner, university professor, internal consultant, and external consultant. He has served as vice president for organization development at Menno Haven, Inc., as a training consultant with Development Dimensions International, and as director of staff development at the Texas Rehabilitation Commission. He has also held teaching positions at Florida State University and Shippensburg University of Pennsylvania.

Dr. Hultman earned his B.S. degree in sociology and an M.A. degree in counseling psychology from Arizona State University. He also holds an Ed.D. degree in counseling psychology from Rutgers University, with a specialization in group dynamics. In addition, he is certified as a trainer by the International Board of Certified Trainers, Inc., and licensed as a clinical professional counselor by the Maryland State Board of Counselors and Therapists. He can be contacted at www.KenHultman.com.

Bill **Gellermann** has over forty years of experience in consulting, facilitating, training, and development. He has been an external organization development consultant with Westvaco, a Fortune 500 company, over a fifteen-year period; a facilitator for the American Management Association's Executive Effectiveness Course for ten years; and coordinator of a process for clarifying the values and ethics of the organization and human systems development profession since 1981. He has had facilitation and consulting experience with a wide variety of organizations—large and small, in both public and private sectors, profit and not-for-profit, including governmental (federal, state, and local) organizations, labor unions, and religious and civil rights groups.

Dr. Gellermann is co-author (with M. Frankel and R. Ladenson) of *Values and Ethics in Organization and Human Systems Development: Responding to Dilemmas in Professional Life* (Jossey-Bass, 1990). That publication includes A Statement of Values and Ethics by Professionals in Organization and Human Systems Development (both in regular and annotated forms), the statement on which the Credo in the Appendix of this book is based. He also served as co-chair of the OD-HSD Clearinghouse of Professional Ethics Information (administered by the Office of Scientific Freedom and Responsibility Programs of the American Association for the Advancement of Science).

Dr. Gellermann received both his B.A. degree in economics and his M.B.A. degree in accounting from the University of Washington. He earned his Ph.D. degree from the University of California, Los Angeles, in business administration. In 1984 he was given the Outstanding Organization Development Consultant of the Year Award by the International Registry of Organization Development Professionals.

About the Editors

William J. Rothwell, Ph.D., is professor of human resource development in the College of Education at The Pennsylvania State University, University Park. He is also president of Rothwell and Associates, a private consulting firm that specializes in a broad array of organization development, human resource development, performance consulting, and human resource management services.

Dr. Rothwell has authored, co-authored, edited, or co-edited numerous publications, including *Practicing Organization Development* (with R. Sullivan and G. McLean, Jossey-Bass/Pfeiffer, 1995). Dr. Rothwell's latest publications include *The ASTD Reference Guide to Workplace Learning and Performance*, 3rd ed., 2 vols. (with H. Sredi, HRD Press, 2000); *The Competency Toolkit*, 2 vols. (with D. Dubois, HRD Press, 2000); *Human Performance Improvement: Building Practitioner Competence* (with C. Hohne and S. King, Gulf Publishing, 2000); *The Complete Guide to Training Delivery: A Competency-Based*

Approach (with S. King and M. King, Amacom, 2000); *Building In-House Leadership and Management Development Programs* (with H. Kazanas, Quorum Books, 1999); *The Action Learning Guidebook* (Jossey-Bass/Pfeiffer, 1999); and *Mastering the Instructional Design Process*, 2nd ed. (with H. Kazanas, Jossey-Bass/Pfeiffer, 1998).

Dr. Rothwell's consulting client list includes thirty-two companies from the *Fortune* 500.

Roland **Sullivan** has worked as an organization development (OD) pioneer with nearly eight hundred organizations in ten countries and virtually every major industry.

Mr. Sullivan specializes in the science and art of systematic and systemic change, executive team building, and facilitating Whole System Transformation Conferences—large interactive meetings with from three hundred to fifteen hundred people.

Mr. Sullivan has taught courses in OD at seven universities, and his writings on OD have been widely published. With Dr. Rothwell and Dr. McLean, he was co-editor of *Practicing OD: A Consultant's Guide* (Jossey-Bass/Pfeiffer, 1995).

For over two decades, Mr. Sullivan has served as chair of the OD Institute's Committee to Define Knowledge and Skills for Competence in OD and was a recent recipient of the Outstanding OD Consultant of the World award from the OD Institute.

Mr. Sullivan's current professional learning is available at *www.RolandSullivan.com.*

Kristine **Quade** is an independent consultant who combines her background as an attorney with a master's degree in organization development from Pepperdine University, and years of experience as both an internal and external OD consultant.

Ms. Quade draws from experiences in guiding teams from divergent areas within corporations and across many levels of executives and employees. She has facilitated leadership alignment, culture change, support system alignment, quality process improvements, organizational redesign, and the creation of clear strategic intent that results in significant bottom-line results. A believer in whole systems change, she has developed the expertise to facilitate groups ranging in size from eight to two thousand in the same room for a three-day change process.

Recognized as the 1996 Minnesota Organization Development Practitioner of the Year, Ms. Quade teaches in the master's programs at Pepperdine University and the University of Minnesota at Mankato and the master's and doctoral programs at the University of St. Thomas in Minneapolis. She is a frequent presenter at the Organization Development National Conference and also at the International OD Congress and the International Association of Facilitators.

Index